THE PRINCESS . . .
"Diana is very charming. But more than charm, what she has is the power to seduce. It's what has accounted for her . . . extraordinary popularity."

. . . AND HER PRINCE
"Nice and kind and concerned as he is, [Charles] is as selfish a person as I have ever met. He does exactly what he wants . . . with never a thought for the effect it will have upon anyone else."

THE MARRIAGE
"The Prince very quickly came to distrust [Diana]. He could never tell when she was telling the truth or when she was playacting."

"There were . . . memorable temper tantrums [by Diana], some of which have been presented as quasi-suicide attempts."

THE PRESENT
"The Queen feels that Diana has publicly slapped her in the face."

"Words cannot convey how betrayed [Charles] feels by what the Princess has done. He is deeply hurt and very, very angry that she could use public opinion against him like that. He would never do something like that . . . not even to a sworn enemy."

"The picture Lady Colin Campbell draws makes so much sense, it must be true."

—Detroit Free Press

DIANA
IN
PRIVATE

The Princess Nobody Knows

Lady Colin Campbell

ST. MARTIN'S PAPERBACKS

First published in Great Britain by Smith Gryphon Ltd.

DIANA IN PRIVATE

Copyright © 1992 by Lady Colin Campbell.

Cover photograph courtesy Globe Photos.

ISBN: 0-312-95051-9

Printed in the United States of America

St. Martin's Press hardcover edition published 1992
St. Martin's Paperbacks edition/December 1992

10 9 8 7 6 5 4 3 2 1

This book is dedicated to my beloved aunt, Marjorie
D. S. Panton, whose constancy, generosity and love
have been a shining example as well as a boon
throughout my life.

♚ ♚ ♚
·

CONTENTS

ACKNOWLEDGEMENTS

*T*his biography would never have come into being had I not had the good fortune to lunch with Alan Frame, whose idea it was. To him, I owe my first debt of gratitude.

No biography of a living person can be written without the help and support of a large body of people who know the subject. Of necessity, some of those have a lot to lose if their co-operation becomes apparent, and for that reason, I was astonished by the kindness and generosity of many friends, relations, acquaintances, and even a few strangers, who spoke to me with sometimes frightening frankness. Naturally, it has not been possible to name all of them, and to those who have to go unsung, including the friends who researched for me, I wish to extend my heartfelt appreciation. Without them, this book would not have been possible.

An equal contribution, however, has been made by the many people whom I can name. All of them accorded me unfailing courtesy when speaking to me, and I would therefore like to thank the following: Dame Barbara Cartland; Her Grace Margaret, Duchess of Argyll; the Earl of Strathmore and Kinghorne; Katharine, Viscountess Macmillan of Ovenden; Her Excellency the Jamaican High Commissioner, Mrs. Ellen Bogle; Jacqueline, Lady Killearn; Richard Adeney; Dr. Gloria Litman; Nigel Dempster; Brodrick Haldane; Tristan Millington-Drake; Duke Alexander di Carcaci; Baroness Izzy van Randwyck; Judy McGuire; Jonathan Dawson; Robyn Hall; Lord Montagu of Beaulieu; Clifford Henderson; Anne Hodson-Pressinger; David Williamson of Debrett's; Lady Teresa Manners; Evrie, Lady Freyberg; the Hon. George Plumptre; Daniel Wiggin; David Hornsby; Ann Cameron-Webb; Lady Renwick; Liz Brewer; James Whitaker; HRH Princess Katarina of Yugoslavia; Roy Miles; Israel Zohar; Terry Dixon; Princess Helena Moutafian; Elke Hundertmark; Murray Arbeid; the Hon. Rupert Fairfax; Pida Ripley of WomenAid; Jamie Jeeves of the English Ballet Company; Bunty Lewis of Birthright; John Coblenz of CRUSAID; Beverley, Lady Annaly of SIGN; Colonel Patrick Reger of Soldiers', Sailors' & Airmen's Families' Association; Alan Sievewright; His Grace the Duke of Northumberland; Anthony Taylor; Lady Cleone Versen; James Buchanan-Jardine; Richard Szpiro; Janet, Marchioness of Milford Haven; Mrs. Henry Ford II; Philippa Gitlin; the late Humphrey Mews; the late James Dorset; Her Majesty's Assistant Press Secretary, Richard (Dickie) Arbiter; and The Princess of Wales's former Private Secretary, Oliver Everett.

Thanks are also due to the Households of Her Royal Highness The Princess of Wales; Her Royal Highness Princess Alice, Duchess of Gloucester; and Their Royal Highnesses Prince and Princess Michael of Kent as well as the Buckingham Palace Press Office, for the unfailing politeness and co-operation with which they dealt with my innumerable queries.

Writing is often an arduous task, and I wish to thank my brother, Michael Ziadie, for making it easier for me by presenting me with every author's lifesaver: a computer.

These acknowledgements would not be complete if I did not say how very fortunate I am to have the most marvellous agent and publisher in Sara Fisher of A. M. Heath & Co. Ltd. and Robert Smith of Smith Gryphon. They have been a real delight to work with, as has my editor, Helen Armitage. Many, many thanks for a happy project.

London
19 January 1992

x

♛   ♛   ♛

CHAPTER ONE

The Antecedents of a Princess

When you meet the Princess of Wales, you are immediately struck by how attractive she is. As she approaches, the first thing you notice is how tall she is: six foot in shoes. Her slender build, narrow trunk, almost flat chest, boyish hips, long legs and arms (which help to give her a natural elegance that people with shorter arms never achieve), all combine with the three extra inches of impeccably cut and deliberately casual hair to make her appear even longer and leaner than she is.

The next thing that strikes you is how animated yet serene she is. She has a perfect social personality: she is warm, witty and down-to-earth; she is natural, with the ease and grace of someone who likes people and likes being liked by them. As she talks, in that light, sweet voice that reveals nothing of the steel lurking beneath the surface, you notice her exceptionally beautiful complexion. Very fine and translucent, its beauty remains even when she has the occasional blemish. I have seen her turn pink from the heat of the moment as well as from the heat of the summer, but it is unfair to maintain, as some writers do, that this is somehow a flaw which detracts. It does not.

For all her attributes, however, the unadorned Diana is not a raving natural beauty, and without her appealing nature, she would never have been perceived as being as attractive as she is. One of her greatest assets is her colouring. To what extent she has improved on nature is apparent when she steps out of the swimming pool, her hair slicked back, her make-up nonexistent. Even then she is an attractive woman, though she gilds her lily. The blonde hair, creamy skin and peachy glow are all owed to one chemical or another, and her use of beauty aids is both proficient and effective.

In repose, Diana's mouth is nondescript. It neither enhances nor detracts from her face. But once more it has a quality of expressiveness that lifts it beyond the ordinary. When her lips tremble with feeling or she starts to chew them, as she often does when she is nervous or has nothing better to do, they gain an appeal which men find enticing and women sympathetic. Her nose could never be called conventionally beautiful except by the most sycophantic of admirers. In person, it is every bit as prominent as it appears in all but the most flatteringly lit photographs. Yet, like Sophia Loren, her minuses conspire to add up to pluses, and nowhere is this better illustrated than with this, the most pronounced of her features. Without it, her face would lose much of its impact and all of its uniqueness. She would be reduced from being strikingly aristocratic to just another plain girl with good skin and pretty eyes.

Her beautiful, big blue eyes are undoubtedly her best feature. They sparkle with warmth and vivacity, and, with the deliberateness that has accounted for so much of her success, she skilfully plays them up. She uses them with the practised expressiveness of the social animal that she is, allowing them to do much of her talking for her. She can flash a look of irritation or warning with as much effectiveness as her more agreeable expressions, though she has not yet reached the heights of intimidation that The Queen commands—everyone who knows Her Majesty lives in terror of The Look. Unlike her mother-in-law, however, Diana also resorts to the tricks of the make-up trade. Through Barbara Daly, she has learnt how to make the most of all her features, though it is from Elizabeth Taylor that she picked up a tip which she fortunately no longer employs as constantly as she did: vulgarizing her appearance by heightening the colour of her eyes with a blue eyeliner pencil on the inside rim of the lower lid.

The two characteristics which accentuate her natural assets and account for much of her attractiveness are not tricks of any trade, however. The first, but less important, is a tremendous sense of style. The second is a winning personality.

Although Diana is by no means perfect—she is sometimes stubborn beyond mulishness, has a terrible temper, is demanding of those close to her, and can be utterly ruthless about carrying out decisions—everyone who knows her well attests to the fact that she is a genuinely kind and decent person. When you meet her, Diana comes across as simple, uncomplicated, and caring. She has real charm and warmth. She touches you, not only with her hand (a disconcertingly unroyal habit, and all the more endearing for it), but with the sincerity of her manner. "She really does like people. She is very warm and caring and thoughtful," says Janet, Marchioness of Milford Haven, whose late husband was Prince Philip's first cousin and the head of the Mountbatten family.

Colonel Patrick Reger, Director of Fundraising for SSAFA (Soldiers', Sailors' & Airmen's Families Association), agrees: "She is a delightful person and very gifted at what she does. I know some people will think, 'He's only saying that because she's who she is.' But I'm not. I'm not one of those people who regard her as a beauty. She's too tall and her nose is too long for me. But she does manage to say just the right thing to the right person, to do the one little thing that lifts an encounter out of the mundane into something more significant. I've watched her closely and I can tell you it's no act. You can tell when people are laying it on. She's not. She came to Swinton for us not too long ago, and she acquitted herself admirably."

"She's changed beyond belief," Lady Cleone Versen, daughter of the Earl of Erne and a friend of Diana's from her pre-marital days, says, "but she was always lovely." Even people who are prepared to dislike her, like a certain well-known architect who would take care not to find himself in the same room as The Prince of Wales, have had their preconceptions dissolved upon meeting the Princess. "I couldn't believe how warm and witty and captivating and flirtatious she is," he says. In the flesh, Diana is indeed very sexual. "She wiggles and winks and blushes and gushes and no one can resist her," he adds. What he should have said was that no man can resist her, for many women, especially the beautiful ones, can find her eminently resistible.

The Princess's attitude to other good-looking women causes mixed feelings amongst her peers. She does not want to have anything to do with them. Even in an official line-up, she always has as few words as she can get away with for the good-looking ones. This was confirmed to me by several well-placed women, including one senior official, who said, "I've met her on a number of occasions. But I can't say I've been able to form an opinion of her. She only ever greets me, then quickly moves on to the man beside me. She prefers men to women, and I'm usually with my deputy, who is [a] tall and handsome [man]. She has no problem talking to him. But to me, she never has anything to say. Not that I'm blaming her. It's all right by me if she prefers men. I'm not so sure I wouldn't be just like her if our roles were reversed. After all, it's far more fun to chat up a good-looking man than speak to another woman."

A former member of her staff attributes different motives to this characteristic of Diana's: "I do wish she wasn't so wretchedly competitive. She has no time for any woman who will steal her thunder. Whether in private or public, she will not tolerate competition. She gives her time and attention only to people who will admire her. To everyone else, she's either completely withdrawn and uncommunicative or, if the situation forces her to be, minimally polite."

Older, more established women, all of whom have a high regard for Diana's accomplishments, also have reservations about the highly flirtatious way the Princess carries out some of her engagements. The eminent charity fundraiser and socialite Jacqueline, Lady Killearn, widow of the wartime High Commissioner to Egypt and mother of the Countess of St. Germans and the Hon. Mrs. [Ian] Ross, is typical of many other women when she says, "I've met her

4

on numerous occasions. I like her and on the whole think she's a force for good. But I do wish she wouldn't carry out her duties as if she were a model."

This is not envy. Diana is a lot more complex and controversial than she appears to be, and those who cross paths with her see a woman with far more to her than the media ever glimpses or conveys. Beneath the highly polished and undeniably glossy exterior is someone who engenders both warmth and coolness, love and hatred, admiration and criticism. She is almost universally revered for her charity work, yet there is now a solid phalanx of people close to and within the Royal Family circle who say that Diana herself precipitated the tenth wedding anniversary "crisis" which caused such an international furore. They hold her responsible for turning the spotlight on to her marriage and the way she and The Prince of Wales conduct their private lives. They blame her for confusing her private and her public priorities, and for wilfully embarking upon a course of action that had the potential to do untold damage to the image of the Royal Family. They have little patience with the myth of the Princess who is made of spun sugar, and are at pains to point out that Diana takes great care to hide all but her most attractive qualities from the public gaze. Yet even they have to admit that Diana is a tremendous personality and her astonishing success is almost entirely due to her own efforts. Not everyone likes her, but everyone has to acknowledge that she is an outstanding person worthy of admiration and respect.

The girl who would grow into this complex woman was born early in the evening of Saturday, 1 July 1961, in an upstairs bedroom at Park House on the Sandringham Estate. Ironically for someone who would later bring such pride to her nearest and dearest, Diana was a disappointment. Her parents, Viscount and Viscountess Althorp, had hoped for a son and heir to replace the boy, John, who had died the day he was born, eighteen months before, on 12 January 1960. Instead, they got yet another girl.

There comes a point when the difference between boys and girls matters to aristocrats, and Johnnie and Frances

Althorp had reached that point. First they had had one daughter, Sarah, by this time aged six, followed by Jane two years later. Desirable as girls were to a sentimentalist like the Viscount, most peers needed at least one son, preferably two, and Johnnie Althorp was no exception. The "heir and the spare," as his cousin by marriage Consuelo Vanderbilt, Duchess of Marlborough, so succinctly put it, were an absolute necessity. For, without the much needed heir, most English titles, including that of the Spencer earldom, would pass out of the immediate family and into the hands of cousins. And with them would go all the wealth and possessions which were entailed upon the title-holder.

The word "entail" is as much a part of aristocratic vocabulary as money is to a banker. What it means is that everything is held from generation to generation by the person currently in possession of the title. It is a way of getting around the inheritance and tax laws, of keeping the estate, the house, and everything within it, out of the rapacious grasp of government after government. Only in special circumstances can an entail be broken, and even then breaking it is never easy or inexpensive.

The Althorps' yearning for an heir was therefore far more than the conventional prejudice towards a son. It meant keeping not only the titles of Earl, Viscount, Lady and Honourable in the immediate family, but also the great stately home Althorp House, with its endless treasures and its vast estate. Losing the title would mean that the Spencer family would, in the following generation, become the poor relations of the grandee who would become the next but one Earl Spencer, and beyond that, they would all be penniless Misters and Misses, possessing neither rank nor wealth.

A babe in arms, however, can have powerful appeal, and the Althorps quickly put aside their disappointment. Johnnie thought the 7 lb. 12 oz. daughter who took over their lives while his wife breastfed her a perfectly magnificent physical specimen, and Frances doted on her the way she had on the other girls. She was registered as the Honourable Diana Frances Spencer, when her parents got around to choosing names for the infant they were so sure was going to be a son. But even her christening, at St. Mary's, Sandringham, on 30 August 1961, indicated the lack of regard paid to Diana's reduced station in life. Unlike her sister Sarah, whose godmother was Queen Elizabeth The Queen Mother, or Jane, whose godfather was the Duke of Kent, she had no royal godparents. She would have to struggle through life with Lady Mary Colman, the Lord Lieutenant of Norfolk's wife; neighbours Sarah Pratt and Carol Fox; her cousin Sandy [Alexander] Gilmour, brother of Sir Ian Gilmour, the baronet MP and later a leading Tory Wet; and the auctioneer, Christie Manson & Woods's chairman John Floyd.

It was not a propitious start. After all, you never know when a regal godparent will become useful, when they will feel compelled to do their duty and help the child climb the ladder of success later in life. And if they do not, the mere fact that the child can boast of having frightfully grand people as godparents in itself often provides an edge when it is needed.

Despite her inauspicious beginnings, the infant Diana was a happy baby in a happy house. Sarah and Jane loved their baby sister, and treated her, as a maid said, "as if she were their own living doll until they were sent away to boarding school" six years later. Contrary to reports which have subsequently been propagated in the popular press, the Althorp marriage was not in trouble at that time, and this has been confirmed to me by people with whom they were friendly, as well as by relations.

Viscount and Viscountess Althorp had the world at their feet. They were young and attractive, well off, well placed, and well liked. He was heir to a grand title and great fortune, thirty-seven, and very desirable. She was the daughter of the 4th Lord Fermoy, twenty-five, and strikingly attractive. Theirs was a love match right from the start. Johnnie, tall, strapping and handsome, with a sexuality that crackled, was unofficially engaged to the tall, blonde and beautiful Lady Anne Coke. Frances was eighteen, also tall, blonde and striking, but with a great deal of spirit and what one of her maids would later call "a certain Irish broadness." In other words, she had overwhelming sex appeal, while Lady Anne had serenity. From the first moment their gazes locked, at Frances's coming-out dance, Johnnie and Frances were propelled towards each other with a passion that neither could resist, and within a matter of weeks he had proposed.

Never one to prevaricate when she could be positive, Frances, who "had been raised to marry as well as she could," according to a family friend, accepted the future Earl Spencer's proposal with a speed that their daughter Diana would later emulate when her turn came. Their union seemed tailor-made for success. Viscount Althorp, born in 1924, was the son of the 7th Earl Spencer and Lady Cynthia Hamilton. His godmother was Queen Mary, and his mother, a daughter of the Duke of Abercorn, had been the love of The Prince of Wales's life before she unwisely accepted Spencer's proposal in 1919. But Johnnie Althorp had no experience of happy family life, and this would later have an effect upon his marriage to Frances. His parents' marriage was a sadomasochistic exercise in which his mother had to endure grinding misery. Her brother the Duke of Abercorn told an eminent stockbroker whom I know: "Cynthia never had a day's happiness with Jack [Earl Spencer]. He was mean and cruel and nasty to her. It was beyond him to be nice or kind or thoughtful or considerate. He was a monster who did everything in his power to make her unhappy, and he succeeded." A misanthrope who was happier locked away in his library, with its 70,000 books, than dealing with people, whenever he surfaced the Earl was invariably "a pig." No one liked him: not his wife, who was regularly beaten by him and remained with him because the solidity of aristocratic marriages has less to do with happiness than other, more worldly considerations; nor his son, whom he despised for his lack of intellectual inclination, and whom he treated with as much kindness as he treated the boy's mother; and none of the many acquaintances who would have despised him had he not had the attractions of great wealth and high position, and who deplored his failings nevertheless.

Despite his tortured home life, the young Johnnie Althorp was an amiable and well-liked boy. It is difficult for a child not to enjoy at least some moments of happiness with the advantages of a comfortable home run by a full complement of staff, and little Johnnie was no exception. He was educated at Eton and Sandhurst prior to serving throughout the Second World War in the Royal Scots Greys, and, with the end of the war, came some unexpected success.

Even though Johnnie Althorp's father had nothing but contempt for a son whose greatest talents lay in the standard gentlemanly pursuits of hunting, shooting, and fishing, King George VI felt differently. Moreover, The King, who had little appreciation of people with a cruel wit, liked Johnnie as a person. He could always be depended upon to be pleasant and charming. He was well-mannered and amiable, without spikiness in his turn of phrase, possibly, as a titled lady who is a Spencer relation said, because "he's thicker than two planks." What also attracted The King to Johnnie was that his long-suffering mother Cynthia was a good friend of Queen Elizabeth's as well as a Lady of Her Majesty's Bedchamber. George VI therefore made him his equerry.

Although relations between father and son were strained, Johnnie and his mother were close, and this had an added appeal for both The King and Queen Elizabeth, since they liked being surrounded by people who gave them a feeling of congeniality and cosiness. The Palace days were happy days, and Johnnie looked assured of leading a satisfying and unblighted future closely allied to the Royal Family.

Frances's parents were also integral members of the inner circle at court. Her father, the 4th Baron Fermoy, was such a close friend of George VI that he was with The King on the shoot that took place at Sandringham the day before His Majesty's death in 1952. Her mother Ruth was one of Queen Elizabeth's closest friends and since 1956 has been a lady-in-waiting. Lord Fermoy had also been on such cordial terms with the late King, George V, that he had been able to rent Park House on the Sandringham Estate from him.

This comfortable, ten-bedroomed house, which is often

called large and rambling by people who have never had access to really big houses, was the setting in which two generations of the Fermoy family would enjoy happy childhoods. Built by King Edward VII to accommodate the overflow of guests at the Sandringham "Big House" during the gun-mad King's shoots, it overlooks the estate's parkland but is secluded from the road by plants and trees. The setting is pretty rather than spectacular, a David Cox painting rather than a Constable landscape. It was here that Maurice and Ruth Fermoy raised their three children, Edmund, the son and heir, Mary, and Frances, and later, after the lease had been turned over by Ruth to Frances and Johnnie, it was where the Althorps centred their family life.

The parallels between the way the Hon. Frances Burke Roche and her siblings were raised, and how she raised her own three girls and a boy, are plentiful. They were all reared to be well-behaved and well-mannered, self-confident and sociable, strong and positive. "You have to remember that the family has Burke blood," another member of the Burke family said. "And the Burkes have always been formidable. The Roches have always been proud of their Burke connection, to such an extent that all the children have carried the Burke name as well as Roche. The significance of being Burkes is that they have always had strong characters—and when I say strong I mean powerful. They are dominant personalities. Very vibrant. Very assertive. Very traditional, but individualistic at the same time. It is a combination that only the Irish seem able to achieve, and they certainly possess it."

Burke men, according to that cousin, invariably marry strong women, and certainly the woman whom Maurice Fermoy chose for himself perpetuated the tradition. Ruth Gill was a product of a military background, the daughter of a colonel from Bieldside in Aberdeen; she was over 25 years younger than her 46-year-old groom when they married in 1931. The celebrated Scots photographer and socialite Brodrick Haldane has known her from before her marriage: "She always had a strong character. Now she's frightfully correct. Not grand. Correct. She knows the rules and plays by them. But in those days she was far more free-wheeling than she is now. She was wonderfully talented, both as a singer and a pianist. She was at the Paris Conservatoire, and was very highly rated."

It was when Ruth was a student at the Paris Conservatoire of Music that she met Maurice Fermoy. She was flattered by his interest, as well she might have been, for he was a rich and noble lord, a friend of The King, and marriage to him would mean a decided step up in the world. The Gills, though a "nice" family, were hardly grand or impressive. A dearth of lords figured in their family tree, though several of its saplings sprang from the wrong side of the blanket. Eliza Kewark, a dark-skinned Indian girl from Bombay, lived with Ruth's great-great-grandfather Theodore Forbes while he worked for the East India Company. Eliza never married her protector, though their union was blessed with progeny, including a daughter, Katherine, who was sent to Scotland for her education; she remained, to marry locally and become an ancestor of Ruth Gill and The Princess of Wales. At that time, the family went to great lengths to cover up Katherine's antecedents, partly because illegitimacy was a disgrace, but even more so because the admission of native or coloured blood, as it was then called, would have disqualified her progeny from marrying white people. I shall come back to this later.

When Ruth married her lord, she was bright and ambitious, talented and attractive. She took to her new way of life the way, later on, Ivana Trump took to Manhattan. As she adjusted to life within the royal inner circle—and became especially friendly with the then Duke and Duchess of York—out went the freewheeling manner, the extended boundaries of the artist. In their place came a rectitude and an awareness of authority that would later bring her into conflict with her daughter Frances and thereby shape the destiny of her granddaughter Diana. In the meantime, however, these new attributes brought her a house on The King's estate and sufficient intimacy with King George V and Queen Mary for The Queen to try to cheer up The King only hours before he expired, with the news that

11

"dear Ruth Fermoy" had given birth to a little girl. The date was 19 January 1936, and the infant was Diana's mother Frances.

Diana's grandmother Ruth, Lady Fermoy was a strict and punctilious mother. But the Burke Roche blood that flowed through her children's veins assured them of sufficient Irish temperament to deal lightly with this. Their father's family, on the other hand, were characters—in that old-fashioned sense of the word conveying so much that is of an elusive quality. They had abundant Irish charm, superb taste—Cahirguillamore and Kilshanning, their ancestral homes, were jewels—and good looks. Once one of the richest families in Ireland, they had lost much of their property through recklessness, fecklessness and gambling. But they were rescued from penury, as so many grand families have been, by a fortuitous American marriage, the effects of which are felt to this day by Diana, her siblings and cousins, all of whom owe their financial independence to their American great-grandmother.

This American connection came through an heiress named Frances, known as Fanny, whose father Frank Work amassed a fortune as stockbroker to many of the richest nineteenth-century American families, including the Vanderbilts. Frank and Fanny Work were as headstrong as later generations of their family—especially Frances and Diana—would prove to be, so their inheritance included spirit and turbulence as much as wealth. Frank Work, however, was a rabid xenophobe with an abiding hatred of foreigners, and when his daughter married the 3rd Baron Fermoy, then the Hon. James Roche, he did not forgive her until she left her husband in 1891 and returned home.

Papa Work was as unreasonable as he was determined, and when the wayward Fanny came back to live with him, he laid down conditions for reinstating her as his heiress that show why later generations of the family, who have inherited his characteristics, have also had trouble maintaining harmonious family relations. In a day and age when the peerage counted for more than it does now, Frank Work blithely insisted that Fanny cease using her title and revert to her maiden name; another condition, reasonable only to him, was that she must never return to Europe. To show the lengths of his control, he then extended this proviso to her twin sons, Maurice (The Princess of Wales' grandfather, the 4th Baron Fermoy) and Francis, to whom he left a share of his fortune solely if they became American citizens and never set foot again in Britain.

Faced with such an indomitable will and so much money, Frank Work's daughter and grandsons took up what looked like permanent residence in the United States, becoming, to all intents and purposes, true blue Yankees; their schooling was rounded off at Harvard University. But not even the £600,000 that each of them inherited could dim the lure of the British way of life in the heyday of the British Empire, with its courtliness, its refinement, its splendour. They applied to the law courts to have their grandfather's will overturned. On succeeding, they returned to Britain, where Maurice set about establishing himself as befitted a gentleman of his rank and station.

By then the troubles in Ireland had altered the position of the Anglo-Irish Ascendancy to such an extent that Maurice, who became the 4th Lord Fermoy in 1921, was not even tempted to return to his native country. He sank roots in England, living what would prove to be a delightful and uneventful life in the lap of royalty. Ruth proved to be a faithful and devoted wife, a conscientious mother to their three children. The fact that Frances repeated the pattern of her childhood when she had her own children is testament to its efficacy and merit.

Park House, which now became the main family home, was a pleasant place to grow up. Norfolk, while undramatic, is the sunniest and driest part of the United Kingdom, and added to the good weather was the good fortune of being brought up on the monarch's private estate. When The King and Queen were in residence, which they were throughout a good part of the shooting season (the Glorious Twelfth of August to the end of February), Lord and Lady Fermoy and their children were treated with all the courtesy accorded to friends and neighbours. Although that did not mean such familiarity that they could drop in on each other uninvited, it did extend to invitations for tea and dinner, to shoot and to chat. It also meant a hive of activity, for when Their Majesties were in residence, so was the court. Private secretaries, equerries, officers of the guard, courtiers, dukes, duchesses, royal cousins and other kith and kin swarmed about this country backwater, providing a buzz that would otherwise never have existed.

For Frances and her brother and sister, this excitement was an early lesson in the workings of the court, as it would also prove to be for her children, especially Diana and Jane. Early on they learnt how and why the human beings who make up the court functioned. Later, this knowledge would come in useful, especially when The Prince of Wales's interest in Lady Diana Spencer had become plain and it looked as if the Fermoy and Spencer families' ambitions might amount to something.

But first, there were other lessons to be learnt. The Fermoy and Althorp children's introduction to school took place at Park House, where a special school was set up for them. They were taught by their own governess, Gertrude Allen, known to Frances as Gert and as Ally to Diana and her schoolmates, who included the local doctor's son and a selection of children from the surrounding countryside. The two generations of children were exposed to a lot more than the fact that the Battle of Hastings was fought in 1066. Their education went on all the time, and much of Diana's character, and many of her attributes, were formed away from school. Indeed, it could be fairly said that the main parts of her education took place outside the schoolroom. Great emphasis was placed on developing the behaviour and tastes of all the children, so that they would emerge as cultivated adults. They were brought up to have exquisite manners, to conduct themselves properly in different kinds of company and a variety of circumstances, never to let the side down and always to be a credit to their parents, to be civilized and well-liked individuals who behaved impeccably in public irrespective of temptation or provocation. Of course, no human being could always behave perfectly, but the message was clearly received that the one thing that would not be forgiven was to behave badly in public. It was an invaluable lesson, one which Diana has neither forgotten, nor failed to apply.

Music has played a large part in The Princess of Wales's life and, contrary to popular misconception, it has been classical more than pop which has brought her the greatest pleasure. She inherited her taste in this field from her grandmother, for whom music has been a consuming passion all her life.

Although Ruth Fermoy had to give up any ideas of a musical profession when she married, she could no more have been separated from her love of music than from her soul. Music remained a large part of her life, and she ensured that her children, then her grandchildren, imbibed an appreciation of it from birth. The result was that her passion enriched them all in unexpected ways. This was especially true after she founded in 1951 the King's Lynn Music Festival, an annual event which regularly attracted such eminent musicians as Benjamin Britten and Peter Pears. Ruth remained the guiding light of this important festival until she had a disagreement with the organizers a few years ago.

Ruth's interest in music had a profound effect upon all her children and grandchildren. This went far beyond merely expanding the narrow aristocratic limits of their lives. They might be ordinary members of an audience, peering past the footlights, or they might mix with the great and near-great musicians and artistes who were perpetually in and out of their homes, and whose erudite and cultivated paths would otherwise never have crossed their own. The musical world is relatively classless, and this, coupled with Maurice Fermoy's American upbringing, had the effect of creating an environment in which people related to one another as if class did not exist. The children and grandchildren were thus equipped with an attitude and a knack which has stood Frances in good stead, for she is liked by just about everyone who has ever met her, with the exception of her late first husband Johnnie, his widow Raine, and Raine's mother Barbara Cartland. She also passed on this aptitude to her own children, and the result has been that Diana has gained universal praise for her classy but classless touch.

Yet it would not be fair to the Spencers to say that Diana's egalitarian touch is due exclusively to her maternal grandparents and their musical friends. Many of the very old aristocratic families have the ability to address a monarch or a pauper as if both are equally worthy of respect. Johnnie Spencer, according to those who knew him well, did this. His manner did not change whether he was talking to a member of the Royal Family at a ball at Buckingham Palace or a working-class tourist from Idaho who happened to buttonhole him on a tour of Althorp House. Diana is the same.

Although ease of manner is inculcated into the scions of the aristocracy, it does not always produce confident adults who are free of emotional turmoil. As the Spencers and Fermoys are typical of their peer group in this respect, the effects of an aristocratic upbringing are worth looking at briefly.

The pressure to be always well-behaved, to be always pleasant and polite, to achieve and maintain a peak of social perfection, can be a double-edged sword. Dr. Gloria Litman, formerly Senior Lecturer at the Institute of Psychiatry and head of the Addiction Research Unit of the Maudsley Hospital, London, confirms that while the child is growing up, the firm boundaries of an aristocratic upbringing will provide confidence, certainty, and the feeling of care that discipline brings in its wake. Accompanying that, however, can be an underlying frustration, a suppressed rage, a resentment that your every thought, word and deed has been mapped out for you to the exclusion of your natural inclinations. Once the child has grown up, the absence of an external authority in conjunction with the natural desire for self-expression can be a combustible combination. The conflicts generated by perfectly natural impulses and the inability to resolve these constructively can lead to alcoholism, drug addiction, melancholia and a host of other emotional difficulties, many of which have shown up in the various branches of Diana's family.

Such problems are and always have been rife amongst

the upper classes. The price paid for privilege is not always a painless one. Her great-uncle George, according to his sister Lady Margaret Douglas-Home, "has been gone for many years." Diana has not been spared the spectre of emotional distress on the maternal side of her family, either. Her uncle Edmund, the 5th Lord Fermoy, was prone to depression all his life, and finally committed suicide in August 1984 in the most horrific way, by blowing his brains out. Even closer to home, Diana's sister Sarah had anorexia nervosa, and this became a matter of public knowledge and some embarrassment while she was dating Prince Charles. Diana herself has "definitely had a real problem with food," according to a former butler in the Wales household, and while she did not suffer from classical anorexia nervosa, her eating habits were neither conventional nor regular. Indeed, she suffered badly from bulimia nervosa from the age of nineteen until relatively recently, and is still not cured. This is an issue that will be dealt with at greater length later.

Nor was Diana's novel approach to food the only manifestation of her family heritage. She has a streak of stubbornness in her character so pronounced that the only charitable way of describing it is to say that its origins are self-preservative, while acknowledging that it has wrought havoc in her life and has definitely proven destructive on occasion.

Nor was this the only destructive Spencer trait which she inherited. Like her father before her, she has her grandfather Black Jack's fierce temper and Johnnie's tendency towards maudlin self-pity, which The Prince of Wales calls "her martyr complex." As a husband, Johnnie was never able to accept personal responsibility for his failings or their consequences, and Diana cannot either. She too resolutely believes that she must be endowed with the mantle of blamelessness and innocence no matter how contrary her conduct is where family harmony is concerned. And she has ensured that the next generation will not be spared either. She has done what her father did, and has turned the children into one of the areas of conflict between The Prince of Wales and herself.

17

👑   👑   👑

CHAPTER TWO

A Marriage Falls Apart

*T*he potent brew of privilege and problems, which the family of Diana's parents shared with many other aristocrats, was bubbling away to undermine the Althorp marriage by the time Frances produced the desperately desired son and heir, Charles, at the London Clinic on 20 May 1964. Although Inga Crane, a nursery maid at Park House for four years from shortly after Charles's birth, when Diana was three, until she was seven, confirmed to a friend of mine that Johnnie and Frances were still "very much in love, very affectionate with each other," Johnnie Althorp was no longer the handsome thirty-year-old with a glorious life in front of him, nor was Frances the jubilant eighteen-year-old, blindingly in love, that they had been at the time of their marriage. Ten years together had taught Viscountess Althorp that her husband would never achieve great heights. Johnnie had neither the initiative nor the innovativeness that she sought, and was, in the words of a cousin, "duller than ditchwater."

But there were other, more profound problems than boredom. Frances had come to learn that Johnnie possessed another expression from the kind and affable face he presented to the world. He had a vicious temper and a cruel streak. His conduct led Frances to conclude that he was using her, and, as she began standing up for herself and demanding the type of treatment she felt was hers by right, their fights escalated. In her divorce petition she would allege cruelty to describe his intermittent behaviour

18

towards her. The marriage was beginning to look more and more to her like a sodden wasteland through which she had to slog with ever increasing difficulty. Although never physically aggressive, in her opinion, there were times when Johnnie could be belligerent in his presentation of an argument. More and more she felt unevenly matched, that she was emerging the injured party in conflicts with him. As she did not regard herself in any way, shape or form as responsible for causing or instigating these, she now felt thoroughly hard done by. Added to this was her increasing belief that her husband did not appreciate her, though, being a proud woman, she took care at that stage to conceal her opinion and the difficulties within her marriage from everyone.

Later, of course, Frances would sue Johnnie for divorce, but at this point she was prepared to put up with the diminishing satisfaction she found in her marriage and bide her time until she had an acceptable way out. So successful was she that even Johnnie would claim, little realizing how damning an admission he was making, that there had never been any indication from Frances that theirs was anything but a happy marriage until her departure, and that she, by inference, had been a good and courageous wife who had stood the shortcomings within her marriage with strength and blamelessness.

"Johnnie was boring beyond belief," a Spencer cousin said, "nice to his friends, soppy and sentimental with his children, but achingly dull. The kindest thing you can say is that he took Frances awfully for granted. She, on the other hand, was everything a woman should be. Elegant, witty, wonderful company. Great fun, and bright. They entertained a lot and were pretty social, but she wanted more out of life than a husband who, putting their personal difficulties aside, really couldn't get his act together to accomplish much of anything. He went to [the Royal Agricultural College at] Cirencester, bought a small [250 acre] farm [at Ingoldisthorpe] and said he was going to farm. Well, that was just ludicrous, and she knew it. I mean, you don't spend your whole life farming one little plot of land, not

19

when you're Viscount Althorp and could do so much more."

As Frances lost respect for Johnnie, she looked about for solutions to her problem. For a woman of her station in life, with four young children, the options were limited. She could just up-sticks and leave, taking the children with her. But what would she leave for? She had no career, nor, in keeping with other women of her kind, did she want one. The idea of leaving for its own sake was simply not done. That was a course of action taken only by the most desperate of women, for instance, those whose husbands beat them up so badly that their lives were threatened. Whatever the conflicts within the Althorp marriage, the situation was by no means at such a point. Moreover, the prevailing attitude for women in Frances's predicament was, and still is, that it is a fair exchange to stay with a man whose attitude leaves a lot to be desired, as long as your way of life remains secure and agreeable in other respects. That was the option which Johnnie's mother had taken, and Frances, being no revolutionary, opted for a variation on the theme.

There was also another lure. They still had that powerful physical attraction between them, although even this would eventually diminish under the vicissitudes of marital strife. "Not for them the 'grit your teeth and get it over with' attitude of so many other nobs and royals, who marry for position and progeny," a well-known member of a ducal family said. "They were both very physical people. Very sexual. You could see it by the way they behaved towards each other. They were very affectionate, but more in an 'I want to get you into bed' sort of way than in a romantic way. There was a certain chemistry between them."

Despite the pleasures of the marital bed, there was no doubt to onlookers that Frances and Johnnie were coming unstuck. Where she sought erudite and scintillating companionship, he went in search of mindless pleasures. A hunting, fishing, shooting countryman, he could not transform himself into an effervescent companion. Defeated by a life that was going nowhere but downhill, Frances took to going up to London, letting Nanny care for the children and leaving Johnnie to trek over the fields of Norfolk in pursuit of game, while she lunched and supped with friends. It was all very innocent, but it was establishing a pattern.

The children, meanwhile, were enjoying a contented childhood. Park House was still a happy house. Frances, whose major attribute was not so much her excellent legs, her handsome face, her cultivated interests, or her undoubted intelligence, as her superb companionship, brought a sense of fun to the commonplace pursuits of life which lifted them, and her, out of the ordinary. Frances set the tone for life at Park House. It was fun. It was orderly. It was down-to-earth. It was warm and affectionate. The basic structure was just as it had been in the days when her mother was chatelaine and Park House had been her parents' home, although much of the formality and the quantity of household staff were reduced. With six servants, it might nevertheless have been an Edwardian household, but for the fact that everyone mingled. According to one of the household staff, who was there throughout the last four years of the Althorp marriage, "Lady Althorp was a wonderful woman. Always laughing. She treated me and the others like friends rather than staff and she spent a lot of time in the nursery. It wasn't a case of children upstairs and adults downstairs at all. She would always be there in the evening for cuddles and bedtime stories and then she and Lord Althorp would have their dinner at 8 o'clock. They did a lot of entertaining and the house was always full of lights and warmth and people in the evenings. In the daytime it was full of noises the children made because of the little school there."

The governess, Gertrude Allen, still came in from the village each morning to teach the children. Diana, like Frances, began her education at the age of four, along with "ten or twelve children from the local farms and the doctor's son."

"The family," according to this member of staff, who still works on the Sandringham estate and sees the Princess, "were not at all snooty. In fact they seemed quite ordinary. Diana was a cheerful child with a good sense of humour and lots of confidence. She had the habit of putting her head on one side even then. It is nothing to do with shyness. Then the troubles started between her parents. Things got bad. There were rows."

A relation states, "Up until that point, Frances had done her level best to keep things sweet. Johnnie says he thought the marriage was happy, but it was plain to see that it was not. In fact, that statement tells you a lot about the sort of person he was, and why the marriage was not happy. Frances wanted a companion, someone with whom she could share life, someone with whom she could enjoy herself, someone who appreciated her and treated her as she required. She's got precious little credit over the years for having kept things together as well and as happily for as long as she did, and a lot of blame for doing what women of less character would have done long before. It's not fair."

A positive and determined woman who would not allow anyone or anything to stand in the way of creating a charmed and charming world for her children, Frances was nevertheless an increasingly unhappy and unfulfilled woman. Their good sexual relationship and a positive approach to her problems had not been enough to prevent her from beginning to despise her husband, and it was inevitable that she would take a way out of her unsatisfactory marriage when it presented itself.

Frances's escape materialized in 1966, in the guise of Peter Shand Kydd. Educated at Marlborough and Edinburgh University, this former naval officer and wallpaper heir was the antithesis of Johnnie Althorp. The only qualities they shared were height, good looks and money. Where the Viscount was boring, Shand Kydd was scintillating, adventurous and entertaining. Where Johnnie was pompous, Peter was refreshingly bohemian, with a liberal attitude towards life and people. He was one of life's contributors. He was not afraid to strike out in new directions, to use his imagination. He had energy and vitality, and when Frances and Johnnie met him and his wife Janet one fateful evening in 1966 at a friend's dinner party, it should have been apparent to all onlookers that the spark of attraction between Frances and Peter would soon ignite, consuming the dead wood of her marriage as well as the thriving contentment of the Shand Kydd's happy home.

Like many another couple who would not otherwise be drawn to each other but for the interest that lies between one's wife and the other's husband, the Althorps and the Shand Kydds struck up a friendship. This allowed Frances's and Peter's attraction to flourish, and flourish it did, especially after they went on a skiing holiday together. Once more, Frances was embroiled in an overwhelming romance. Here was the answer to her prayers, the realization of her dreams. Here was a man who had all the passion, the sparkle, the interest, the appreciation and the liveliness that she needed.

For his part, Peter's position presented him with a dilemma. He loved his wife. They were happy together, as she would confirm to friends before the divorce became final. "I still find it hard to believe," Janet Shand Kydd said, and was so traumatized by what happened that she has never remarried. But Peter was in the grip of a passion over which he had no control, and on that skiing trip the romance with Frances changed gears. Janet was not blind to what was going on right under her nose, but Johnnie, "in his complacent and bumbling way, was," as one friend put it.

The Althorps and the Shand Kydds, despite appearances to the contrary, did not have a great deal in common, aside from wealth and the occasional mutual friend.

Married in 1952, Peter and Janet Shand Kydd had been living the life of a wealthy and privileged young couple in London, but a scratch on the surface would reveal that their social position was precarious to say the least. They were generally acknowledged to be rich and agreeable but common, a damning indictment for a couple who were as socially active as they were.

They gleamed more brightly, however, when Peter's half-brother Bill married Christina Duncan, whose sister Veronica was married to the elegant and witty Earl of Lucan. Bill and Christina were dedicated party-givers, and soon the name Shand Kydd was appearing on society mantelpieces with their engraved "At Home" cards. Despite also being thought "common," they were now much in demand, and all but the most snobbish of the social world's elite flocked to partake of their hospitality.

Peter and Janet, meanwhile, produced three children: Adam, Angela and John. Although less "fashionable" than Bill and Christina, they were also in demand, and it seemed to onlookers that their life would continue in its elegant and unruffled way forever.

In 1963, however, Peter changed direction totally. He withdrew from the family's wallpaper business, turning it over to his brother Bill. He bought a thousand-acre sheep farm in Australia, and took his family to live in the middle of nowhere. Home was now what one Australian who knows the place calls "an average sort of Australian farmstead house: tin roof, boringly functional furniture, verandahs. In the grip of the drought there's nothing but shrub. Even the sheep look depressed. The centre of the universe it's not. The closest place of any consequence is Canberra. The town has two pubs and two shops, but what it lacks in sophistication it makes up for in a great surfing beach at Mollymook which Diana used to go to."

After three years, the family had a surfeit of primitive living and moved back to Britain. Within months of their return to Britain, Peter and Janet's marriage was under severe strain due to Frances's provocative presence.

So too was the Althorps' union. Frances has usually been portrayed as a "bolter," an impetuous woman who abandoned home and children in a mad rush to seek satisfaction in her lover's arms. This could not be further from the truth. Although both Frances and Peter knew that their feelings for each other were strong and deep, neither was sure initially where their hearts would lead them. This is not exceptional. Most married men and women who find themselves in love with someone other than their spouse feel their way gingerly. Unless they are stupid or irresponsible, which Frances and Peter most decidedly were not, they take care not to dismantle the structure of their lives until they are absolutely sure what they want to replace it

24

with. So it was with Frances and Peter. From their meeting in 1966 until well into 1967 they maintained the status quo. They were no different from thousands of other men and women who find themselves in love. Like other women in the same position, Frances obviously asked herself, "Will he leave his wife for me? Dare I leave my husband and take the chance? What if I end up without husband and lover? And what about my reputation? Do I throw caution to the winds and grab this chance of happiness, or do I play safe, and move only when it's all right to? Or when I have to?" Peter also obviously asked himself, "How can I leave my wife? She's been a good wife. She's done no harm. How can I hurt her? Will this romance last? Do I really love Frances? What if I leave Janet and I then discover that I made a mistake? How can I disrupt my life until I'm absolutely sure what I'm doing?"

For over a year Frances and Peter watched and waited while their feelings for each other grew. It was not, for all its passion, excitement, and rewards, the happiest of times, filled as it was with uncertainty and conflicting loyalties. Then in September 1967 the two elder Spencer girls, Sarah and Jane, were sent to boarding school at West Heath. Diana was still at school downstairs at Park House, being taught by Gertrude Allen, while Charles was just coming out of the toddler stage.

Shortly after the departure of the girls, Johnnie and Frances had a tremendous quarrel at a party. Outraged and humiliated, Frances stormed off, saying how tired she was of the marriage. The next day she packed her bags and left Park House, Diana and Charles following the day after. Unable to bear her marital purgatory any longer, Frances had embarked upon what she and Johnnie deemed a "trial separation."

Moving into a flat in Cadogan Place, a short walk away from Sloane Square and one of the smartest areas in London, Frances enrolled Diana in a day school and Charles in kindergarten. Violet Collinson, a housemaid from Park House, came to act as cook (she worked with Frances until her retirement), and soon they were all settled into a comfortable and agreeable routine.

"Frances was a passionate and devoted mother," a well-known relation says. "The idea of abandoning her children, for any man or for any other reason, would have been unthinkable. It has been particularly galling for her that the world believes, to this day, that she just upped and left, dumping the children like compost in a storage shed. She did not. She took them with her, and fully expected to have them forever."

For the remainder of 1967, Diana and Charles lived with their mother in London while their father continued residing on the Sandringham Estate at Park House. "He appeared not to be devastated by her departure," someone who knew them at the time confirmed. Nor indeed did the children seem particularly distressed by the disruption in their lives. "Diana was a delightful and mischievous little girl. Very self-confident. Always laughing, like her mother. Charles was very young, of course, but he too was a well-adjusted and happy little boy," that same relation confirmed.

Events, however, were rapidly moving to an unpleasant, and, to those who knew Frances, unjust denouement. "Frances is essentially a very civilized person. She's also very fair and correct, and it never occurred to her that there would be a problem with Johnnie if she behaved with her usual rectitude. So she took the children back to Park House for Christmas. It was a fatal error. By this time Johnnie knew the game was up, that the marriage was well and truly over. Frances wanted a divorce. She wanted to regularize things with Peter, and even if their romance petered out, she still wanted her freedom. No matter what, she had had enough of life with Johnnie. His response was to dig his heels in—I believe initially in the hope that she would come back. He refused to let her take the children back to London with her when the Christmas holidays came to an end."

Stunned by Johnnie's behaviour, Frances tried everything in her power "to get him to change his mind." Neither patience nor civility, time nor reasoning proved to be on her side, however. Rooted to the spot with a stubbornness which his youngest daughter would later emulate, sometimes with equally disastrous results, Johnnie enrolled Diana and Charles at Silfield School in nearby King's Lynn. A small school, similar to what the children had known under Ally, it was run by Jean Lowe, the headmistress, and classes contained a maximum of 15 boys and girls. Diana was enrolled into the first form, for five- and six-year-olds.

Ms. Lowe was favourably impressed by the education which Diana had received to date. She could read and write well. She also seemed a happy and well-adjusted little girl. Bright without being academic, cheerful and mischievous, she took part in all the outdoor games with relish: rounders, netball, and all the other activities which took place on the tennis court or in the garden.

Pleased though Frances was by how well the children were adjusting to life without her, she was profoundly distressed by being kept apart from them. However, too much had happened between herself and Johnnie for her to contemplate returning to him, so she took the only other course of action open to her. She began legal proceedings for custody of the children and the dissolution of the marriage.

The children, meanwhile, were beginning to be affected by the separation from their mother. The effects would only increase with the passage of time. Charles, by nature a more sombre personality than his older sister, became positively taciturn, while Diana, always so willing to please anyone she liked, started showing signs of churlishness and rebelliousness. Her nanny, Mary Clarke, remembered how seriously affected she was at that time. She took to locking the maids in the bathroom, throwing their clothes out of the house, and chattering, for the first and only time in her life, non-stop.

Diana also, rather touchingly, became a surrogate mother to her baby brother, and one relation believes that "her definite affinity with small children and the vulnerable stems from this period. She took Charles firmly but lovingly in hand, making him tidy up his room, pack up his books at school, and do the myriad things that little boys are meant to, but often do not, do. She became a real little mother hen, and you can still see the evidence of that when she stoops to speak to an AIDS victim or squeezes the stump of a leper's hand."

Life for the two Althorp children who were at home with their father was grim. Gone was the sunshine which their mother's presence had brought, clouded by their father's desire to have control of them. It was not that Johnnie did not try, for he did. Nanny Clarke remembers him joining them for tea in the nursery, which was the children's province at the top of the house, and the place where they spent most of their time. But the special relationship that they had with their mother just did not exist with their father, and it was all very hard work. He was not relaxed with them and they were uneasy with him. He would ask them about their day at school. They would give him a specific reply, lapsing into silence until he asked his next question, to which they would once more provide a precise answer before falling silent once more. They never initiated conversation with him. Finally, in desperation, Nanny suggested bringing the whole painful procedure to a close by enlarging the boundaries of their existence. Diana and Charles were allowed to join their father downstairs for lunch, and gradually, with Frances's regimen altered, and with new habits introduced, they all began to relax more and more in each other's company. But the joyousness for which Frances had been responsible would never return, and no matter how used everyone got to the new situation, it was a poor substitute for the old one.

If life was not working out for Frances in one way—she was torn apart by what was happening with her children—in another direction it was. On 10 April 1968, Janet Shand Kydd sued her husband for divorce. Peter would soon be free, even though the price was high. The grounds were adultery and Janet named Frances as the co-respondent. The newspapers eagerly picked up this latest episode of the aristocracy being caught with its trousers down, but it was hardly a major scandal, more a minor but highly embarrassing sensation. Where it was harmful, however, was in Frances's custody hearing.

In divorce actions involving minors, the custody of the children is usually decided before the divorce itself is dealt with, and so it was in the case of Althorp *versus* Althorp. This was heard behind closed doors in the Family Division of the High Court, as is usual in such cases. Protecting the privacy of the parties was not a favour granted to this aristocratic couple, but a legal device by which all children in Britain, no matter how well or humbly born, are shielded from the prying eyes of the public and the airing of their parents' dirty linen.

It was just as well that the law took such care, for the case of Althorp *v.* Althorp would prove particularly nasty, though not for one second did Frances imagine that she could lose. In 1968 women were automatically granted custody of their children unless the court deemed a mother, in the very rarest of circumstances, to be so unfit, by virtue of extraordinary and extenuating circumstances, as to be an actual threat to their welfare. Obviously, there was no such danger where Frances, Viscountess Althorp was concerned. She was a good and loving mother. She was a reputable and well-known member of society. The only blemish to her reputation was her association with Peter Shand Kydd. It is interesting to wonder whether the whole course of the divorce might not have been different had Frances run off with a duke instead of a wallpaper merchant, albeit a rich one. However, as even prostitutes were customarily awarded custody of their children, as long as they were not shown to be child-batterers, it was inconceivable that any court could find a reason for depriving Frances of the same right.

What happened next would shatter the Althorp and Fermoy families for all time. Ruth, Lady Fermoy chose to support Johnnie's side rather than her daughter, Frances. She viewed her mother's actions as a betrayal, and has never either forgiven her or forgotten that Ruth helped to deprive her of her children.

Although Barbara Cartland would later tell the wife of a deposed head of state that "Lady Fermoy bravely supported Johnnie against Frances," Ruth Fermoy's stand in the divorce action drew widespread criticism. Richard

29

Adeney, the eminent flautist, says, "I met Lady Fermoy when I went to play at the King's Lynn Festival and stayed with her as a houseguest afterwards. She was charming and very hospitable. Later on I mentioned this to a friend of mine who was professionally involved in the divorce. He said he strongly disapproved of her stand."

It takes no great imagination to see that, if strangers should feel so strongly about a mother behaving towards a daughter in such a manner, Frances, Ruth's own daughter and the person so disadvantaged by her actions, was hardly likely to take a more lenient view. And Frances did not. "She is a great letter-writer and wrote a vitriolic letter to her mother over the court case," Barbara Cartland said, revealing that Frances did not take her mother's stand lying down, but put the mirror of a daughter's outrage to Ruth's conscience. Thereafter, she uttered not one word to her mother for several years, and while they now speak, their relationship has all the warmth of an Arctic winter.

But why did Ruth do what she did? A famous and aristocratic connection of the Royal Family explains, "You must understand how people like Ruth think. She has a dyed-in-the-wool courtier mentality, and many of them, I hate to say, become so caught up in the atmosphere surrounding the [Royal] Family that they become pseudo-royals themselves.

"At that time, it was unthinkable for a member of the Royal Family to be divorced. This, remember, was pre Princess Margaret's divorce and Prince Michael's marriage. So the courtiers, aping the royals, considered divorce unacceptable for themselves. I could go on and on about the many other ways in which they emulated the royals, but this is the one that's material here.

"Frances, of course, got caught out when Mrs. Shand Kydd cited her in her divorce. As a result, she broke Cardinal Rule No. 1: never be found out; never frighten the horses; never let your private matters spill out into the public arena. I personally don't believe that she would have been banished from the royal presence the way Lord Harewood [The Queen's first cousin] was, when he was divorced and it emerged that he had fathered an illegitimate child by Bambi Tuckwell, who is now his Countess. To be blunt, Frances wasn't important enough to the royals to warrant ostracism by them." But she was important enough to her mother, and Ruth, fired up with indignation that any daughter of hers would allow herself to be placed in such a predicament, took steps to distance herself.

Respected by one and all, from the Queen Mother downwards, for her grasp of and adherence to the correct way of behaving as a member of the charmed royal circle, Ruth joined forces with her son-in-law the Viscount to deprive her own daughter of permanent custody of her four children. The one question no one asked was: why would a mother take her son-in-law's side against her own daughter in a divorce, unless that daughter was so depraved as to be an actual threat to her grandchildren's safety? As this was patently not applicable in Frances Althorp's case, the onus for Ruth's actions should logically have fallen upon Ruth, not upon Frances. But life, as Frances was learning to her bitter cost, was not always logical nor fair, and the onus fell upon her.

CHAPTER THREE

After the Spencer
Divorce

*T*o Frances, the loss of custody of her children was devastating, and was a wound which she will take to her grave. No one needs much imagination to appreciate how furious and betrayed she felt. But Frances was not her mother's daughter for nothing. She also had spirit and backbone, resilience and indomitability, and once she got over the shock, her equilibrium and optimism returned. Her petition for divorce on the grounds of cruelty was due to be heard in December 1968. She was confident that once that succeeded, she would regain custody of the children.

Sadly, it was not to be. Frances was about to learn a lesson that aristocratic woman after aristocratic woman has had to endure throughout the ages. Nor was it a lesson that was lost on her children, especially Diana, who gained valuable insights into how her world functioned, with the result that she was worldly wise beyond her years, and would later have the advantage of perspicacity lurking beneath a veneer of youthful blandness, when she became involved with The Prince of Wales.

There are some whose loyalties go where they perceive the greater part of the privilege and social cachet to be. In aristocratic circles, when a couple is divorcing, those people therefore often take the man's side. Johnnie Althorp, after all, was the one who was a viscount, the heir to a great earldom, a beautiful stately home and countless treasures therein. He was the one with the greater social position, and it would only increase when his beastly father obliged him, and everyone else, by dying. Thereafter, his supporters would be able to enjoy the rewards of friendship, amongst which would be the delights of staying in one of England's greatest stately homes. I know from personal experience that, inconceivable as it may seem to people who do not live in such a world, many socially prominent people will do anything to be invited for the odd weekend in a big house. It is one of the more astonishing features of a privileged existence, and one which I still cannot understand. You would imagine that true friendship, real decency and loyalty are more important than the perks of nobility, but not, experience and observation have taught me, to your average ignoble nob. Nor were these lessons in treachery being learnt by Frances exclusively. Diana and her sisters were also receiving an eye-opening exercise in the workings of a world that can be as cynical as it is seductive. The result was that they had an appreciation of what worldliness really is all about at a much younger age than most other children. Diana especially became aware of the pitfall of public opprobrium as well as the technique for manoeuvreing an enemy into it, and these early lessons would stand her in good stead later on in life.

The social world can be as harsh and heartless as any courtier's heart. Its rules, though more complex and sometimes more tolerant than a courtier's, are equally straightforward. The name of the game, not to put too fine a point on it, is position. You either have one or you do not. Depending upon where you are in the pecking order, you either rate a lot, not much, or not at all. At the top of the heap, in order of precedence, is the Royal Family. Younger royals such as The Prince and Princess of Wales count for more than older royals like The Duke of Edinburgh or Queen Elizabeth The Queen Mother, though The Queen remains resolutely in the premier position. Glamour also counts for more than rank, which is why Princess Michael of Kent is more of a crowd-puller than the Duchess of

33

Gloucester, but in any toss-up between two royals, the more popular is always the more desirable, irrespective of rank.

Immediately beneath the Royal Family are the ducal families. The richer and better known dukedoms such as Westminster and Beaufort mean more than the poorer or more obscure ones like Manchester or Somerset. But the ducals are very much like the royals: they all rate, no matter what. Below them, divided into two basic camps, are what can be called the upper and the lower aristocracy. The former includes families like the Spencers, the Pembrokes, the Howard de Waldens and the Baths, while the latter features families whose names are known only to those who read old copies of *Tatler* or Jennifer's Diary in *Harper's & Queen*. While the uppers count for a lot socially, the lowers, bearing third-rate titles like Countess Alexander of Tunis, are on a par with second-string celebrities like Michael Winner the film director. In the fiercely hierarchical world that the popular press calls "high society," that is only a cut above having no position at all, and while any position, no matter how ignominious, is better than none, the lowers invariably end up being placed somewhere between the salt and Siberia at grand dinner parties—present because of who they are, ignored because of who they are not.

Not everyone, of course, cares about who occupies what place in the social pecking order. Many people who have valid places in society choose their friends because of what sort of human beings they are. Others, however, have very strong herding instincts. They like their own kind. They are uncomfortable with faces that do not fit. And, knowing that others judge them by the company they keep, they try broadly speaking to keep the best company they can. They therefore pad out their drinks and dinner parties, their weekend house parties and dances, with as many social luminaries as they can attract. And if they can have a royal or a ducal instead of a lower, they most certainly will.

Frances was about to learn just how expendable the lower rungs of the social ladder are when the socially aware are confronted with a choice between a lower and an upper. The timing of the lesson was 12 December 1968, when her divorce petition came up for hearing. The cruelty of the world which she had inhabited, and to which she had added so much light, would give her quite a jolt. It made the law of the jungle, where animals never kill for anything but survival, seem tame in comparison, and the mauling Frances received left deep and abiding marks on this woman whose chief crime had been to hang in too long with a bad marriage.

Johnnie laid the ground by fighting her application with a vigour and an ability that surprised many who knew him, calling upon a variety of character witnesses, amongst whom were some of the grandest names in the country, to vindicate him of her accusations. While Frances was naturally enough embittered by so many of her friends and her own mother acting against her interests, and there is no doubt that the motives of some of them were questionable, others were undeniably motivated by genuine friendship for Johnnie and true disapproval of Frances's departure.

Of course, the reality of most marriages takes place behind closed doors, and this was as true of the Althorp marriage as it is of any other troubled union. No one could speak with absolute authority about what had transpired between the couple, except themselves. But this did not prevent some of the character referees from putting aside such considerations, along with the loyalty that they owed to Frances, and coming out in favour of the next Earl Spencer to the detriment of the future Mrs. Peter "social nonentity" Shand Kydd. Once more Frances felt she was drinking of the poisoned chalice of betrayal. This time, however, the draught was public. Very public. Johnnie cross-petitioned for divorce, citing adultery with Peter Shand Kydd in Queen's Gate. To that, of course, she had no defence, for Peter had as good as admitted adultery in his divorce by not defending Janet's action.

All the less august segments of the press carried the story of the Althorp divorce, allowing their readers to consume Frances's distress with their morning coffee. A titled schoolmate of Diana's remembers, "Her parents' divorce was a big thing. Everyone knew about it. It was there, incredibly messy, this really awful thing. Diana and the others [Sarah and Jane] knew everyone knew. The effects lingered for ages, as these things do."

Embarrassing and upsetting as Sarah, Jane, and Diana found the mud-slinging and muck-raking—Charles was still too young fully to appreciate what was happening—their distress was nothing compared to their mother's. Frances's petition for divorce, which she had hoped would regain her custody of the children, failed due to the stance of her mother and some of her friends. On the other hand, Johnnie's petition, not surprisingly in the light of the *de facto* admission of adultery in the Shand Kydd divorce, succeeded. In the eyes of the world, Viscount Althorp was vindicated. He was seen as the victim, his wife the culprit. He was seen to have suffered at her hands, not vice versa. The myth of Frances the Bolter and Johnnie the Victim was born. Even worse, from her point of view, was the fact that custody of the children was to remain with Johnnie.

"Although the children did not seem to take sides, they actually did," a relation said. "They were definitely pro their mother." One other bright spot illuminated this bleak period of Frances's life. On 2 May 1969, one month after her divorce became absolute, she married Peter Shand Kydd. They took up residence in Sussex and settled down to a happy married life. Anonymity became the cornerstone of their existence, but they were not hiding away from the world, not even when they went to Australia for months at a time, as they did each year.

"They were too contented, and Peter's always been too much of an individualist, for them to worry what 'society' was thinking of them," a family friend says. "But Frances was very bitter about what had happened. In her opinion, it was a disgrace."

The victorious father and grandmother, meanwhile, were finding that responsibility for children in a motherless household could be daunting. Sarah was often virtually uncontrollable. Once she even brought her horse into the drawing room. Jane, although more pliant, felt the absence of her mother acutely, as did the rebellious Diana, whose refusal to toe the line at home continued to worsen. Charles, being still less than five years old, was the only child whose behaviour and attitude remained relatively trouble-free although he also missed his mother acutely. Diana remembers him crying himself to sleep at night, and this has influenced his adult view of family life, resulting in him being an exceedingly devoted father. Both Johnnie and Ruth, who spent as much time with the children as she could, exercised tolerance and indulgence. One of their household staff noticed that "They ignored most of their antics, even when Sarah brought the horse inside. You could see that they thought, 'If I ignore this, it will go away.' So they acted as if everything was normal, even when it wasn't. And it usually wasn't."

With hindsight, it is possible to see that indulging the children in their bad behaviour was not the wisest course of action to pursue. Sarah and Diana especially grew up with the notion that they should be allowed to do exactly as they pleased. In their opinion, anyone who sought to curtail their activities or stand in their way was mean, ghastly and seeking to deprive them of their God-given right. Self-indulgence, in other words, became not a failing but a right, and this is an attitude which has created untold havoc in The Princess of Wales's marriage and in her life. "She was always a spoiled brat," a school friend said. "Sweet when everything was going her way, but spoiled. She's still the same. A real angel until you cross her, then watch out. She becomes a real demon."

This lack of discipline at Park House was not helped by Frances, who was understandably intent on re-establishing any maternal influence she might have lost as a result of the divorce. "Although she had not wanted the children to become the battleground between Johnnie and herself, now that they had become precisely that, she was not about to stand by and see them slip from her grasp," a cousin says. "So she stood her ground." The children, for their part, felt her influence and imbibed her opinion of their father.

Being old enough to understand more than Charles, but young enough still to be at home, Diana saw more of her

37

mother than her elder sisters, who were safely away at boarding school. After each visit to Frances, it would take days for Diana to settle down and treat her father with love and affection. The bond between mother and children remained as strong as it had ever been, and Frances would always continue to be the dominant influence in her four children's lives.

Upper-class girls and boys are inevitably sent to boarding school, however, and in September 1970, a year and a half after her parents' divorce, Diana was dispatched to Riddlesworth Hall in Norfolk. Over an hour's drive away from Park House, Riddlesworth is a large and attractive neo-classical house in the depths of the country. Like the Sandringham Estate, its aspect is bright and sunny, but the terrain is neither hilly nor interesting.

Riddlesworth was a comfortable place for Diana, an extension of the world she had known since early childhood: lovely surroundings, well-tended, well-staffed, and agreeable. The house itself had high ceilings, intricate mouldings, impressive panelling, just like countless other houses owned and visited by members of the aristocracy. The tone of the school was similar to that set by Silfield and Park House both before and after Frances: you were expected to have good manners, to think of others, to behave in the aristocratic tradition. Admittedly, Diana had had a glimpse of the savagery beneath the veneer, but she was still expected to conduct herself with charm and grace, kindness and consideration. To her credit, she usually did.

Riddlesworth also had a good academic record. Its headmistress, Elizabeth Ridsdale (the girls all called her Riddy), was a solid chip off the traditional block of education. You learnt by rote. You were taught the significance of history as it had always been handed down, remembering dates and why they mattered. English literature and language were also subjects which the girls were expected to grasp well. They would not leave Riddlesworth failing to know who Wordsworth was, any more than they would depart without appreciating the subjunctive. Similarly, they would be drilled in mathematics, geography, and all the other subjects in which they would have to be knowledgeable, three years hence, when they sat their Common Entrance examinations for public schools like Benenden, where Princess Anne was a pupil from 1963 to 1968, or Felixstowe.

It quickly became apparent, however, that the Hon. Diana Spencer, though quick on the uptake, would never shine academically. Moreover, she took a while, as do all but the most unusual children, to adjust to life away from home. She was dreadfully homesick at first, but once she made the adjustment, Diana shone in the field of human relations, as she would later, after she became The Princess of Wales and darling of all but a few who meet her. Vibrant, enthusiastic, and energetic, she was friendly and eager to please, and before the end of her first term, she had made several friends. Significantly, she did not have a best friend, preferring to spread herself thin. This is a pattern that has lasted throughout her life, and an early indication of self-reliance and cautiousness.

One of her school friends remembers, "She was very self-confident, loads of fun. She laughed a lot and got along with all sorts of people. What she never did, though, was break new ground. She never took the initiative. She was a follower, someone who would come into a situation, adapt to it, then make it work to her advantage. She's still like that. In fact, her adjustment to being Princess of Wales has been similar in many ways to her adjustment to Riddlesworth. She had a fitful start with both, felt her way tentatively, got her footing, then grabbed the ball and ran with it."

So well did Diana run with the ball that at the end of her first year, she was awarded the Legatt Cup for helpfulness. "Always one to please," as one of her nannies has said, she had learnt the value and rewards of pleasing.

Riddlesworth was typical of schools of its kind. It paid due attention to how its girls performed out of the classroom, not only with regard to their general demeanour, but more particularly to their physical education. It was here that Diana excelled. A gifted and impassioned dancer, she "fell in love with ballet" by her own admission, to such an extent that she took extra lessons in the subject.

In winter the girls played hockey and netball, but in summer they switched to tennis and swimming. She loved tennis, but it was swimming which she took up with a vengeance. A born athlete, with the fiercely competitive personality of a winner, Diana was not afraid to work hard when she wanted something. Swimming became her primary athletic passion, and she spent many an hour improving her strokes and perfecting her dive, until it was ripple-free. In her final year, all the hours of practice, all the energy of competing inside and outside the school, paid off, when she and the other members of the Riddlesworth swimming team won the Parker Cup. She never won any prizes for tennis, but that did not prevent her from enjoying the game, and taking her love of it into adult life.

Her attitude towards sport was an indication of how her character was developing. "Aside from being competitive, she is extremely determined and will take great pains, go to any lengths, to get what she wants," says someone who has known her well over the years. Duties apart, she still swims every morning of her life, driving over to Buckingham Palace at seven o'clock and doing twenty lengths in the pool before returning to Kensington Palace for breakfast. She also plays tennis whenever she can, usually at the Vanderbilt Racquet Club in London.

Having settled in at Riddlesworth, Diana was relieved that her parents did not disrupt the harmony. Everyone, as we know, had heard of the scandal of the Althorp divorce, but no one, not even the teachers (who were on the lookout for such things), could find fault with the way Frances and Johnnie now conducted themselves. They always came to visit separately, on alternate weekends, making sure that there was no further cause for conflict. Finally, they were holding true to the aristocratic dictat of not spilling their messes into the public arena.

For her part Diana, like many other children whose parents divorce, developed a dignity that was impressive in someone so young. She always acted as if there was nothing amiss, and quite possibly, as one of her school mates said, "that is because, to her, nothing was. This was infinitely preferable to being tugged to and fro and fought over, with everything appearing in the gutter press." Her teachers also noted this, though they felt that she would never have revealed what was going on behind her agreeable façade even if she had been upset. "Even then, Diana was very controlled," one commented.

In 1973, Diana sat her Common Entrance examination. It was not one of those pass or fail examinations. Certain of admission to West Heath, her mother's Alma Mater, she prepared to leave Riddlesworth and move south, to Sevenoaks in Kent.

West Heath is housed in yet more agreeable surroundings. Once more, it is pretty and well run, well cared for and well situated. A large Georgian house, surrounded by verdant and undulating countryside, serves as the main building. It is a small school, with some 120 pupils, drawn from varied but privileged backgrounds. Queen Mary had been a student there when she was Princess May of Teck, though she did not achieve the peaks of Diana's mother, Frances Burke Roche, who was captain of everything. Diana's sisters had also attended West Heath. Both set excellent academic examples for her to follow. Sarah, a noted equestrienne who had inherited her grandmother's talent on the piano, passed six O Levels. Jane, who was a senior and a prefect when Diana arrived, whizzed through eleven. Diana was no dunce, but the school watched to see if she would display a greater interest in academia than she had shown to date.

The headmistress of West Heath was Ruth Rudge. An Australian, whose avowed aim was to instil character and confidence, she made all West Heath girls do community work. Diana's undoubted talent for speaking to the aged and infirm was developed at this stage, when she had to visit an old lady in Sevenoaks every week, doing chores for her such as shopping and light cleaning. She also looked in on handicapped children at a home nearby. Miss Rudge remembers Diana as having a mixed standard of behaviour. Sometimes she was well-behaved, sometimes she was not. She had, in short, a perfectly normal deportment record, though another West Heath girl recollects, "She could be really nasty. That look, which everyone now

41

thinks is so sweet. If everyone had been at West Heath, they'd know it's anything but sweet. She used to make the younger girls tremble with that look. It meant, 'Watch out, you're in big trouble.' It always meant that she was really furious about something someone had done. She had quite a temper, believe me, and she made sure she always got what she wanted."

Just as Diana's determination manifested itself early on, so did an eating pattern that would waver between abstention and indulgence. She was prone to put on weight, but she also liked her food. As she herself admits, "I have a huge appetite." Each morning at breakfast, which the girls ate at eight sharp, Diana would help herself to three or four helpings of All Bran. Nor could she resist baked beans, and would not stop eating until she had polished them all off. Diana's sister Sarah had also been prone to overindulgence, although her taste ran to something rather stronger than food. It resulted in her departing from West Heath under a cloud, for Sarah, though abstemious now, had a highly developed taste for alcohol in those days. By her own admission, she drank anything she could get her hands on: whisky, cointreau, sherry, or, most usually, vodka, because it could not be smelt on her breath. She marked this habit, which she shared with preceding members of her family, down to boredom. One day, however, the fumes which she thought she concealed so well did prove to be detectable, and she was duly dispatched from the school with a haste that was as unseemly as it was final.

Athleticism was something all the children inherited from their mother. Like her sister Diana, Sarah excelled at tennis and diving, even more so than her youngest sister, whose greatest passion was, and would remain, dancing. It was while she was at West Heath that Diana learnt the first of several bitter lessons in disappointment. Her ambition was to become a ballet dancer, but, as her height kept on increasing to such an extent that she became a veritable asset in netball, she realized she would never achieve her wish. She had grown too tall for a career as a dancer, though this did not stop her from still throwing herself into her ballet and tap classes, a love which she has retained to the present day.

At West Heath, Diana excelled no more in academic life than she had at Riddlesworth. "The trouble was," a school friend remarked, "that she spent every prep reading Barbara Cartland romances. There was a vast pool of her novels at West Heath, and Diana was one of the prime contributors. The girls bought stacks of the books and rotated them. They just devoured them as quickly as they could, before handing them on for someone else to read. We all hoped that we'd grow up to live a life like a Cartland heroine. She often got in trouble for reading after lights out: we all did.

"It wasn't that she was stupid. Anyone who knows Diana knows how quick-witted she is. But she had this emotional hunger for passion and romance, for being wanted and needed, and didn't give a stuff about passing exams or keeping up with the school work. She had absolutely no intellectual curiosity, no interest at all in improving her mind or learning about issues. All she wanted, all she has ever wanted, was to be liked and loved. She's still like that. The fact that she's now begun to develop her mind is as a result of becoming involved in work that brings her what she needs emotionally: public approval, being liked and loved. That's what motivates her. That's what always motivated her. But, now that her brain has been awakened, she's learning that it can be fun to be knowledgeable. Not that she's intellectual or ever will be, for she won't. She's a creature of the heart, not the mind."

Her headmistress did not remember Diana as being of an intellectual bent either, though she did assess her as of average intelligence. Where Miss Rudge remembered her pupil as being outstanding was in the area of dress sense. Even at that early age, Diana had a superb eye for colour and the knack of wearing striking clothes that flattered her. Her meticulousness about her appearance came naturally; it was an integral part of her character and extended into other areas of her life, as did the simplicity which she brought to selecting eye-catching clothes. Even when weeding, the Rudge punishment for minor infractions of

43

the West Heath rules, her headmistress recalls her looking glamorous.

West Heath was a school with clearly defined conventions, as the stylish singer Baroness Izzy van Randwyck, a contemporary of Diana, remembers: "Younger girls never spoke to older girls unless spoken to. I was three years younger than Diana so we weren't friends. One never is when there's a large age gap, but the school was small, so everyone knew everyone else. She was sweet, but she was no angel. She could get up to things like anyone else." Other contemporaries included such disparate girls as the former tennis star, Annabel Croft, and Lord Ampthill's daughter, Vanessa Russell. Vanessa and Diana, being the same age, struck up a friendship. But they also had another bond. Vanessa's father had been the subject of a scandalous divorce, in which his father had unsuccessfully tried to disprove his paternity while he was still a baby, and during the girls' school years together, the ugly question of Lord Ampthill's paternity once more reared its head. His younger half-brother took him to court in an attempt to prove that he, and not Vanessa's father, was the rightful Baron Ampthill, providing lurid scandal and speculation. The Ampthill case titillated the British people and the massed ranks of the aristocracy in much the same way that the Althorp divorce had done, and the one person who comprehended what Vanessa Russell was going through was her good friend Diana Spencer. But while Vanessa developed a dislike of being the centre of attention and thereafter never had a taste for publicity, Diana, who understood only too well publicity's interweaving threads of attention and anguish, glamour and vulnerability, had acquired a predilection for being the centre of attention and did not, in the slightest, fear publicity.

♔   ♔   ♔

·

CHAPTER FOUR

The Coming of Raine

*D*iana's teenage years were spent at West Heath. By this time, her life had assumed a rhythm and she split the school holidays between her parents. Her step-sister Angela Shand Kydd recalls their happy upbringing together and how, "My father and Frances originally lived in Sussex for four or five years before going up to Scotland where he farms." This farm is located in Perth, but there is also a house deep in Campbell country in the Highlands of Scotland near Oban, situated on the Isle of Seil. The island is separated from the mainland by a narrow stretch of water that is technically the Atlantic Ocean, and a short and narrow humpback bridge joins the two bits of land in what is often and fancifully referred to as "the only bridge over the Atlantic." While strictly speaking this description contains a measure of accuracy, it is hardly the Golden Gate Bridge and would never have rated comment from anyone had Frances Shand Kydd's daughter not married The Prince of Wales. As so often happens when royalty become involved, however, delusion and illusion run riot with fact and good sense.

According to Angela, "Diana and I grew up together with all the others. We spent our holidays together until we were in our late teens. Both lots of children spent equal time with both lots of parents, except that I think Diana and the Spencer children spent marginally more time with their mother. Perhaps more like 60/40. Anyway they were all enormously close to her and we all got along very well.

Frances is very good with people. Everyone always likes her and Diana certainly takes after her in that respect."

Life had settled down, but not for long. In June 1975, just before Diana's fourteenth birthday, her grandfather died. Her father became the 8th Earl Spencer, brother Charles took over as Viscount Althorp, and she and her two sisters all became Ladies. When school was out, Diana went home to Park House to discover the chaos of all the family's possessions being packed into crates and boxes for the move to Althorp. Having not been to her ancestral home since her parents' divorce eight years earlier, Diana was daunted by the prospect of moving to a strange place. So anxious was she that she fled to her friend Alexandra Loyd, whose father was the Queen's land agent at Sandringham. Scooping up all the peaches in the house in a quest for comfort, the girls headed for the family's beach hut at Brancaster, which had been the scene of many happy outings over the years. They polished off all the peaches, Diana consuming more than her fair share.

Althorp, to which the family moved, was a magnificent house set in a 600-acre park on an estate of 13,000 acres six miles north-west of Northampton. As with boarding school, once Diana made the adjustment, she settled in well. The servants remembered her as a happy and well-behaved teenager without airs and graces. She often came into the kitchen to talk to them, and practised her dancing for hour after hour on the black and white marble floor of Wootton Hall. She "lived in jeans, seldom wore make-up, and, in summer, could be found swimming if she wasn't dancing." Diana had her own bedroom and bathroom, in what had once been the night nursery, on the first floor near her father's suite of rooms. Her quarters were simple and comfortable rather than luxurious, as befitted any aristocratic teenager. In her bedroom there were twin beds, a sofa, and bookshelves containing her vast collection of Barbara Cartland romances, while her bathroom was pure Edwardian.

Diana's bedroom was sparsely furnished, in sharp contrast to most of the other rooms in the house. Whether they were the larger guest rooms, the state rooms, or the family's private rooms, all were unabashedly luxurious. Althorp had one of the finest collections of eighteenth-century furniture in the country, and it was difficult to sit or sleep on something that was not worth several thousand pounds. The pictures were also spectacular—portraits and landscapes by the finest artists of their day: Reynolds, Gainsborough, Kneller, Van Dyck, Rubens. Most of these treasures had been left by Diana's ancestor, Sarah, the first Duchess of Marlborough, to her favourite grandson, John Spencer. They were ideally housed, for Althorp is a beautiful setting. Built in 1508 by Sir John Spencer, who made his fortune from sheep farming, the house was extensively altered between 1787 and 1790 by Henry Holland, the Prince Regent's architect who was responsible for much of the architecture associated with his patron's name. It was Holland who added the white brick façade, which, though weathered by the years, gives Althorp its light and distinctive air.

Inside the house was even more beautiful than out. The rooms were large and well proportioned, with high ceilings beautifully moulded. From these hung stunning chandeliers, whose lights were reflected on the marble floors. With the exquisite tapestries, the eighteenth-century silk curtains, the paintings, furniture, porcelain, rugs, books, and silver, Althorp was a singular treasure: all who knew it say it was truly magnificent.

Into this bower of eighteenth-century delights came Raine, Countess of Dartmouth. She was having an affair with the new Earl Spencer. The wife of the Earl of Dartmouth and eldest child and only daughter of Barbara Cartland, Raine had been a well-known, indeed highly controversial, figure for years. As a vociferous Tory councillor for Westminster and a member of the GLC's Historic Buildings Board, she had acquired a reputation as a powerhouse and did what she believed in, brooking no opposition from those who stood in the way. One famous incident started at Heathrow when she rattled the British Airports Authority about the cleanliness of teacups at the airport, creating a hue and cry that played and played in the gutter press. Raine was, and still is, tall and striking, with clear alabaster skin and auburn hair. She is always impeccably dressed, overdressed, her detractors would say, but, in fairness to her, it must be acknowledged no more so than any other good-looking and aristocratic woman of her generation.

My stepmother-in-law, Margaret, Duchess of Argyll, has known Raine since she was a little girl. "Barbara and I have been friends ever since I was a deb [in 1930]. She's a good friend. She's very loyal. Always there when you're in trouble. Everyone likes Barbara. On the other hand, Raine has never been popular."

According to a close friend of the family, "Barbara, as you know, is brilliant with publicity, and I believe she's always advised Raine on hers. If something's written about her she rushes to Barbara and says, 'Mummy, what should I do?' Barbara says do this or that.

"Dartmouth's a nice man. Forgettable, but nice. And Spencer, well, we all know about Spencer."

More than one person told me that Raine had set her cap at Johnnie. But, whatever her motives, Raine went for it, and her husband divorced her for adultery after a tragicomic scene at the Dorchester Hotel.

"Raine and Johnnie had been having what we can politely call a tête-à-tête," a member of one of Britain's most scandal-ridden aristocratic families said. While they were deeply involved in their private discourse, "he was suddenly taken ill with his first stroke. Not the major one, but a warning. They had to call an ambulance and take him to the hospital, with Raine standing by, looking bedraggled and forlorn. It was obvious what they'd been up to. After that, the divorce was inevitable." Despite her professed stand on the sanctity of marriage, Barbara Cartland supported her daughter during the ensuing divorce, in an admirable lesson in loyalty that Ruth, Lady Fermoy, might have done well to notice.

Having lost one earl, however, Raine was disconcerted to discover that the other one was curiously reluctant to slip a wedding ring on her finger. Nothing she said or did seemed to make a difference. Johnnie, as Frances could have told her, was not the easiest man to budge.

Raine turned to her eldest son, Viscount Lewisham. William Lewisham has never ranked high on my list for Brainbox of Britain. Nor did I consider perspicacity to be amongst his attributes, until one evening over dinner he recounted how his advice helped his mother to entice Earl Spencer. "Get yourself asked on someone's yacht and go cruising for two weeks," he recommended. "Make sure he can't reach you."

"But William, I can't do that," Raine protested. "It won't be any good unless he can speak to me."

"It won't be any good if he can," William counselled. Raine took his advice, and shortly after her cruise, in July 1976, Johnnie Spencer married Raine at Caxton Hall Register Office in Victoria, London. None of his three daughters and son, nor her three sons and daughter—William, aged thirty-one, Rupert, twenty-nine, Charlotte, eighteen, and Henry, twelve—was present.

The reign of Raine has been a long-running saga that has provided constant gossip for the aristocracy and intermittent entertainment for the masses. Sarah, Jane and Diana disliked their stepmother from the word go. "I would sooner take up residence in Lenin's Tomb, cuddling his corpse for warmth, than have Raine Dartmouth for my stepmother," Sarah said before the wedding.

Barbara Cartland declares that the girls used to tell their father, "You can marry anybody except Lady Dartmouth," whenever the subject of marriage was mooted. "But Johnnie and Raine had a passion which, in the end, he found irresistible," claims a famous socialite who knows the family. "They were so hot for each other that once, en route from I believe it was London to Althorp, they had to pull into an inn and have it off before continuing their journey. They remained highly attracted to each other, after years of marriage, until his death."

Being a stepmother is never easy, and Raine just might have had a difficult time with her stepchildren even if she had been a different sort of person. For instance, there was the occasion of her son's fortieth birthday. A friend of William Lewisham recounted: "William told me his mother didn't even send him a birthday card. She forgot it was his birthday. I felt so sorry for him. Can you imagine a mother forgetting her eldest son's fortieth birthday? There's no love lost between his sister Charlotte and Raine either." But neither Raine nor her ever loyal mother could see that her behaviour and attitude might have contributed in any way to the antipathy which Sarah, Jane and Diana showed her.

According to Raine, during this period Sarah deliberately snubbed her at every turn. She gave orders over her head to the servants, was hostile, and pointedly rude. Jane, on the other hand, took the opposite course of action. She refused to acknowledge Raine's existence, even when she brushed past her on the stairs. For two years, not one word to Raine escaped through Jane's pursed lips. Diana, she now says, was more friendly, though only Charles, who was still very young, could be fairly said to have been truly pleasant. Time, however, would alter that happy state as well.

There is an alternative interpretation as to why the girls behaved the way they did, and it is supplied by yet another well-known figure: "The possibility is that Raine swept in, the way she always does, reordering everyone, everything, and everywhere, to her taste and predilection. The girls, especially the elder ones, would take strong exception to such a woman taking over. If you haven't seen Raine in action, you cannot believe her. She's like a tank rolling over ants. Like many powerful people she doesn't realize the effect of her strength of character. Naturally, the children's mother told them to stand up for themselves. Any mother would, though a fat lot of good it did them."

Barbara Cartland gave a glimpse of the family's life in the early days. "I would see Diana when I went to Althorp for lunch on Sunday. She was then a little girl of sixteen and she used to seize the pile of books I brought with me and run off and read them. Of course Raine had four children herself. It was always arranged that they would come at different times to Johnnie's children and therefore they were never particularly good friends."

What Barbara Cartland did not say was that the divisions within the family went further than that. Nor did time heal the breach that quickly developed. Sarah and Jane saw as little of Raine as they could. So too did Diana, who took to visiting Althorp and staying with Jane at her house on the estate, instead of in her room at the big house. Only too soon, all the girls were going up to Althorp only when they absolutely had to do so. Whenever she had weekends away from school, Diana often went up to London to stay with Jane or Sarah rather than board the train northwards. "The girls still loved their father, but they tried to see him only when they did not have to encounter Raine," a family friend said.

Raine, meanwhile, continued to prevail. "She should be fried in hot oil for what she's done to the house," a Spencer cousin said. "And if they [the four Spencer children] are bitter about the destruction to the house and the dispersal of their heritage, as they indeed are, they should be."

Raine's admirers claim that Johnnie owed over £2 million in inheritance taxes on Althorp when she married him. "Of course they [the Spencer children] should be very grateful to Raine because she saved them millions of pounds," says Barbara Cartland. Lord Montagu of Beaulieu, then Chairman of English Heritage, begs to differ. "The government has a scheme whereby they will accept works of art of a high calibre in lieu of death duties. I have no doubt they'd have accepted pictures by artists such as Van Dyck up to the amount of the death duties. And the paintings could have remained at Althorp, hanging on the walls."

Whether or not the cash raised by Raine to pay off the death duties was money well spent, the indisputable fact is that she brought her considerable energy to bear with all the forcefulness she had displayed as a Greater London councillor. To raise further revenue, she opened a gift shop, to sell souvenirs to visiting tourists; undertook schemes to increase the income from visitors to the house; and even went to the lengths of organizing dinners for paying guests. But, knowing that these measures alone would never be enough to allow her to fulfil her ambition of leaving her mark on Althorp House, she cast around for alternative sources of revenue.

Raine needed to look no further than the walls. Althorp's magnificent art collection would come to her rescue and provide her with the means to decorate the house as she saw fit. So she set about dismantling one of the finest collections of Van Dycks in either private or museum hands, disposing of eleven out of twelve of the treasured paintings. She further organized for Wildenstein, the art dealers, to buy Andrea Sacchi's *Apollo Crowning the Musician Pasqualini* for £40,000. This painting, which had been bought by the first Earl in 1758, was promptly resold to the Metropolitan Museum of Art in New York for £270,000, casting very serious doubts on Raine's financial acumen.

Although the Spencer children were up in arms, accusing Raine of flogging off their birthright for knockdown prices, Johnnie was firmly under Raine's thumb. He could only sing her praises. Tristan Millington-Drake, whose first cousin Duke Alexander di Carcaci is married to Raine's daughter, Lady Charlotte Legge, gave the family interpretation of Raine's abilities. "She is a very shrewd businesswoman. There's no doubt she was a tremendous help to the old boy, who was a real sweetheart and absolutely adored her. If it hadn't been for her, the house would have fallen down around his ears. I admire Raine. She's got guts and spirit. She speaks fluent Japanese, you know. She decided that they had to court the Japanese. So she went out and learnt their language, to be able to deal with them on their level. I think that shows amazing pluckiness."

Johnnie Spencer himself echoed that opinion when a cousin brought up the subject of the vanishing treasures. "She's doing a marvellous job," he said. Politeness alone prevented the person from asking, "Of stripping the house of its treasures or of maximizing your assets?"

As painting after painting, old master drawing after drawing, irreplaceable eighteenth-century china and furniture, even books, flooded out of Althorp, Johnnie's heirs questioned to what use the money was being put. True, the overdraft was cleared, but was it really necessary to continue divesting Althorp of over 300 priceless works of art so that Raine could regild every bit of gold leaf in the house and advise purchasing bungalows at Bognor Regis?

"They were sick when they saw that Raine had flogged an old master and replaced it with a truly appalling portrait of herself, all pink candy floss and sugar and spice. Her taste, I can tell you, leaves a lot to be desired," a most famous arbiter of taste said. "She's her mother's daughter in that respect. You know, plastic flowers in huge arrangements, that sort of thing. All frightfully vulgar. An upmarket version of ducks on the walls."

The Spencers justified expenditure on a scale amounting to millions of pounds by saying that the house had been run down, was in need of structural repairs, and would have fallen down if they had not undertaken the work they did. "I don't agree that Althorp was run down or in need of structural repairs," a Spencer cousin says. "Black Jack [Johnnie's father] might have been a monster who cared about few things, but the one thing he did care about was Althorp. He kept up the house and had superb taste. He also had the intelligence to call in capable people to execute the work Althorp required. In the sixties he got Stephen Dykes-Bower, who was the surveyor of Westminster Abbey, to completely overhaul the place. So when Johnnie inherited, everything was in pristine condition. It sparkled, like the well-tended jewel it was.

"Raine, however, was dissatisfied with Althorp. Its taste was too subdued, too mellow for her. She wanted somewhere that socks you between the eyes with the statement, "I've got money. I've arrived. I'm a grand stately home owner." You know, nouveau aristo taste. So out went the old log fires crackling fragrantly in the elegant fireplaces. In came the fakes that Raine found so pleasing. Wall-to-wall carpeting was laid, concealing beautiful floors and replacing fine rugs. The walls were painted Barbara Cartland pink, or bright blue and riveting green. They went from being walls to a feature that jumped out at you." Having been bitten by the decorating bug, Raine, who claims to have the gift of being able to close her eyes and visualize what an undecorated room should look like down to its last detail, received an added impetus in the refurbishment of

Althorp. Diana married Prince Charles, and Raine and Johnnie became pseudo-royals. She decreed that Althorp, enjoying a resurgence of prosperity due to a rollicking trade in visitors, needed to sparkle as never before. So she called in Partridge (Fine Arts) Limited, the eminent fine-art dealers of New Bond Street, to redo the entire house.

Clifford Henderson, the Chief Executive, is a neighbour of mine, and he was gracious enough to break a long-standing silence as to the exact role played by Partridge in the decoration of Althorp House. "We were responsible for the entire restoration of Althorp, in other words all the furniture, ormolu, picture frames, porcelain, that sort of thing. It took eight years. It was a wonderful job for us.

"Raine is very easy to deal with. She is highly professional. Most times she knows what she wants.

"What the press has never said and don't know is that she was guided by Peter Thornton, who was the head of the decorative arts section of the V & A [Victoria & Albert Museum], and by David Laws of Colefax & Fowler. The criticism has been most unfair. The press doesn't know what it's talking about. They just love to criticize her."

Through that long and happy association, Clifford Henderson became good friends with Lord and Lady Spencer. "Yes, I was on very good terms with Raine and Johnnie. Yes, I had my fiftieth birthday party at Althorp. It was for 100. It was their suggestion originally. I paid for it, but they organized the whole thing from A–Z. It was beautifully done, faultless, and I'm not just saying that. It really was. They could not have been nicer. Johnnie received all my guests and said goodnight to them at the door. He didn't have to do that. It was a cold February night, and the party didn't break up until 12:15. They really gave me the works."

To finance the restoration of Althorp, which the Spencer children and many other people who knew the house felt was completely unnecessary, Raine and Johnnie sold yet more priceless works of art, yet more pieces of irreplaceable furniture. "I used to go and stay with Anton Kristensen [a popular society antique dealer] at Althorp," says Liz Brewer, the socialite and public-relations consultant who specializes in launching people and products into society. "He rented a house on the estate and helped Raine sell stuff."

So too did Clifford Henderson, although he said, "We have a golden rule. We never comment on who buys or sells with us. Obviously you would never want anyone to know if you sold anything through us, so you can appreciate why we have that rule." Nevertheless, back copies of the Partridge catalogue reveal piece after impeccable piece with the unchallenged provenance of Earl Spencer, Althorp.

"The items never realized their full value," claims a titled lady, whose late husband was a friend of Johnnie Spencer. "Their approach was all wrong." This was borne out by Christie's, the auctioneers, who told me that the surest way of maximizing value, especially if you have a well-known name and a variety of pieces to sell, is to hold a sale and bill it as a collection. Had Raine done this, she would have needed to sell only a fraction of the treasures with which she parted subsequently. By this reckoning, she was therefore not a good businesswoman, despite the assertions of her family to the contrary, and the Spencer children were right to bemoan the drain on their inheritance.

Nevertheless, the refurbishment has come in for admiration from some unexpected sources. The Dowager Lady Torphichen's daughter, art restorer and interior designer Anne Hodson-Pressinger, said, "Having heard so much about it, I expected a nightmare. But it's really beautifully done."

Tristan Millington-Drake agreed. "Raine had a dance to celebrate Charlotte's marriage to Alex in May 1991. They opened all the rooms at Althorp and it was a magical evening. I was amazed to see that the place really looks great. It wasn't at all what one had been led to believe. The main criticism has been that the gold leaf is too bright, but Raine is very practical and a good businesswoman. While you can dampen down the brightness, that takes years off its life, and she shrewdly decided to let time do it for her, on the basis that it would then be that much longer before it had to be done again, and also because when the house was first built, it would also have been as bright as it now is. But it doesn't look garish at all. It looks very beautiful. Raine's improvements have been a great success."

No sooner were the refurbishments complete than Johnnie and Raine started selling off the cottages on the estate to raise yet more capital. This was also seriously in breach of the code of conservation by which most responsible aristocrats live. You never sell anything you cannot replace unless your solvency depends upon it. And you certainly never, but never, sell anything irreplaceable to spend the capital realized on something transient or of lesser merit, like selling old master paintings to regild picture frames with gold leaf, or selling cottages to finance a Thirties style of living.

The Spencer children hit the roof. The country-house circuit has its own brand of bush telegraph, and everyone was agog at what was going on. It was virtually impossible to stay in any big house without the subject of the Rape of Althorp arising. This was how Simon Blow, the society journalist and grandson of the eminent turn-of-the-century architect Detmar Blow, came to write the article in *Connoisseur* that once more blew the lid off the animosity within the Spencer family. He was not tipped off by any member of the immediate family, and they did not, according to them, have a family meeting at which they discussed leaking the story to the press.

"Nevertheless, once the story was out, they were all delighted," a Spencer cousin says. "They hoped it would have the effect of staunching the flow." The other side of the family, however, found the publicity painful and appalling. I spoke to Raine's son-in-law Alex. While he was most forthcoming about the feelings of the family, he asked me not to quote him, for it would make life awkward for him. As the only reason he spoke to me was that I am a friend of his father, the Duke of Carcaci, I agreed to respect their privacy. But Tristan Millington-Drake, his cousin, summarized everyone's feelings by saying, "It was a real sore spot with them. They just wished the press would leave Raine alone. They found the whole thing very upsetting."

For his part, Johnnie was furious with Diana and his son Charles, and was quoted as criticizing them as being ingrates. Diana, he also alleged, was too young to understand about money, a comment which said far more about his connection with the realities of life than her financial acumen.

Johnnie Spencer, meanwhile, remained happy with his wife. So what if she was responsible, as his children seemed to feel, for the dispersal of a great part of the Spencer heritage? She was just what he needed. She could control him, and control him she did. Time, however, was not on Raine's side. On 29th March, 1992, Johnnie Spencer died suddenly of a heart attack. He had been taken ill earlier that week and was hospitalised, but was so much on the mend that his daughter Diana felt free to accompany her husband and children on a family holiday to Austria. While she was there, he passed away. Within twenty-four hours Raine vacated Althorp House. She now lives in what would once have been called a "town dower house" in Mayfair, which means that it was bought with her husband's money and reverts back to his family upon her death. Her stepchildren never come to call, nor does she visit them. And, irony of ironies, her stepson Charles, the new Earl Spencer, announced in June 1992 that he would have to sell yet more treasures to pay for the inheritance liabilities of his father's death. "Now that he's in the hot seat, that's how he copes," Raine commented acerbically to a friend when she heard the news. "He's doing exactly what he criticised hs father and me for doing."

CHAPTER FIVE

An Ambition is Formed

Within a year of her father's remarriage, Diana, who had acquired the knack of ekeing out a happy existence for herself no matter the turmoil surrounding her family life, approached the next milestone in her life: her O Levels loomed. But, there was also something more significant happening in June 1977, as she was about to sit and fail her examinations. The happy teenager with a large circle of friends gained a new feather in her cap: her sister Sarah became Prince Charles's girlfriend.

It all began when Sarah became reacquainted with Prince Charles at Royal Ascot. Sarah, Jane, Prince Charles and Princess Anne had been childhood friends. They had gone to each other's birthday parties. Whenever the royals were at Sandringham, they all played together. Frances used to take care of Charles and Anne at parties, and the Spencer children, for their part, all knew The Queen as Aunt Lilibet. But although Charles and Anne, Sarah and Jane had drifted apart with the passage of the years, at Ascot, Prince Charles and Sarah discovered that they had a real rapport. Soon she was his latest in a long line of girlfriends. The Spencers and Fermoys were jubilant. According to a noblewoman, whose brother-in-law occupies one of the most senior positions at court, "Like all courtiers, they have a heightened awareness of royalty. Nirvana lies in a royal connection. Just working for the royals induces an ecstasy exceeding anything else on earth, so how much more heavenly is a personal connection, especially a marital one?"

The Spencers, it seemed, were finally going to go legitimate. Throughout the centuries, the family had had many honoured but illegitimate personal connections with the Royal Family. Three of Diana's antecedents were mistresses of King Charles II: the Duchesses of Portsmouth and Cleveland and Lucy Walter; another, Arabella Churchill, was mistress of his younger brother, James II; and yet another, Frances, Countess of Jersey, of George IV. All except Lady Jersey produced royal bastards, with the result that Diana's children became the first royals to combine the disparate threads of the Stuart and Hanoverian lines, thereby fusing the old and the new Royal Families.

But Diana's family's obsession with the Royal Family did not stop there. Her ancestor Sarah, Duchess of Marlborough was popularly suspected of being Queen Anne's lesbian lover, and during the reign of George II, Sarah offered Frederick, Prince of Wales £100,000—a vast sum in those days—to marry her favourite grand-daughter, Lady Diana Spencer. George II and his heir, universally known as Poor Fred, were tempted. In the eighteenth century, the British monarchy was not as rich an institution as it is now, but the prime minister forbade the marriage. Instead, Frederick, Prince of Wales was married off to the seventeen-year-old Princess Augusta of Saxe-Coburg, and Lady Diana Spencer became the Duchess of Bedford. The Spencers would nevertheless have to wait nearly 250 years for another Lady Diana Spencer to fulfil their lofty ambitions.

In the interim, the Spencers kept up their connections with the crown. Lady Georgiana Spencer, the beautiful and exotic Duchess of Devonshire who was addicted in equal doses to producing illegitimate children and incurring staggering gambling losses, blessed her illicit union with that generation's Prince of Wales (Prinny, the Prince Regent, later King George IV), much to her husband's fury, by producing a little bundle of joy. Thereafter, the closest the Spencers ever came to the throne was to serve it, being honoured in the process by having royal godparents such as King Edward VII.

"When Lady Sarah Spencer started going out with The Prince of Wales," says a noblewoman with senior connections at court, "you could see how elated her whole family was. This was their chance finally to acquire a legitimate royal connection."

Lady Sarah Spencer, however, was not one for fulfilling people's expectations. Although she had come a long way since the West Heath débâcle, and had given up drink, Sarah was having serious problems in coming to terms with life as she was expected to lead it. She was in the middle of waging a battle against anorexia nervosa. This condition is brought on, in large measure, by extreme external pressures exacerbating personality problems stemming from childhood, so it was hardly likely that someone who was already struggling to gain a healthy equilibrium would have the internal resources to handle the pressures that are inevitable with any royal romance.

"Sarah now says with the benefit of hindsight that she didn't fancy Prince Charles and that she was never interested in him as anything but a friend," says a member of one of the great aristocratic families, with connections to the Royal Family. "If you believe that, you'll believe anything. Of course she was interested. And she would have hung in there for as long as it took to get him, but for the fact that her emotions got the better of her. She wasn't strong-minded like Diana or Jane. She was insecure and sensitive, and the strain reached her.

"You have to understand the way the Prince treated his girlfriends to see why she wasn't up to the job—of waiting, I mean. He blew hot and cold, not only with her, but with all of them. One minute he'd be very charming and attentive and the next it would be as if you did not exist. After you'd seen him steadily for several days, you might not hear from him for weeks. It put a terrible strain on anyone, no matter how tough. And Sarah Spencer was not tough."

As the romance spluttered and coughed, Sarah evidently vacillated between hopefulness and assumed disinterest. In November 1977, while she and Prince Charles still harboured hopes for their romance, she asked him up to

Althorp for a shoot. He spent the night, rising early the following morning to join the shoot.

Shooting is primarily a male sport. The ladies join the guns, as the men are called, for lunch. If they are particularly enthusiastic, these women trail after them, picking up the game they shoot and generally doing their best to keep out of the way of gunshot. "A good woman is quiet and invisible," a Scottish friend of mine said. "A gun shouldn't have to notice her unless he wishes the distraction."

The sixteen-year-old Diana Spencer, who was up from school for the weekend, had been reared in this world. She lived by its rules, and still does. That is why, on that Monday morning, when Sarah presented her youngest sister to The Prince of Wales in the middle of Nobottle Field, their first meeting since Diana was a baby, there was nothing outstanding about Diana except her natural prettiness and her height. She was dressed in as low key a manner as every other female on a shoot. Although Prince Charles noticed in a vague sort of way that she was a sweet and fetching young girl, he was not bowled over by her beauty or charm. "All his adult life, you must remember, people have put on their best clothes and manners for him. He does not understand what it is to encounter the whole spectrum of the average personality. It's not his fault. He's simply never exposed to it. Everyone—his private secretaries, his staff, the people he meets in a private or official capacity, his friends, even his cousins—all put their best foot forward," a cousin remarked.

Diana, for her part, found meeting Charles a real thrill, but that should hardly have come as a surprise. He was the world's most eligible bachelor, the Heir to the Throne, and, in person, he has a lot more appeal than he appears to possess in photographs or on the television. He crackles with a wonderful physicality, is warm and charming, with a seductive quality that owes much to his earnestness and intensity. The Duke of Rutland's daughter, Lady Teresa Manners, speaks for many of Charles's admirers when she says, "I can understand why any girl would fall in love with him. He is the nicest, kindest, most delightful man."

He was also Diana's sister's boyfriend. That meant that

she could not dream, not even lightheartedly, about what it would be like to be The Prince of Wales's girlfriend. "When Diana married the Prince, Sarah said that they clicked in that ploughed field, that Mr. Right met his Miss Right. With hindsight, one could stretch a point and make it so, but that's not the way it was," a friend of Sarah's says. "All her life the family [the Spencers and Fermoys] had Diana earmarked for Prince Andrew. They were quite open about it, and it didn't seem at all unlikely. They'd known each other since childhood. Diana was even called Duchess in anticipation of the day when she would become The Duchess of York, which everyone in royal circles knows is the title customarily given to the Sovereign's second son. Andrew and Edward used to go over to Park House to swim in the pool that Lord Spencer built there. They were all pretty chummy. But no one envisaged her for The Prince of Wales. No one. It was just, well, inconceivable."

And so, after this brief and inconsequential meeting, whose significance has been so exaggerated over the years, the shoot continued until lunchtime. Everyone then repaired to the stable block at Althorp to eat. They were served stew with mashed potatoes and brussels sprouts, followed by every public schoolboy's delight, treacle sponge. That evening there was a dinner party which Lord and Lady Freyberg, friends of Lord Spencer, attended. She remembers the occasion well. "My husband and I were at Althorp the night Charles met Diana. We weren't there for the shoot, but for dinner afterwards. She was absolutely sweet. Lord Spencer was very proud of her. He said it was her first grown-up do. I was not aware of Prince Charles noticing her in any special way."

The great romance had not begun.

In December 1977, Diana resat her O Levels. Once more she failed. There was no question of a further education. She would have to leave school. This was not the disaster it might have been for a girl from a less privileged background. Even though Diana had no qualifications, she had assets, and these would stand her in good stead whatever the future held for her. She had a decent-sized trust fund, thanks to her headstrong American ancestor, Fanny Work. She was well connected. And she was personable. If Prince Andrew did not marry her, some other well-born young man would. That would take care of her future.

Confronted with what to do with their daughter until she was old enough to settle down to something definite, Johnnie Spencer and Frances Shand Kydd opted for finishing school. There she would not be stressed academically, but would be safely out of trouble while learning all the useful subjects which might make her future more agreeable: French, skiing, cooking. It was the option they had taken with Sarah after her precipitate departure from West Heath, and it had worked. So, in January 1978, half-way through the school year, Diana was dispatched to the Institut Alpin Videmanette near Gstaad in Switzerland. She had never been abroad before, nor had she ever been on an aeroplane.

Over the years, many rumours have grown around her stay there. But Heidi Yersin, the headmistress, puts paid to some of them. "People say she was homesick and that is why she left early but this is not so. Diana was only ever booked in for one term. She had a good time and wasn't homesick at all. All the pictures of her—that we have at the school—make her look very happy. She studied intermediate French and made fair progress. Her humour made her very popular and she made lots of friends. She wasn't shy at all. More modest. Although she was modest, she could always cope well with everybody.

"Diana only ever went out to the cinema with all the other girls. They were allowed to go into Gstaad and meet up with the boys from a boys' school but Diana never went. We know this because we have checked the records."

Out of a total of sixty pupils, there were nine English-speaking girls at the school. Diana immediately fitted into the group, striking up in particular a close and lasting friendship with Sophie Kimball. Sophie remembers, "Diana wasn't a scrap shy at all. In fact, she was great fun to be with. The school had a chalet in the mountains and we could go skiing for the whole day but then we would have to work very hard the next day at our French." They also learnt other practical subjects such as dressmaking, typing and shorthand.

Sophie Kimball also supplies one of the reasons for Diana's apparent reclusiveness: "There was no social life in Rougemont. It wasn't a large village. We could go into Gstaad, but that just meant sailing around in one of the large *après-ski* places." This sort of activity no more appealed to these well-bred girls than joining up with a load of strange boys whom they did not know. The aristocratic tradition of mixing only with your own kind, and of desiring friendship with no other—not even foreigners who were similarly privileged—was too strong to be broken down in a few short months. This might have changed had the girls faced a stay of years before them, but, as it was, they were happy to stick together for the short time they were in this foreign land.

Later that term Sarah arrived in nearby Klosters on a skiing holiday with The Prince of Wales and the Duke and Duchess of Gloucester. The romance was going well enough for them to be together, but not so well that the impetuous Sarah felt secure or inspired to further patience. "If Prince Charles asked me to marry him, I would turn him down," she declared to a reporter. "I wouldn't marry a man I didn't love, whether he was a dustman or The King of England."

A friend has made sense of her extraordinary behaviour. "I believe she hoped to knee-jerk him into snapping to attention. It didn't work. He was bitterly wounded—he's very easily hurt—and he retreated to his old sources of consolation. But he was interested in her. He was actively looking for a wife and she was definitely a possibility. You know, nice girl, good family, that sort of thing."

Sarah had well and truly blown it. She had humiliated the Prince and broken quite a few upper-class taboos in one fell swoop. Never frighten the horses. Keep things within your circle. Keep your mouth shut in public. And never, but never, speak to the press. Although she remained friends with Charles, she thereafter had no chance of becoming Princess of Wales. Once more, the Spencer dream of a legitimate, marital connection to the Royal Family had been dashed.

Soon afterwards, Diana went home for the holidays. She did not return to the Institut Alpin Videmanette, but Sophie Kimball provides a more down-to-earth explanation than the subsequent and fanciful press speculation about severe homesickness and other such poignant reasons: "Most of the English girls only stayed a few months because the exchange rate was dreadful and it was really very expensive." Diana did not go home to her father. Despite Lord Spencer's hard-won right to custody, it was to Frances's house in Cadogan Place that Diana headed. Thereafter, this would be her primary home until she had one of her own.

Once more, Diana's parents were confronted with what they should do to fill in their sixteen-year-old daughter's time until she was old enough to strike out on her own. Her period of muddling through, of trying to find something to do with her life was just beginning. She did have the help and support of her family, however. Without them, she would never have done any of the things she did, nor would she have achieved the heights which she subsequently scaled. "Diana has never been an independent person. She is headstrong and fiery. She is self-willed and stubborn. But she has never, not once in the whole of her life, ever achieved anything without the help and efforts of others," a courtier remarked.

Her first job she got with friends of the family. It was at the Land of Nod, a house in Hampshire where she worked as a mother's help to six-year-old Alexandra Whitaker, daughter of Major Jeremy Whitaker, a photographer, and his wife Philippa, whose brother Willy von Straubenzee is still a friend. Here she stayed for three months and the Whitakers sing her praises to this day.

After a summer holiday and odd-jobbing as a cleaner, Diana decided to do a cookery course, wisely reasoning that she might as well learn how to cook properly as it was something she could always put to good use in the future. "She was always fantastically domesticated," a friend says, "to a degree that is impossible to exaggerate." So she enrolled with cookery teacher, Elizabeth Russell, who said, "She came in September 1978. We loved her. She was a very good pupil. The course is ten weeks and is designed so that anybody doing it can earn her living from it afterwards."

Her ambition was to dance, not to cook, however, so, after finishing her cookery course, Diana approached Madame Betty Vacani, niece of the famous founder of the Vacani Dance School in South Kensington, who had once judged a dance contest at West Heath which Diana won. "Diana wrote to me and said she had been at West Heath and wanted to train as a dancing teacher. At her height she could never have become a dancer. She was about seventeen at the time, a shy, quiet, nice girl. However, she only stayed a month. She went off skiing and never came back. I think that she felt that the training—three years and until 6:30 in the evening—would be too all-embracing. She never gave a reason for not returning. I imagine that she felt teaching at the kindergarten would not be so demanding." Significantly, Diana did not ask this venerable old lady, who then lived in retirement in Sussex, and who taught The Queen, Princess Margaret, The Prince of Wales and The Princess Royal, to the wedding.

"Diana does not tolerate guilt or failure. Not in herself and not in anyone else," says someone who knows her well, explaining her behaviour towards a woman who was kind enough to give the young, unproven Diana a chance. Nor was this the only manifestation of that particular syndrome. Diana was, and remains, a cleanliness and tidiness freak. Most psychologists claim that one of the classic symptoms of people who do not wish the world to see their shortcomings is a mania for cleanliness or tidiness. Nor was this a trait Diana developed with age. At Riddlesworth she "had to endure the torture of bathing on alternate days," she once told a friend, but by the time she reached West Heath, which allowed only three baths a week on a rota basis, she was sufficiently self-confident to break the rules. Refusing to tolerate what this friend recalls she described as "the grime," she bathed nightly, after lights out, often going to bed with wet hair, for she also refused to be

66

restricted to one shampoo a week, and washed her hair as she bathed. "Even now, she goes absolutely spare if everything isn't spotless. This extends to all areas of her life. Everything must be done exactly as she demands. The house has to be dusted just so. The ornaments placed just so. Her clothes ironed just so. And if they aren't, she makes her displeasure felt. Very forcefully. Very."

At the age of sixteen and seventeen, however, she had no one to bawl out. She was the maid, which was a socially acceptable way of earning money and an effective channel for her disposition. Her sister Sarah was sharing a flat with Lucinda Craig-Harvey, a Hampshire landowner's daughter who later became a theatre producer, and Diana worked for them three days a week. She had to do everything: clean, dust, wash up the dirty dishes, scour out the bath and lavatory. "If she hadn't been good, Sarah would have got rid of her," a friend of Sarah's commented.

This, however, was not enough to occupy her time or bring in the income required to keep up a decent standard of living in London, so sister Jane helped Diana get another job. Kay Seth-Smith, a fellow West Heath old girl whose sister Janie had been a contemporary of Jane's, ran the Young England Kindergarten in a church hall at the corner of St. George's Square and Lupus Street in Pimlico. Hearing that Diana needed work and was good with children, she offered her a job assisting with the new group, for younger children, which the kindergarten had recently started three afternoons a week. Diana's duties included helping the children with their pictures, bricks, and other games, teaching them basic dancing, changing them when they soiled or wet themselves, and cuddling them when they cried. One mother says, "She was really wonderful with the little ones. She had a real empathy with them. It's a gift she has."

Diana still needed more income, however, so she put her aptitude for physical activity to further use and signed up with several temping agencies, including Solve Your Problems, Universal Aunts, and Occasional Nannies. "She came to us with references from the Whitakers and Young England," Jan Govett, formerly of Occasional Nannies, said. "Both were very good. She came to us in October 1979. When she filled out the application form, she crossed out Mrs., leaving Miss. She did not put in Lady. She said that she could swim, play tennis and dance. Also that she could drive and had her own car. She said she would look after children aged between one and ten because, of course, she had no formal training and that made it difficult to care for young babies. One of her references said she would be prepared to help with anything—washing up in particular. As she had no training, she was after being more of a mother's help than a nanny.

"She asked for £1.00 an hour. The first job we gave her was in November 1979 with the Jarmans at Prince of Wales Drive [in Battersea]. Then in January 1980 she got her second job, with Mrs. Patrick Robinson at Belgrave Square, the American wife of an oil executive. She had to give their child lunch, walk it in the park, and give it a nap in the afternoon. She only wanted to work two days a week.

"One of the girls in the office remembers the first time she came in. She was wearing a bright red jersey, a white shirt and jeans. She blushed very easily and smiled too much."

Life was not all work. In fact, Diana made sure, like most well-bred young ladies, that her work revolved around her social life. "Diana was a perfectly normal young girl-about-town," a relation says. "She did all the things young girls of her age did. She had beaux. She went to dances. She went to the cinema with friends, gave and attended dinner parties. She was fanatically neat and was famous for jumping up and washing up the dishes as soon as dinner was over. She'd have washed up your dishes after each course if you gave her half a chance, but she was not prissy. She had a very good sense of humour, was very witty and often had her tongue firmly in her cheek. She was good company and absolutely normal, with all that implies, though she was never much of a drinker and didn't smoke at all.

"There was occasionally talk about her possibly marrying Prince Andrew, but at that stage it was very much just talk. He was still at school, or had just left—no, he was still at school—and they were really too young for anyone in their right mind seriously to expect either of them to settle down."

Diana's fully fledged boyfriend was the Hon. George Plumptre, the third son of an obscure peer, Lord FitzWalter. Eight years older than her and very much a sophisticated man of the world, with all the tastes and demands of his breed, he was the most significant of the relationships she had prior to her marriage. But he was not the only one.

"Daniel Wiggin is the son of baronet Sir John Wiggin. He works with W. A. Ellis the estate agents in the Brompton Road and shared a flat with her brother Charles for a while," says a friend of mine who knows him. "He's godfather to baby Kitty [Diana's niece, daughter of Charles Spencer and his wife Victoria]. He's very attractive: dark, sturdy, not too tall but not short, and sexy. Girls find him devastating. He told me he was definitely her boyfriend even though he's a bit younger than her. He actually said he was *The First.*" Simon Berry of the St. James's wine-merchant family has always publicly denied that he was ever a boyfriend, but I was told that he was briefly a beau. "They didn't hit it off in the romance department, but liked each other, so they became friends," a friend said.

At this point in her life, Diana was living the life of your average, privileged teenager. She spent most weekends in the country, staying either with friends or, very occasionally, on her father's estate in Northamptonshire. She never went alone, and was invariably accompanied by her boyfriend George Plumptre and either with or without a girlfriend or two in tow.

The nuts and bolts of Diana's life during the brief period between leaving school and getting married reveal the typical lifestyle of a young noblewoman. The first car she drove was her mother's blue Renault 5. After passing her driving test on the second attempt, she was given a Honda Civic by Frances. This was soon traded in for a pale blue Volkswagen Polo, and when she crashed it at the height of the press siege in 1980, Charles duly arranged for the Duchy of Cornwall to replace it with the famous red Mini Metro.

For the first year of life in London, Diana operated out of her mother's house, but when that was sold, she got a place of her own. No. 60 Coleherne Court was a spacious three-bedroomed flat. Its bathroom facilities might not have been up to the exactitude of American standards—even though an attempt was made to cheer it up with bright red wallpaper—but the flat had a comfortable sitting room and Charles Stonehill, a friend, remembers "a beautiful, completely modernized kitchen where Diana cooked for her very smart dinner parties."

The flat cost Diana £50,000 in 1979, bought with money which she inherited on her eighteenth birthday from her American great-grandmother, Fanny Work. She spent the next few months happily doing up the place with her mother's help: choosing furnishings, wallpaper and fabrics. "The flat was pretty," says someone who knew it well. "It was tastefully furnished, and charming." In the process of doing it up, Diana discovered something that she would never forget: shopping gave her a tremendous high, a great sense of release and, when she looked at her acquisitions later, of accomplishment.

Sophie Kimball and Laura Greig were Diana's first flatmates. They would eventually be replaced by Carolyn Pride, a student at the Royal College of Music; Virginia Pitman, an Asprey's shopgirl; and Anne Bolton, who worked for Savills the estate agents. All the girls were intent on having a good time. These were the late seventies, when young ladies tested the water before plunging into the pool of marriage. There was no pressure put on them, the way there had been in their mothers' generation, to get married young. The mood of the times was for them to enjoy their youth and freedom, to explore their sexuality gently and discreetly. There was none of the hysteria about virginity of fear of pregnancy, and, as AIDS had not yet been heard of, no fear of death through sexually transmitted diseases. Young ladies were expected to dabble with undemanding jobs and desirable young men until they were well into their twenties, at which point it was hoped they would meet suitable men three or four years their senior, who would offer them marriage and the shelter of the shires or the City.

Thereafter, life would be very much the same as it was for their parents. There would be a weekly round of dinner parties, three children and a nanny, weekends in the country for the urbanites, nights in London for the ruralites. They would do their shopping at Peter Jones in Sloane Square, the General Trading Company just off it, and Harrods or Harvey Nichols when they wanted to splash out. They might appear in *Tatler* once or twice in their lives. But only if they hit the jackpot in a really big way—say, by marrying a duke, a marquis, or, God willing, a royal— would they be catapulted out of the anonymity of the British Establishment into the stratosphere of celebrity. Although Diana's flatmates were not particularly ambitious, she was. "She made no secret of the fact that she wanted to become a member of the Royal Family," a friend said. "She made little comments about it fairly consistently over the years."

Unusually for a creature of the late seventies, Diana wanted to be married as soon as possible. By inclination and aptitude, she was equipped for nothing else. "She knew that she was facing a boring life unless she married well, and she was intent on doing the best she could and as quickly as possible."

Although Sarah had scuppered her chances with Prince Charles, Jane proved to be both a successful role model and a potentially useful tunnel through which shone the beacon of hope. Despite being what one aristocrat described as "so plain even a mouse would look like Joan Collins if it stood beside her," in April 1978, the 21-year-old Jane married Robert Fellowes, the 36-year-old son of Sir William Fellowes. "His father has been The Queen's Land Agent at Sandringham and he was an assistant private secretary to Her Majesty, with all that implies," reports a noblewoman with a well-placed brother-in-law. "That marriage certainly kept the family's royal flame burning brightly. You know, access to The Queen herself; invitations to Balmoral and Sandringham, that sort of thing. It was, in social terms, a very good match. If you can't get a royal or a duke—and there weren't any of those around—the next best thing is, of course, a permanent member of The Queen's staff, which is what Jane bagged. Later he became Deputy Private Secretary, and when Sir William Heseltine left in 1990, he succeeded him as Private Secretary. They were married in great style at the Guards' Chapel. The reception was held in St. James's Palace, and he and Jane took up residence at Kensington Palace."

Jane had always been Diana's favourite sister, although Diana also enjoyed a close, albeit competitive, relationship with Sarah. She was Jane's chief bridesmaid and commented to one friend after visiting her newly-wed sister, "It would be wonderful to live at KP."

Diana's heady ideas about living in Kensington Palace had to take a back seat for a while, however, when Earl Spencer suffered a severe cerebral haemorrhage in September 1978. At fifty-five, Johnnie had seemed a strapping specimen of rude good health. Ecstatically happy to be under the care and control of his indomitable wife, he was preparing to celebrate Althorp coming out of the red when he fell ill. He was rushed to the local hospital in Northampton.

"I know for a fact Raine had a stand-up row with the doctors at Northampton," one of the doctors at the hospital, where he was subsequently taken, told me. "She wasn't right. They would have moved him to a hospital where he could get the treatment he needed." That Raine fought the doctors tooth and nail has now entered the public mythology, and whatever the truth of that matter, there is no dispute concerning the speed with which the perilously ill Earl, given up for dead by the local doctors, was removed to London. "I have to say," the doctor continued, "if it hadn't been for the move, he wouldn't have survived. As much as people kick at Raine, if she really was instrumental in getting him moved—and I am not convinced her fight was necessary—she probably was responsible for saving his life.

"Johnnie was in the hospital for nearly four months. He

was a very, very ill man, as you know. For much of that time, he was drugged up to the eyeballs and when he came out of the coma was not able to speak very clearly. At first he wasn't aware of what was going on at the periphery [with the family]. Only later did he get *compos mentis,* by which time Raine and the rest of the family, who were at daggers drawn, had sorted out different visiting times.

"Raine was very protective of Johnnie. She didn't even want his first family visiting the bedside at the same time as her, though she always brought her youngest son, who was a young lad then, about twelve or so, with her. So they visited around her. They all came. I saw Jane quite a few times. Robert Fellowes was with her. Sarah visited a lot, as did Diana. I saw Charles [then Althorp] several times. Again when Raine was not there. He and Diana were very much a unit—them versus Raine.

"Diana was very upset about everything, understandably. She had had the message spelled out to her that her father was in danger of his life and she was very distressed about it. She struck me as a very nice girl. Not jolly hockey sticks, but a young Sloane around town."

Whatever her motives, Raine went to great lengths to save her Johnikins, as she called her husband. A cousin of the Queen Mother confirms that "The Duke of Portland himself told me that she asked him to arrange for an experimental drug from Germany called Aslocillin to be used on him. They were having trials in Surrey, I believe, otherwise it wouldn't have been allowed into the country. He said that Johnnie Spencer would almost certainly have died without the drug."

For the remainder of his life, Johnnie himself could not praise Raine's spirit and courage enough. One friend said, "He owed his life to her. She literally willed him to live. When he was in his coma, she played his favourite opera, *Madama Butterfly,* over and over again. She'd hold his hand for hours on end and talk to him, telling him he mustn't, he couldn't, die. All the McCorquodales have energy: Raine, Barbara [Cartland], Ian [Raine's half-brother]. She turned on the energy tap and let it flow until he opened his eyes."

The Earl himself told a relation, "She's a miracle. I owe her my life. I'd have died if it hadn't been for her." He remained "very much in love with her for the rest of his life. I've seen her at her worst and her best, and I love her no matter what. As long as I can be with her, I'm happy."

Whatever the merits of the role Raine played, and the evidence points to it being considerable and decisive, Johnnie recovered. "Everyone thinks the stroke affected him and he was radically different than he was. That's not so. He always fumbled and doddered and was slow. It made very little difference," says someone who had known him for decades.

On the very day that Johnnie was released from hospital, in January 1979, Diana and Sarah were at Sandringham for a shooting weekend. "A lot of nonsense has been written about The Queen being so fond of them since childhood that she asked them up for the weekend off her own bat. That is not so. Had Jane not been married to Robert Fellowes, The Queen would not have thought to ask them. They were asked because they were the sisters-in-law of her Assistant Private Secretary, not because they were Johnnie Spencer's daughters and he was ill."

Sister Jane's marriage was standing them in good stead. "She was thrilled to go up to Sandringham that first time. It was like being asked to heaven," a friend said. Diana, moreover, was no Sarah. She had already told a friend, "If I'd had the chance Sarah had [with Prince Charles], I'd never have blown it." All that remained to be seen was whether she would get that chance. And, if she did not, whether she would somehow be able to manufacture it.

The courtship of The Prince of Wales and Lady Diana Spencer was not a straightforward affair. Indeed at first there was not even a friendship, and on that first stay at Sandringham, Diana's high came more from just being there than from any romantic possibilities. Staying at Sandringham, according to a friend of mine who is closely related to the Royal Family, is fun: "The Queen is always very relaxed when she's there. I know you must have heard how she is a countrywoman at heart, but it really is true.

She partakes of all the simple country pursuits, like picking apples herself, and she's never happier than when she's taking a long walk with a friend or relation, the corgis and dorgis running riot, her hair concealed beneath one of those headscarves that she so loves. Or riding. She does a lot of that at Sandringham, regardless of the weather.

"She never loses her dignity, not even with her closest relations, but that doesn't mean that she's stuffy or can't take a joke. She has a wonderful sense of humour and loves a good laugh. Nor is she averse to sophisticated humour. You can talk about anything you want. As long as it's done tastefully, there are no forbidden areas of conversation, which is just as well, for we all know how salty The Duke of Edinburgh and The Duke of York can be.

"The Queen makes everyone feel at home. The public's concept of her being someone who keeps everyone on tenterhooks couldn't be further from the truth. She's a very warm person, cosy almost, though, of course, majestically so.

"When she's at Sandringham, she's surrounded by the people she most cares for. It really is a family home, and house parties there always reflect that. Before his marriage, Prince Charles was often there with a flame, and so was Prince Andrew. The Queen is not an intolerant parent. On the contrary, she's always indulged all her children. I think she feels that their lives are so restricted and duty-bound that she shouldn't add to the restrictions.

"You can tell a lot about a hostess by the atmosphere she creates. The Queen likes her house parties to be harmonious, happy, full of laughs and fun. As a personality, in her private life she is remarkably easygoing and fun loving. Not at all the Miss Piggy of popular myth."

It was into such an environment that the seventeen-year-old Lady Diana Spencer came that January day in 1979 when she and Sarah joined their sister and brother-in-law, who were in residence with The Queen. Diana, of course, had grown up with some knowledge of the court. Her early childhood had been spent on the Sandringham Estate, so she had memories of the excitement which inevitably accompanies the Monarch. She expected heaven and that indeed is what she got.

Most people, even such established and blasé figures as presidents, heads of state and other visiting dignitaries, can find the whole experience of staying as a house guest in one of The Queen's residences thrilling. When questioned later, they invariably comment that it will remain one of the high points of their lives. Even years afterwards, they reminisce about each and every detail, their memories as clear as if they had been guests only yesterday.

"That first stay at Sandringham showed Diana just how heady and agreeable life in the royal circle can really be," a friend said. "She was impressed. It's fair to say she regarded the experience as even better than she expected. But contrary to what some writers have said, there was still no question of this being the starting point of her romance with Prince Charles. To him, she was still little more than a child. Of course, he was very partial to young people even then, but his interest went no further than in being kind and paternalistic."

Diana evidently returned to London and the Vacani Dance School with a host of conflicting emotions. According to this same friend, in some ways she was smitten by the Prince; the small kindnesses he had shown her had fired her imagination. Here truly was a hero from one of the novels whose storyline she hoped to embody in her life. Charles was the most eligible bachelor in the world. Any woman who was lucky enough to become his wife would thereafter occupy one of the most splendid positions on earth—with room for eventual promotion. He was also physically attractive and a genuinely nice person, to such an extent that he had paid a measure of unexpected attention to the adolescent sister-in-law of his mother's Assistant Private Secretary. In other ways, though, despite having her head in the clouds, Diana's feet remained squarely on the ground. She knew that there was no point in dreaming. The Prince had not seen her as an object of desire. Nor did there seem any likelihood that he ever would. The age gap seemed an insurmountable barrier, not because twelve and a half years was so much, but because he was interested only in witty and sophisticated women of the world. And Diana, though witty, was an unsophisticated girl with the scent of school still clinging to her. So she pushed her dreams to one side and threw herself into life as a budding Sloane. It was a poor substitute for the nirvana she had glimpsed at Sandringham, and she told Simon Berry, with whom she went on a skiing trip, "It would be nice if I could be a dancer—or The Princess of Wales."

Like all teenagers whose talents do not match their ambitions, Diana was having problems finding a role that would bring her the attention, activity and satisfaction she sought. Learning to be a dance teacher, especially, had not lived up to expectations. It had been humiliating and taxing, and after she had given it up, without even bothering to provide Madame Vacani with an explanation, and returned to charring, many people, including The Queen, expressed reservations about her staying power. Yet, whatever Diana's failings, laziness and lack of resourcefulness are not amongst them. When she was not cleaning flats or babysitting, she was game for anything that would occupy her and bring in a bit of extra money. One of her jobs was with William Worsley, son and heir of landowner Sir Marcus Worsley, Bt, the Lord Lieutenant of Yorkshire who is the Duchess of Kent's brother. Diana painted the ground-floor room of his Bourne Street house, and "did it pretty well too."

Fortunately, her social life was proving to be more rewarding than her career, even if the set she was moving in was not the most glittering in society. Her circle of friends, though well-born and nice enough for her to have contact with to this day, was certainly not the smart set. They included the Hay brothers, the Earl of Erne's daughter, Lady Cleone Crichton, Rory Scott, Sophie Kimball, and Laura Greig. They did not have the impact of great status or fame, and the same was true of her. She was just another pretty well-connected girl, like thousands of others who make up the padding of the Establishment and go on to spend the whole of their lives in comfortable obscurity.

To describe the budding Diana as immemorable might

seem harsh, but that is precisely what she was. I know this to be a fact because occasionally I ran across her at large parties given by mutual friends. I have absolutely no recollection of her, even though I recall her name in connection with her father and stepmother. Yet there are other girls of the same age whom one remembers, either because they were outstandingly beautiful or had striking personalities, or because they were naturally charismatic or just ugly enough to stand out.

It seems, if her friends can be believed, that Diana had not yet gained entry into the charmed inner circle of The Prince of Wales. He was not taking her out at this time. "I've read that she used to go to the theatre and the opera with him occasionally. That's absolute nonsense. He didn't ask her out, not even to make up numbers. Diana was very open about what she was up to, and I'm sure I'd have been told if she had been seeing him," says a friend. "Look at it sensibly. Why would a busy man about town of thirty, who has more friends and acquaintances than he knows what to do with, take out an eighteen-year-old girl who he's not even interested in bonking? It's just too ridiculous for words."

So Diana's life continued on its pleasant but dull and aimless course. The high point was her eighteenth birthday and the purchase of Coleherne Court, until in July 1979 Diana received another invitation to join the Royal Family, this time at Balmoral. Once more, this was directly due to her brother-in-law, Robert Fellowes, and sister Jane, who were justly availing themselves of the perks of his position. But there was also another purpose in asking Diana. "All their lives the girls had been told that Diana was reserved for Prince Andrew. Having her around was a way of keeping the flame alight, of keeping her under his eye, so that, when he was ready for marriage, he'd need look no further than her. It was a speculative and long-term thing rather than short-term and calculating—the way it sounds when I'm telling it. It was deliberate but not cold-blooded," a Spencer cousin remarks.

Diana gave every indication of enjoying herself at Balmoral, according to a member of the royal circle who was there. She fitted in well and was as much an asset as you could expect of any eighteen year old, thrust into older and more sophisticated company. She had a good sense of humour, was ready and willing to join in the fun, and, without being pushy, was gently flirtatious. It was also on this occasion that she began to think more about Prince Charles. "It was still more a dream than anything else, but her interest did grow, and she developed what I suppose you could call a crush on him. I believe what appealed to her was a mixture of him being The Prince of Wales and actually taking the trouble, yet again, to be nice to her," says a friend of hers. "She was really thrashing about for somewhere to cast her anchor. Remember, her life away from the Palace set wasn't exactly intriguing. When she wasn't charring she was rattling around London having a rather more low-key time than she wanted. Royal life had a very powerful appeal for her, with all its glamour and comfort and status.

"This was when thoughts of a marriage with Prince Andrew receded into the background. She started saying that she'd love to become The Princess of Wales. It seemed to be the position and all it offered that attracted her, as well as Charles the man. I'm positive she would have felt the same way if he'd been a lot less nice, but his niceness made it easier for her. There isn't any doubt that she was exceedingly ambitious, far more so than her abilities warranted, and while I have no doubt that she did fall in love with him —she's very romantic and wouldn't allow herself not to be madly in love with whomever she set her cap at—I am also sure that she would never have given him two moments' pause if he hadn't been who he was."

A former member of the Royal Household who knew and remembers her well from this period concurred. "At that time, she would have fallen in love with any unattached Prince of Wales as long as she stood .000007 per cent chance of becoming Princess of Wales. Even if he had three arms, was a Cyclops, and spat when he spoke. Is that love, or love of position?"

But Diana was not yet really in love with Prince Charles. Although he was officially available, he was not unattached, and she knew it. So she hovered, like a skier at the top of the slope, waiting for the propitious moment to push off in one direction or the other. If she spotted a chance of getting the heir to the throne, she would zoom off towards him. But if she did not, she would hold herself in reserve for his younger brother. Only when she knew it was safe to move would she allow herself to fall in love. She was, it seems, remarkably perspicacious, sensible and self-protective for all her romanticism.

At the end of this royal visit in 1979, Diana once more returned to London and a life that, for all her undoubted efforts, seemed to be irretrievably bogged down in a morass of ordinariness. Unbeknownst to her, however, things were about to look up. A happy series of divergent activities brought new meaning to her life. There was the thrill of doing up her first flat. There was the joy of the jazz, tap and keep-fit classes which she took at the Dance Centre in Covent Garden, where she had enrolled after leaving Vacani's in March, and whose meaning to her cannot be exaggerated. Diana herself says she adores dancing, and she never failed to leave Covent Garden without the glow of doing something she loved. In September, she started her work at the Young England Kindergarten, which she describes as "a very happy time." Her social life, despite not being high calibre and exciting enough to satisfy her ambitions, also kept on throwing up friends whose companionship delighted her. They gave and attended dinner parties in each other's flats, dined in Sloane hang-outs like Topolino d'Ischia in Draycott Avenue, Foxtrot Oscar in Royal Hospital Road, and La Poule au Pot in Ebury Street, where the food is good and substantial, the décor upper class and understated, and the atmosphere redolent of quiet wealth and accustomed privilege. Diana did not go to a great many parties, but she was often at the cinema with friends like Simon Berry and her boyfriend George Plumptre, and with the passage of time she has come to value the friends of her youth in a way she did not when she first became Princess of Wales.

"Diana is very practical. She was biding her time until she could get what she wanted. In the meantime, she was enjoying herself. She didn't see the need to force the pace.

She was young—too young really for what she wanted—and the one virtue she has always had is patience," says a friend. An aristocratic relation gives another interpretation. "Watchfulness might be a more appropriate word than patience, but there is no doubt that she is the sort of person who knows exactly what she wants, then waits until she can get it. If she'd been a wild animal, she'd have made an excellent hunter."

CHAPTER SIX

The Goal Draws Nearer

*I*n May 1980, Sarah Spencer married Raine's cousin, Neil McCorquodale, a farmer, at Great Brinkton Church on the Althorp Estate. Diana was chief bridesmaid. She was also acerbic about a marriage that would prove to make her sister happy, allowing her to indulge her passion for horses and giving her the emotional security she craved. "It's Westminster Abbey for me—or nothing," she commented acidly, unimpressed by the ordinariness of upper-class country life: the life which yawned before her unless she could manage a royal union.

It did not seem very likely with The Prince of Wales. Everyone in royal circles knew he was desperately in love with Anna Wallace, whom he had met in 1979 while out hunting with the Belvoir. This is one of the finest hunts in the country; its ground is on the Duke of Rutland's estate in the Vale of Belvoir. That same month, James Whitaker, the noted royal journalist, whose proud boast is that he never leaves his house without a pair of binoculars, zeroed in on Charles lolling about on a blanket with the sensual Anna by the banks of the River Dee at Balmoral. This was behaviour that was very out of character for a man who would normally have been fly-fishing. When Charles realized he had been spotted, he sent Lord Tryon, the husband of his confidante Kanga, to chase away the reporter and

Ken Lennox, who was trying to get photographs. Anthony Tryon did so, telling them to clear off with a four-letter word, but it was too late. They already had the picture they needed. And Whitaker, who understood the significance of what he had witnessed, duly conveyed it to the world.

Diana could not have failed to know what was going on. But, as she was not yet actually in love with Charles, it did not affect her unduly.

Over the years, there has been a considerable amount of conjecture about the Prince's relationship with Anna Wallace. Accounts in the press and books have differed widely, with some writers claiming that it was not a big romance, some saying it was not even a proper romance, and others saying that he wanted to marry her. So I asked a member of the Royal Household who was on the scene at the same time as Anna. "She used to come to the Palace constantly. She knew her way around it—his office, his apartments, how to get to them from the side door, which everyone uses. She was often there, out of view of the press and public.

"He was deeply in love with her. He proposed to her. She didn't turn him down. They had agreed that she should think about it. It was while she was doing so that they broke up. I was sorry about it. He definitely should have married Anna instead of Diana. He'd have been much happier with her. She was right for him; Diana isn't. He and Diana have the same needs. That's their problem. They're both after the same thing. They can't give it because they both need it. Anna could satisfy his needs though. Anna is far more intelligent and less needy emotionally than Diana. And The Prince of Wales is an intensely sexual man with overpowering sexual needs. Diana couldn't cope. How do I know? Because of something she told me. Obviously I can't quote her. That wouldn't be suitable. But she definitely said that he was too highly sexed for her.

"But you could see, just from watching them together, that he and Anna shared a great and successful passion. I was often with them. When they were in the same room together, the air just crackled with desire. He couldn't take his hands off her, and the way he looked at her was enough to make your heart flip. It really was very touching."

A prominent merchant banker explained what it was about Anna that men, Charles included, found so captivating. "I had a short but intense affair with Anna Wallace. It only lasted about six weeks, but I can see why Prince Charles fell in love with her. She has a tremendous amount of personality and character. She's great fun, very intense and intelligent, interested as well as interesting, passionate. She's got a beautiful face and a flawless figure. There's a very down-to-earth side to her. She'll say exactly what she thinks, and it's people's problem if they don't like what they're hearing. It's absolutely true that he proposed and that she wouldn't say yes. What was the effect? It only made him keener."

Anna was an expert equestrienne who shared Charles's love of hunting. Her nickname was Whiplash, not because of her ability to wield a hunting whip, but because of her tongue, which she did not hesitate to use when she became angry. And she had a quick temper. "If she didn't like something, she said so," says the former courtier. "The Prince wasn't used to people treating him in what the Americans call so 'up-front' a manner. It perplexed and enchanted him. To her, he was just another man, even though he was The Prince of Wales and she was never disrespectful. But she gave no quarter because of his rank. That really intrigued him. All his life people had been influenced because of who he was instead of what he was. This was the first time he'd ever had anyone who was really totally unimpressed with Charles the prince but loved Charles the man."

Charles the prince, however, botched it up for Charles the man. "He always blew hot and cold," says the same informant. "One day he'd be all over the latest girlfriend like a rash, then she wouldn't hear from him for three days, sometimes even a week. He was totally selfish. It wasn't that he intended to be hurtful. Ever since he was a little boy, life had revolved around him. Having his own way, thinking only of himself, of what he wanted and how and when he wanted it—and being very cross if he didn't get it

—was a way of life for him. He'd never had to think about anyone but himself. It wasn't a question of people letting him get away with it. This was the way life had always been for him, and all his other girlfriends had complied with the way things were. But not Anna. She wasn't putting up with any nonsense from anyone, not even The Prince of Wales."

There were some funny and some notable scenes. Once, at Windsor Castle, she asked Charles for champagne. He returned with a glass of brown ale and said to the disbelieving Anna, whose father Hamish was a sophisticated Scottish millionaire landowner, "Mummy's got the key to the drinks cupboard." Then there was Queen Elizabeth The Queen Mother's eightieth birthday party, which also took place at Windsor, and ended on a rather sourer though equally unimpressed note for Anna. Charles, mindful of his duty to mingle with as many of his grandmother's guests as he could, left Anna to her own devices for most of the evening. At first, she was tolerant. She knew where his duty lay and was not about to lambast him for doing it. However, she became increasingly annoyed as time flew by and still Charles kept himself scarce. She was not about to tolerate anyone treating her in a cavalier and disrespectful way, and prior to flouncing out she snapped, "Don't ever ignore me like that again. I've never been treated so badly in my life. No one treats me like that. Not even you."

Had that been the end of the romance, Lady Diana might have breathed more easily. But it was not, not quite. What finished it off totally, and ruined any chance of revival, was Prince Charles's conduct at Lord Vestey's ball at Stowell Park, Gloucestershire. Instead of paying court to Anna, he spent half the evening dancing with Camilla Parker Bowles, who, up to the time he started taking out the Whiplash, had been considered the great love of his life. Anna stormed out in a fury. Shortly afterwards, she became engaged to the Hon. Johnny Hesketh, younger brother of Lord Hesketh, the Tory politician and motorcycle manufacturer. "She married Johnny Hesketh on the rebound. Getting involved with someone else was her way of ensuring that she wouldn't be lured back into continuing the affair with Prince Charles. She didn't want to be messed around again. She knew she'd made a mistake within a week. Johnny Hesketh wasn't right for her," says the banker who had the romance with her.

Charles was disconsolate. "He was very, very depressed when Anna left him," says the former member of the Royal Household. "He'd really loved her and he'd ruined it."

One person, surprisingly enough, who did not regret the demise of Anna's relationship with The Prince of Wales was her former employer, Lady Renwick. Better known as Homayoun Mazandi, the Caviar Queen of Belgravia, who, upon arriving in London from her native Iran, amused everyone in fashionable circles by travelling in a chauffeur-driven Rolls Royce with a hired black cab leading the way so that her chauffeur could learn how to get around town, she has had a veritable string of glittering social secretaries. Aside from Anna, these have included Princess Michael of Kent when she was Marie Christine Troubridge. Homayoun told me, "Anna is a very good girl. She was a good social secretary and did her job well, but he [The Prince of Wales] chose the right person for the job. Anna wasn't up to it. She's very trustworthy, a good girl, but for sure she couldn't be Lady Di. Lady Di is good with people, with children and adults—she has the right touch. Anna doesn't. Although she gets along with some people, if she doesn't like someone, she shows it. She's too black and white. She's a very good person. She's not tricky. She's outrageous but straight, maybe too straight. She's a girl you can rely on, but she loses her temper very quickly. She gets along with animals, especially horses, better than with people. Nor did she get much support from her family for whatever she was doing. Her problem is that she has bad taste in people, and this and her temper have affected her life. No. Anna wasn't up to the job. In the end, The Prince of Wales chose the right person." That conclusion was one which Lady Renwick arrived at in early 1991, before the events surrounding Diana's thirtieth birthday party in July 1991 and the publication of the Morton book in June 1992. Since then, The Princess of Wales's reputation has eroded considerably in Royal circles. It is no secret that she was behind both attempts to elevate herself at the expense of her husband's reputation. While she has succeeded in winning column inches and support from the general public, who do not fully appreciate her part in those episodes, she has tarnished her halo to a considerable degree, and is presently as *declassé* amongst the *cognoscenti* as it is possible for any Princess of Wales to be. But more of that later.

That summer of 1980, while Charles floundered around morosely, Diana's chance presented itself. "Robert and Jane knew that the romance had busted up and Diana was keen to have her opportunity with the Prince," says the courtier. "Jane had just had a baby and so they asked her up to Balmoral in July."

She went and, according to a member of the royal party at Balmoral, "played Charles like Nigel Kennedy plays the violin. She has absolutely wonderful instincts. She knows just what to say or do at any given moment to make people like her or to achieve whatever else it is she's after. She may have been only nineteen but, believe me, she was an expert. She used all the tricks in the book: the regular things like dressing attractively and being entertaining, but also the more unusual ones. She shrewdly realized that he is the sort of man who cannot resist a pretty woman adoring him, and she followed him around like a lovesick puppy. She had no shame, none at all. She didn't care who thought what. As long as he kept her in his range of vision, she was succeeding.

"Everyone in the house party could see for themselves what was going on. She made herself utterly available and sent out very clear messages of worship. The Prince was flattered and enchanted. He's always been drawn to vulnerability. But he didn't take her seriously. To him, she was just an adolescent, even if she had made him realize that she was a charming and attractive one."

Diana had made enough headway, however, to be included in the Prince's party shortly thereafter when Charles played polo at Lord Cowdray's club, Cowdray Park, on the Cowdray Estate in Midhurst, Sussex, though not so much that he asked her to join the Royal Family on the *Britannia* for Cowes Week. She was still nothing more than padding, a bit of fluff on the periphery of the Prince's circle, and the desire for a romance with this child who hovered uncomfortably near the age of consent had not yet occurred to him, according to friends of both Charles and Diana.

But Charles had underestimated Diana. This was just as well, for had he done otherwise, she would most likely have frightened him away. As it was, she now set about enticing him with a vengeance. "Diana is very strong-minded. In that respect, she's like her sister Jane. If Sarah had been one tenth as determined as either of them, she'd now be The Princess of Wales," says the former courtier. "Diana did all the running. She knew he wasn't a scrap interested in her, but she also saw that he was vulnerable. She wouldn't get a better chance than this. So she was as cute as a kitten and cunning as a fox. She tracked her man and she must be admired for doing it so successfully. After Balmoral, she saw that she'd have to inveigle herself into his circle. She'd never get him if she wasn't constantly around. So she got herself invited to join the family for Cowes by the simple expedient of cultivating Lady Sarah Armstrong-Jones."

Princess Margaret's daughter and Diana had been friends since childhood. As children, they had played together, with Prince Andrew and Prince Edward and her brother Viscount Linley, when the court took up residence on the Sandringham Estate. They attended each other's parties, swam in the swimming pool that Diana's father built in the grounds of Park House, and partook of the myriad activities that children undertake together.

Although Sarah and Diana had drifted apart in the five years since Lord Spencer had succeeded to the Earldom and moved to Althorp, they rekindled their friendship at Balmoral. This has stood the test of time, though the closeness of those early days prior to Diana's marriage has lessened with the passage of the years and the divergence of their lifestyles. Sarah is now a serious artist who shares her life with a budding actor, Daniel Chatto (the illegitimate half-brother of the actors Edward and James Fox), while Diana, as we all know, was well on her way to becoming the Royal Family's answer to Mother Teresa, with a dash of Mrs. John F. Kennedy thrown in for good and stylish measure.

Cowes Week is one of the high points of the social calendar. The calibre of people with whom Diana mixed while staying as a guest on the royal yacht certainly put her Coleherne Court circle in the shade. Aside from the cream of the sailing fraternity, most of whom are multi-millionaires, she mingled with the most famous socialites in the world, some of whom flew in from the four corners of the earth.

Diana, however, had no interest in the social scene. She was very focused in her attention. Although she remained warm and friendly towards Sarah, and was as sociable as every situation demanded, she did not bother to hide where her priority lay. Wherever Prince Charles was, so was she. Whatever he did, so did she. When he went windsurfing, so did she. She took every opportunity to show off her swimming and diving skills, "taking great care to let him notice what a good figure she had. She would hover until she knew he'd seen her. She always stretched just that little bit more than one would normally do, or stroked herself just that much longer, sending him subtle subliminal messages. She undoubtedly set out to stimulate him sexually, to seduce him," says someone who observed her.

Diana must often have been disheartened, for, no matter what she did, Prince Charles still did not take her seriously. It can be fairly said that seldom since female liberation has a girl worked so hard to have a man view her as a sex object. But she departed from *Britannia* with no more to show for her endeavours than when she arrived.

Diana, however, was now completely caught up in the game. Having shoved off from the top of the mountain, like a skier hurtling down a slope she could not stop. The mountain was too steep, and until she crashed or passed the finishing line, she would have to ski for her life. Now that she had finally chosen to love one of the two princes, she was the living embodiment of a Barbara Cartland heroine, bravely yet abjectly enticing the princely, but elusive, object of her desires.

"She could not ask Jane to have her up to Balmoral again," a friend said. "That would have been far too obvious a move for Jane to make. Everyone would then have known that Diana was chasing Prince Charles." So she got her grandmother, Ruth, Lady Fermoy, who was staying with the Queen Mother at Birkhall, her home on the Balmoral Estate, and who knew of her desire to become Princess of Wales, to arrange an invitation for her. Ruth was naturally only too eager to oblige in anything that would increase her family's attachment to the royals, and Diana duly headed northwards once more.

"There is little doubt that Diana would never have married Prince Charles had it not been for her family," says the noblewoman whose brother-in-law is a senior courtier. "They did their utmost to incorporate her into the Royal Family circle, and you must emphasize how easy it was for them to do so. The royals are so cut off from life. The result is that, to a large extent, the courtiers end up being the only other group of people, aside from relations, who are close to the Royal Family. This is because they are the only group of people who have unlimited access to the royals. Far from being mere servants, they therefore become friends, and usually end up being very close and trusted ones at that. Their opinions are treated with great respect. Their feelings are given a consideration accorded to only the most beloved royal relations. Because they are in such close and constant contact with the royals, they wield a degree of influence that no one else does, including royal relations.

"Diana hadn't been at Birkhall for more than a few days before everyone at Balmoral was saying how lovely she was. It was a short hop from that to how suitable she was, and how wonderful it would be if The Prince of Wales married someone like her."

Diana, however, had to play her part if she was going to win the game of being "royalized." At Birkhall, she did this to perfection. "She stuck to him [Prince Charles] the way deodorant sticks to your armpit," says someone who was there with them. "She had abandoned all reserve. It could almost be said that she humiliated herself. She was abject in her unspoken supplication to him. You could tell by the way she looked at him, how she spoke to him, how she followed him around, how she laughed that little bit too much and in general behaved towards him. She did not behave badly. Far from it. She was very careful how she trod. But it was plain for all to see that she was throwing herself at his feet, metaphorically speaking of course, and saying, 'I'm in love with you. Acknowledge me or abandon me.' It was just the right tactic to use with Prince Charles, because he really is very soft-hearted, and would never knowingly hurt a fly."

Confronted with this openly adoring and attractive eighteen-year-old, The Prince of Wales, whose great-aunt Princess Alice, Duchess of Gloucester opined that he is perhaps too sensitive for his own good, was soon seduced into viewing Diana as an object of desire. "The first time he kissed her," says a former member of his household, "his fate was sealed. Remember, he is an intensely sexual man. Once Diana whetted his sexual appetite, the power shifted. Up until that point, she'd done all the running. Now she ran in another direction. She was all lovey-dovey and gamine, but thereafter she let him chase her. Again, those superb instincts of hers were spot on. It was just the right thing to do.

"I remember once, after the romance was under way, he'd been away and didn't phone her right after he got back. Diana didn't do what every other girl would have done. She didn't phone him and she wasn't extra sweet to him when he phoned her. She took her phone off the hook. And kept it off for two days. By the end of it, he was in a frenzy. She's a pastmistress, I tell you. A real natural at animal cunning."

♛   ♛   ♛

.

CHAPTER SEVEN

Charles's Loves

*T*he man Diana Spencer was pursuing so ardently was at a crossroads in September 1980. His whole life was in a state of flux.

The most serious uncertainty for The Prince of Wales was what role he should be assuming now that he had left the Navy. At the end of 1976 he had resigned his commission and departed from the antiquated HMS *Bronington,* a 365-tonne minehunter which rolled so badly that much of Charles's ten months as commander was spent in the throes of seasickness. In 1977, the year of The Queen's Silver Jubilee, the Prince headed his mother's Jubilee Appeal. Occupied with that, his anxiety was masked for a year, but since then, it had been increasing. "He didn't know what to do with himself," says a member of his household. "I vividly remember a conversation we had. He was very dejected and said, 'I don't have a role. Everyone else has a role. All my friends are at the top of their professions. By the time I have a proper role, I'll have one foot in the grave.' I strongly disagreed and told him, 'Sir, you're The Prince of Wales. That's a role in itself. You don't need another role. You can do anything you want. You can make a real impact on the world. You can make any contribution you want. You can even change things if you want to. The Prince of Wales has one of the most influential positions in the world. It's yours by right of birth. All you need to do is use it to make your mark. That'll take care of your role." He looked astonished. He had that quizzical expression that he often has when he's not sure about something. 'Do you really think so?' he asked. You could see he was hoping I'd meant it. I said I did. That was only the first of many conversations like that. I'm not saying I'm the only person he spoke to along those lines. There were one or two others. But what we said did help him to carve out a niche for himself, and he's done that very successfully over the years."

The professional sphere aside, Charles's personal life was a further cause for anxiety. "It was terrible, just terrible," says one of his cousins, a member of another royal family. "The poor guy simply couldn't escape the pressure. Every day the papers were full of news about the latest girl in his life. Sometimes they didn't even bother to get their facts straight. They had him marrying girls he'd never even met.

"The Duke of Edinburgh was also piling on the pressure. He can be very waspish, and every now and then he'd sting Charles with a comment. Sometimes he'd be quite funny, which wasn't particularly pleasant for Charles, who was made to feel rather like a bit of a retard. He didn't really have any defence against singeing wit like Prince Philip's. And of course Charles knew The Queen was also keen to see him settle down. No, she never piled on the pressure. That's not her style. She simply wanted him safely tucked up. You didn't need to be a genius to see that she disliked all the press speculation. She regarded it as undignified. She's dedicated her whole life to the nation. She felt it was his duty to find a nice wife and have some children. Take care of the succession and make a family life for himself." Queen Elizabeth The Queen Mother was anxious as well. She wanted her favourite grandchild to provide her with great-grandchildren before she died.

Throughout the 1970s, there had been no shortage of girls in the Prince's life. His first proper girlfriend was Lucia Santa Cruz. The daughter of the Chilean Ambassador to the Court of St. James's, she was three years older than Charles. They met while he was a student at Trinity College, Cambridge. The striking brunette was working for

Lord Butler of Saffron Walden, Master of Trinity, as a research assistant on his memoirs, *The Art of the Possible*.

"Rab" Butler was a noted Conservative politician. He had been the Member of Parliament for Saffron Walden from 1929 until his elevation to the peerage, and was frequently called "the best Prime Minister Britain never had." A close friend of The Queen and Prince Philip, he subsequently sold the Monarch his Gloucestershire house, Gatcombe Park, for Princess Anne and Captain Mark Phillips in 1976. Prior to that, as Master of Trinity, he was responsible for the care and welfare of the heir to the throne.

Knowing the problems Charles would have adjusting to college life, he set aside forty-five minutes each evening in which they could talk about whatever concerns Charles had. He also gave the Prince a key to the side door of the Master's Lodge, for him to pop in whenever he wished. Both privileges Charles used to the full: the former, to increase his knowledge of current affairs, as witnessed by a brilliant and clear-speaking man who had been at the centre of British politics for nearly half a century; and the latter, to have privacy. Charles's other abode was Room 6, on the first floor, staircase E, in New Court. It was refurbished by Buckingham Palace, with new carpets, curtains, and elegant but comfortable furniture, as soon as it was allotted. It was even provided with its own telephone line, a security necessity but one which nevertheless caused some envy and fuss. Nevertheless, Charles was not intoxicated by his quarters, which were cramped and too accessible to all and sundry. The Prince had never lacked space or privacy before. Lord Butler came to the rescue and was as hospitable as he was open-minded. For this Charles was especially grateful once he struck up the romance with the sophisticated Lucia, which Lord Butler sanctioned, to such an extent that she was also given a key to the side door of the Master's Lodge.

Able to conduct their romance away from the public gaze, Charles, by his own admission, fell in love. The relationship lasted for several months, coming to an amicable but inevitable end. Charles was too young to contemplate settling down, and even if he had done so, he could never have considered a Roman Catholic. Such marriages are specifically forbidden under the terms of the Act of Settlement of 1701, the Parliamentary decree which was responsible for inviting Charles's forebears to sit upon the throne of England. The Prince and Lucia Santa Cruz have nevertheless remained friends, and after her marriage he even became godfather to her first child.

Lucia Santa Cruz was the only brunette that Charles knowingly took out. Her successor, in 1972, was Georgiana Russell, a brown-eyed blonde with a penchant for wearing eye-catching clothing like transparent tops with opaque pockets strategically placed. The daughter of the British Ambassador to Spain, Sir John Russell, and his wife Aliki, a former Miss Greece, Georgiana was as sweet and funny and unaffected as she was pretty. Impeccably behaved, she would undoubtedly have made an excellent Princess of Wales. She is now Lady Boothby, the chatelaine of a Welsh castle, works for the Almeida Theatre, and is a brunette. If her hair colour has changed, her taste in clothes has not. Recently I saw her, at a party at Tiffany, the Bond Street jewellers, as exotically dressed as ever in one of her suggestive blouses. She also remains as pretty and sweet and funny as ever.

Although Charles was usually drawn to girls who knew how to make a sartorial splash, his next girlfriend was never in danger of making the Best-Dressed List, even though she had the looks and the means to do so. Lady Jane Wellesley was the daughter of the 8th Duke of Wellington. Bright and lively, with an inquiring mind and agreeably unstuffy views, Jane shared a paradoxical quality with Georgiana: they both manage to be bohemian and conservative at the same time. The first inkling the public had of the relationship was when Charles first joined Jane and her family for the excellent shooting on the duke's three-thousand-acre estate near Granada in southern Spain, given by the Spanish nation to the Iron Duke after his victory in the Peninsular War in 1814, in gratitude for ridding them of Napoleon's elder brother, King Joseph. Charles was comfortable with Jane. She was used to the ways of the court. She was intelligent, thoughtful, inquisitive and responsive. They continued to see each other on and off for over three years, and she was his guest at Sandringham for New Year 1975. The relationship, however, was going nowhere, mostly because Charles had discovered the pleasures of being in demand and had no wish to sacrifice his freedom, while Jane also valued that commodity and did not wish to give it up for the gilded cage of Princess of Wales. She also opined that, as she already had a title, she did not need another one. By this time, she was working in the cut-throat world of television for the BBC, and she went on to become her section's representative for the National Union of Journalists, where she acquired a reputation for ability and toughness.

Meanwhile, Charles took advantage of the temptations that destiny threw into his path. In 1975 he met Laura Jo Watkins, an admiral's daughter, at a yacht club in California when his ship, the *Jupiter,* docked there. Only too delighted to succumb to temptation that came in such a beautiful package, the Prince gave full rein to his passion for the lean, sun-streaked blonde who, being American and therefore ignorant of the expected modes of behaviour towards royalty, treated him more naturally than he had ever been treated before. Not that Laura Jo was ignorant of the niceties governing ordinary social exchanges. She had good manners, was personable as well as intelligent, and so captivated him that he asked her to fly to London to witness him take his seat as a peer of the realm in the House of Lords. "That should have been an accurate enough indication of how much she meant to him, but most royal-watchers missed the clue," a friend of his said. Long-distance relationships are notoriously difficult to sustain, however, and this one proved to be no exception. It petered out, though they remained on good terms.

"The Prince of Wales is an intensely dutiful man. From earliest childhood he was raised to do what was expected of him, and marriage, he knew, was what the family and public alike wanted. Although he had and would continue to have ambivalent feelings on the subject, he sacrificed his private reservations and continued keeping an eye open for his future wife," says a member of a foreign royal family, a cousin of Charles.

His next girlfriend seemed acceptable, even if she did not have the glittering lineage of the Duke of Wellington's daughter or the stunning looks of Laura Jo Watkins. Charles met Davina Sheffield, a major's daughter whose grandfather was Lord McGowan, in 1976, at a friend's dinner party in Fulham. He was immediately taken with the tall, slim, busty blonde. She had a ready laugh and a twinkle in her eye. She also had character. Her mother had been brutally murdered at the family home in Oxfordshire, but Davina did not allow this to warp her view of the world. Charles admired the way she coped, and was drawn to the vulnerability with which this trauma left her. He quickly fell in love and began considering her as a serious contender for the future throne. All the family liked her, especially The Queen and the Queen Mother. He asked her up to Balmoral, to see how she coped with the demands of the rustic Highland life. She coped rather too well for his somewhat chauvinistic liking, it emerged, for Davina insisted upon breaking out of the feminine mould and accompanying him on a stalking expedition, despite his suggestion that she stay behind. He ensured that she would thereafter remember her place, and accompany him only for luncheon served from the back of a Range Rover, by deliberately dragging her through all sorts of rough terrain, so that, by their return to the castle in the evening, she was too exhausted to come down for dinner. The end of their romance coincided with her ex-boyfriend, James Beard, revealing in a Sunday paper that she had lived with him, though that was not the reason for the split. "Of course he did not expect to marry a virgin. None past the age of twelve existed, unless you included monstrosities, lesbians and frigid men-haters. And anyway, you know as well as I do how sophisticated everyone in that set is," says a relation of Charles's.

One of the most famous gossip columnists in the world, a close friend of Princess Margaret and at least one other member of the Royal Family, confirmed this, "There weren't many virgins in Charles's generation. He fucked most of them."

Whether he did or not, the Prince did not let the absence of a hymen interfere with him and Davina Sheffield. Nevertheless, "they broke up by mutual consent. Having had a taste of the rigours of royal life, being Princess of Wales held no appeal for her. From the Prince of Wales's point of view, that was fine. He was in a no-lose situation. If he got married, he did his duty, and if he didn't, he kept his independence."

"I fall in love quickly," Prince Charles once said while speaking about romance and marriage. He might also have said, "My hormones insist that I fall in love regularly. I don't like being without a woman for long." Without an "official" girlfriend, with only his tried and true confidantes, Lady Tryon and Mrs. Parker Bowles, for female companionship, and mindful of the dangers of relying too heavily upon married women—the spectre of the previous Prince of Wales, his great-uncle David, the former King Edward VIII and subsequent Duke of Windsor, was never far from Royal thoughts—Charles looked around for some luscious unattached filly with whom he could dally.

Like thousands of men of his generation, Charles's imagination had been captured by the actress Susan George. He had seen her raped in *Straw Dogs* and *Mandingo,* two films that established her as one of the most popular sex objects of the decade. Unlike most of her admirers, however, the footloose and fancy-free heir to the throne was in a position to do something about it. So he duly arranged for her to be sent an invitation to his thirtieth birthday party at Buckingham Palace. Susan was duly presented to The Queen, the Queen Mother, and The Duke of Edinburgh, whose appreciation of a pretty girl had long been the bane of the courtiers' lives at Buckingham Palace. It was the son and not the father, however, who asked for her number at the end of an evening that she found glorious. She gave it, was rung up and asked to dinner at the Palace in Charles's suite of rooms, and that same evening began what proved to be a passionate and satisfying romance for both of them. Much of it was conducted in the privacy of Windsor Castle, though inevitably, a relationship that was going nowhere had to come to an end. Once more, the Prince's knack for remaining friends with his exes held true. Susan has remained on good terms with him. She attended Queen Elizabeth The Queen Mother's eightieth birthday party in 1980, Charles's wedding in 1981 as well as the wedding breakfast at the Palace afterwards, and I saw her at Prince Philip's seventieth birthday party in June 1991 at Windsor Castle, with her husband, the actor Simon MacCorkindale.

Susan George, however, was not Prince Charles's only foray into the delights of show biz. "He had a long and enduring romance with Sheila Ferguson of the Three Degrees," says a friend of mine who knows her. "They were crazy about each other. Her house is a shrine to him. Everywhere you look, there are pictures of them together. No, not only official pictures: private photographs of them together. Very obviously together as a loving couple. I know the public think the Three Degrees were his favourite group, and that's the end of the story. But there's more to it than that, much, much more. The romance lasted for years. Even though Sheila and Charles haven't been romantically involved for years now, they're still on cordial terms and she still adores him."

No matter how fond The Prince of Wales was of Susan George or Sheila Ferguson, and he was genuinely attached to both, neither of them could ever have been anything more than a fling. "An actress or an entertainer of any complexion simply wasn't suitable," says a British connection of the Royal Family. "The question of marriage never even entered into it. It would have been Wallis Simpson all over again. He's had it inculcated into him from when he was knee-high to a grasshopper by Queen Elizabeth [The Queen Mother] that Wallis Simpson and his Uncle David were on a par with Satan himself."

It was just as well that The Prince of Wales had such a clear view of who would make a suitable bride, for there were two girlfriends from this period who would have made rather more interesting queens than the British people bargained for. The first was the Hon. Fiona Watson,

Lord Manton's daughter. She ruled herself out of the running, despite a suitable background and good looks, when it emerged that she had given several million readers of *Mayfair*, a down-market girlie publication, an intimate glimpse of her aristocratic body. Contrary to received and inaccurate wisdom, though, this was not the end of the romance. "He always phoned up at the last moment and expected her to be available," says a friend. "She got fed up with this cavalier treatment and decided to teach him how to behave. Once, when he rang up, she said she could not go with him. That was the last she ever heard from him. Whether he wasn't that interested or simply couldn't take the rebuff, I don't know. Nor does she. They speak when their paths cross. They just don't cross that often. They're not particularly friendly."

The aristocratic morsel was replaced by a divorcée, Jane Ward, who became the reigning paramour for a few months during 1979. They met as a result of polo. She worked in the office at the Guards Polo Club. For a while, it looked as if their romance would go the way of all the others, but it ended bitterly, with Charles sending his detective to order her out of her workplace, which happened to be on the grounds of his mother's estate. They never healed the breach.

Jane Ward was not the first girlfriend to experience the royal deep-freeze. Sabrina Guinness, the free-spirited brewery heiress whose adventures had included a close relationship with Mick Jagger and a period in Hollywood in Ryan O'Neal's house as Tatum's nanny, discovered that staying at Balmoral could be both terrifying and discomfiting. The Royal Family did not like the idea of the Prince developing an attachment to this well-bred scion of a household surname that evoked almost as many images of wealth as Windsor did. So they breached every cardinal rule of hospitality, providing a display of bad manners that began before her clothes were even unpacked.

Sabrina, who is charming and delightful, innocently remarked that the car that had picked her up at Ballater station resembled a Black Maria, the vehicle used in those days to convey criminals to and from court. It was obvious that she meant no offence, but before the sentence was properly out of her mouth, the notoriously waspish Duke of Edinburgh unnecessarily and pointlessly retorted that Black Marias were something she should know all about.

If she expected The Queen to make her feel any more at home, Sabrina was due to receive an object lesson in disillusionment. When she went to take a seat, Her Majesty informed her with all the charm of a Victorian schoolmistress that she was not to sit where she intended, as it was Queen Mary's chair. The fact that The Queen's grandmother had been dead for twenty-five years was not lost on anyone. To add insult to injury, Charles ignored her for her whole stay, pursuing his activities as if she were not his guest.

But Sabrina had still not been exposed to the full force of royal courtesy. This came when the Prince asked her to accompany him to a dance given at the magnificent stately home, Wilton House in Wiltshire, by its owner, the Earl of Pembroke, the tall, thin and handsome movie producer who was responsible for putting the seventeen-year-old Koo Stark into his racy film, *The Adventures of Emily,* thereby depriving her of the chance to become Duchess of York. The trouble was, Charles asked Sabrina's twin Miranda along as well. He then crowned the solecism by paying little attention to either, before dumping them and making off into the night on his own. So much for a gentleman seeing a lady safely to her door.

There were, of course, two other girlfriends, aside from Lady Sarah Spencer. But these belong to a different category, as they married and went on to become confidantes. The first on the scene was Dale Harper, whom Charles met in her native Australia in the late Sixties. She was young, cute, blonde, buxom, and charming. She had, and still has, an Australian accent that would make Crocodile Dundee feel right at home, hence the name Charles endowed her with: Kanga. Incidentally, I know of none of her friends who call her anything but Dale. Kanga seems to be the exclusive province of the Prince and the press (although she has utilized the name for her exclusive dress shop in Beauchamp Place, Knightsbridge).

As often happens with very young people, Charles and Dale moved on to other partners after their initial flurry, even though the virtues that attracted them to one another remained constant. She married Lord Tryon, whose father was Keeper of the Privy Purse to The Queen, and took up residence in England. Dale's personality, always her greatest asset, continued to stand her in good stead, and accounted for much of the success she quickly began enjoying in royal circles. One of the nicest and warmest people anyone could hope to meet, she is also bright, breezy, capable, and utterly natural.

It was only a matter of time, once she and Charles reforged their friendship, before it evolved more closely and deeply. Eventually, they became so close that she received the accolade of confidante. This is a special role, an honoured and esteemed position in royal circles, which I shall deal with more thoroughly later. Suffice it to say that Dale could never have occupied such a pre-eminent position had she not been securely married. The fact that her husband was a friend of the Royal Family only enhanced this security, and made it possible for the husband, wife and Prince to pursue many pleasures without fear of untoward criticism. Among these were trips to Iceland and Scotland, which continue to the present.

Dale shares the Prince's passion for fishing. She is also a fine horsewoman, and Charles, of course, delights in equestrian activities. So many shared interests have only strengthened their regard for each other, as have the children. There was her firstborn, a beautiful daughter, Zoe, to whom Charles was an adoring "uncle." She was followed, in the early days of the friendship, by Anthony's son and heir. He was named Charles, in honour of the Prince, who even then was close enough to the Tryons to become godfather. Later, after Dale had assumed the coveted position of royal confidante, she gave birth to twins. These were duly given royal names, Edward and Victoria, two monarchs who had been great-great-grandfather and great-great-great-grandmother of the Prince.

No one in the smart set has been surprised that Dale still enjoys a solid friendship with her former boyfriend and all the older generation of the Royal Family. She and her husband frequently stay at the various royal residences as guests of The Queen, and while Diana might not drop into Dale's for tea when she is in Wiltshire, Queen Elizabeth The Queen Mother does. And the children have grown up secure in the knowledge that Anthony, Dale, and the Royal Family all love them.

The other girlfriend who became a confidante after her marriage is Camilla Parker Bowles. She is the sister of Mark Shand, an intrepid traveller better known for having lived with David Bailey's ex-wife Marie Helvin than for writing books about his exotic adventures such as crossing the Indian subcontinent on an elephant. She is also the niece of Lord Ashcombe, and thus a member of the family which built much of Belgravia, the smartest area in London, for the Duke of Westminster's Grosvenor Estate. The Shands have never been known for their beauty, and Camilla does not have the allure or style that Dale does. What she has, however, is confidence allied to the right ancestor, and this helped to kick off her romance with Charles. They met when they were both in their early twenties, and hit it off at once. There was also an ancestral link, which made their romance all the more poignant while also lending it an air of cosiness. Camilla's great-great-grandmother, the Hon. Mrs. George Keppel, had been Charles's great-great-grandfather King Edward VII's last mistress. Her position was acknowledged to such an extent that Queen Alexandra sent for Alice Keppel to join her by The King's bedside as he lay dying.

But Charles's and Camilla's romance proved to be neither straightforward nor smooth. Like Diana, whose timing was more fortuitous, Camilla wanted to get married. She was not interested in having a career. Charles, on the other hand, was ambivalent about settling down. He loved her. But how could he be sure she was right for him? What if someone else, another girl who would be even more perfectly suited for him, were around the corner? Should he take the chance? Or should he keep his options open? "He is very indecisive," says a member of his staff. "Contrary to his reputation, he is not a man of action. He is more of a thinker than a doer. He's a real ditherer."

Unable to make a commitment but unwilling to let her go, Charles seemed to be leading Camilla up the primrose path. She, however, was not prepared to be kept dangling forever, and when Andrew Parker Bowles, a handsome army officer with the right pedigree, began showing interest in marriage, she encouraged him. They married and Charles realized the mistake he had made. It was too late to make Camilla his wife. But she could become his confidante, a position which she fulfilled in even more peace and harmony than Dale. Andrew Parker Bowles was even more patient and generous of his wife's time and interest than Anthony Tryon, although both husbands were mindful of the honour being done to their wives.

With both husbands according their wives varying degrees of cooperation in the pursuance of their friendships with Charles, Dale and Camilla were free to play a rich and vibrant part in the bachelor Prince's life. This they did with relish. They were the constant threads in the fabric of his existence, irrespective of whichever latest girl happened to capture his interest, and this happy state of affairs continued even when Lady Diana Spencer came on to the scene. By then, whatever romance there had once been was nothing but a distant memory, and Camilla was Charles's closest friend. Life without her would have been inconceivable.

How Diana coped with this friendship is instructive of her *modus operandi*. In the early days of her relationship with The Prince of Wales, she was only too happy to accept the status quo and Camilla's offers of friendship and hospitality. Later, of course, all this would change. As soon as her engagement was announced and she had moved into Buckingham Palace, Diana began the process of chipping away at all of Charles's relationships that predated her. "Camilla was not the only person she perceived as a threat," a former member of the Royal Household said. "In fact, Camilla was not even regarded as the greatest threat. Not at that stage, at any rate. Stephen Barry was her first bug-bear. Only later did she become obsessed with destroying the Prince's friendship with Camilla. That was after her marriage had started to go sour. You must remember that Diana is not the sort of person who ever considers herself to be in the wrong. She has a pathological belief in the rightness of anything she says or does. Yes, you could say she lacks insight. It never occurred to her that she might be responsible, if only partly, for the way her marriage was going. It had to be all the Prince's fault. She is also intensely competitive. She's the sort of person who has to have an enemy. She thrives on the competition. Ergo the need for someone like the much-maligned Camilla Parker Bowles, who in Diana's mind became the living embodiment of all her frustrations and jealousies."

Whatever Diana's feelings about Camilla, The Prince of Wales did not desert his friend. At least not for long. There was a period of greater distance, between his engagement and the marriage hitting the rocks, but since then Camilla has been restored to her position of pre-eminence.

Moreover, Camilla is someone who is respected by all the Royal Family. Her conduct has always been unimpeachable, as has her husband's, with the result that both have been the recipients of Royal largesse. During the 1980s, Colonel Andrew Parker Bowles was made Commanding Officer of the Household Regiments. He was then made Silver Stick in Waiting, an honorific position at court which basically means that he is The Queen's ceremonial bodyguard, and was elevated to the rank of Brigadier. In 1991, his fiefdom was enlarged to include responsibility for all the dog-loving Monarch's canines, with his appointment as the Honorary Colonel Commandant Royal Army Veterinary Corps.

As far as Camilla's favour with the Royal Family is concerned, no more accurate gauge is possible than The Queen's conduct towards her at the height of speculation about the Waleses' marriage in June 1992. At the Queen's Cup polo match at Smith's Lawn, Windsor Great Park, the Parker Bowleses were received as her guests by Her Majesty in her box. No louder acclamation in favour of Camilla or her consort could have been possible in royal circles. Nor could there have been a more public reproach to Diana.

CHAPTER EIGHT

Baiting the Line

*A*ll great enterprises succeed because of a combination of skill, application, and luck. While landing The Prince of Wales might not have been on a par with the discoveries of Christopher Columbus or Alexander Graham Bell, it was undoubtedly a great enterprise, if only because it would give the conquering heroine a lifelong tenure in the two most pre-eminent positions open in the world to a woman. She would be first The Princess of Wales, with all the glamour, cachet and opportunity that that had to offer, then the Queen Consort of Great Britain, Northern Ireland, Canada, Jamaica and the many other Commonwealth countries which remain monarchies.

For the rest of her life, Christmas Day would be every day. The difficulty would be not deprivation, but the inevitable sating brought on by consuming Christmas pudding every day of the year, and having Father Christmas permanently in residence with a sackful of treasures. Certainly there would be problems. Too much of a good thing can induce stresses and strains. And there would, of course, be a price, paying back the nation for the bounteous privilege that would thereafter be one's due. But, compared to the concerns of the rest of humanity, a Princess of Wales or Queen of England would have no right to complain. What she would have would be a positive and indubitable obligation to spend the rest of her life showing appreciation to everyone and everything that had made her good fortune

106

possible. Any other reaction would not only be unrealistic and ill-advised, but also churlish and insane.

When the nineteen-year-old Diana Spencer crossed the bridge from seductiveness to romance with The Prince of Wales at Balmoral in September 1980, she too was aware of the enormous desirability of the position on which she had set her heart. "There can be nothing more desirable in the world than being The Princess of Wales," she said to a cousin of Charles, who noted that her choice of words revealed a measure of ambition.

That is not to say that Diana did not love Charles. She was, according to everyone who knew her, definitely head over heels in love with him by this time. The issue, from the vantage point of some of the royal relations, was not whether Diana was in love with Charles, but whether she would have felt that way had he not been a Prince of the Blood Royal. One connection of the Royal Family surmised that she was as in love with the position as with Charles: "The Prince of Wales was taken in, but the blinkers fell off later, and, I can tell you, when they did there was an almighty thud."

Not everyone, however, shared that interpretation. One of her closest friends said, "She was really in love with him. Totally. What happened later broke her heart." And Lady Teresa Manners said, "Diana herself told me that she had always been in love with Prince Charles," though a cousin of the royals by marriage attributes Diana's use of the word "always" to an attempt to rewrite history and eliminate previous male objects of desire.

Meanwhile, she marshalled her forces. "Diana has always been a tremendous flirt," says a schoolmate. "She has also always been extremely manipulative. Getting Prince Charles was a piece of cake for her. Sure, she had to keep her head and make all the right moves, whether towards or away from him didn't matter. She was pulling the strings, don't kid yourself. And she had a lot of help—from her family, from her friends, from the press, even from his family."

Someone who observed her at Balmoral says, "Diana set out to be noticed. She's very good at attracting attention, and she made sure she attracted The Prince of Wales's. She employed all the little tricks that girls have."

On her autumnal visit, Diana's tactics were a variation and repetition of those employed on previous royal visits: "looking striking, entering a room with just the right amount of flourish, beaming approval, laughing at all his jokes with just that extra bit of relish, being witty and flirtatious," says her observer at Balmoral. "And trailing him like a private detective in an American television series! She wasn't sure when she'd be asked back—indeed, if she'd ever be asked back. This might be her one and only chance. She knew it, took it, and succeeded so well that, when she got back to London, she was already The Prince of Wales's girlfriend."

Luck certainly was on Diana's side. Not only was Charles at a low point emotionally, and therefore more amenable than he would otherwise have been to external pressures, including a seductive and appealing teenager, but those very pressures were conspiring to further her cause. There was, as we have already seen, the approval orchestrated by Diana's family. "Once the romance was under way, Queen Elizabeth The Queen Mother actually stopped being cantankerous long enough to be positively exultant," says a connection of the Royal Family. "The Duke of Edinburgh was also very taken with Diana. The Queen was more reserved in her judgements. But she wasn't anti-Diana. The Queen seldom takes a strong stand with her children [if they wish to adopt a course she is not in favour of], as you know. And there were Robert and Jane Fellowes and Ruth Fermoy's sensibilities to consider, so she was neutral more than anything else. It's fair to say her attitude created a vacuum which had no effect whatsoever on the surrounding atmosphere. What had more of an impact was Queen Elizabeth [The Queen Mother]'s attitude. I needn't tell you how pro-her The Prince of Wales has always been. Her opinion counted, a lot—yes, a tremendous amount."

Yet another fortuitous occurrence fell into her lap to help Diana solidify her position with Charles. On 8 September 1980, the *Sun* broke the news of the latest Prince Charles romance. "He is a very decent and responsible person," continues Charles's relation. "The last thing in the world he'd do was romance a nice girl then dump her." Harry Arnold, by breaking the story of their relationship so early in the day, changed its gears prematurely. "The publicity made the romance more serious than it might otherwise have been. It removed some of the element of choice, from The Prince of Wales's point of view."

Diana was ecstatic. "She didn't care how she got him up the aisle, as long as she did," says her schoolmate. When she returned to London from Balmoral and took up her duties at St. Saviour's Church Hall, Pimlico, she made no pretence of what she was up to. Kitty Waite Walker, who was at Young England Kindergarten as well, remembered, "Diana made the running. She used to come to school and admit it. Of course she was in love, and just set out to get her man."

Confronted with a public image for the first time in her life, Diana showed how mature and worldly wise she was beneath the puppy fat. "She learnt early on that fools rush in where wise men fear to tread," says the schoolmate. "She's always been very deliberate about how she behaves. She is genuinely nice and well-mannered, but there's a whole heap more to her than that. What the press mistook for shyness was simply Diana being clever enough to hold her counsel and hide behind a modest demeanour until she was sure of how to play things. She's always had that tentative quality, the nous to test the water before jumping into the pool, to hold back until it's safe to plunge in. She was like that even when she was at school. It's nothing to do with shyness though. If anything, it's a combination of caution, calculation and deliberateness. It's not even a question of insecurity. She's never been afraid that she can't do what she wants. If anything, she's supremely self-confident and a bit of a perfectionist who likes doing things well. She just has the common sense to recognize that you have to start carefully if you're going to be a strong finisher. And Diana is a strong finisher. She has the will-power of ten devils."

Almost immediately, Fleet Street christened Diana Shy Di and churned out countless paragraphs attesting to how demure she was. "Princess Diana is not shy," Dame Barbara Cartland said at a luncheon I attended at Camfield Place, her Hertfordshire house near Potters Bar, shortly after the wedding. "The press thought she was because she tends to look down and hunch over, but she does that because she's so tall. It's nothing to do with shyness." Sophie Kimball agreed. "Diana wasn't a scrap shy," she said, while Simon Berry explained the secret of her success: "The thing is that she is an ordinary, terribly nice, unexciting girl who was clever enough to treat the press very well."

Preoccupied with hooking Charles, Diana spoke to everyone, including Vikki, an assistant at Headlines, her hairdressers, where she not only had her hair cut, styled and washed, but also her legs waxed, her eyelashes dyed, and her facials. "It is amazing looking back when I think that I used to give her advice about her boyfriend. Diana is no fool—never think that. She is very astute about people. She was so obviously in love and you know how girls talk to each other. And we had a lot of friends in common. But of course I never knew who he was until the announcement was made. I have always been aware that the client is in a vulnerable position lying here naked and it seems easier to find out what they are really about."

Diana, according to Barbara Cartland "had a distinct personality and was not a person, whether she spoke or not, whom one could ignore." Stephen Barry went further and admitted how intent Diana was on capturing the Prince's hand in marriage. "She went after him with single-minded determination," the Prince's valet confirmed, prior to his death: "In all my years, I've never seen anyone as tricky or determined as she was. She was like a jellyfish. You couldn't see her coming but, my God, the effect of the sting. Looking back, I can see he didn't stand a chance. It's funny to say this, but he was like a lamb to the slaughter. What a butcher she would've made, with that sharp blade and a grasp like a steel vise!"

"Diana is *very* charming. But more than charm, what she has is the power to seduce," says the aristocratic sister-in-law of a senior courtier. "It's what has accounted for her quite extraordinary popularity. Her looks and glamour have contributed, undeniably, but they're the icing on the cake. Believe me, her force of character, and the ability to mask its less attractive features, are the key to her success. That's also what won her The Prince of Wales."

"The Prince of Wales doesn't like women who demand anything of him emotionally. He likes confident, worldly women who are good listeners, who encourage him. If anyone's doing the propping up, it must be them, not him. That's one of the reasons why his marriage to Diana hasn't worked well. It's also the reason why Camilla Parker Bowles has gone from strength to strength," says someone who worked with him for years.

In the period after her return to London, Diana was so intent on pleasing her Prince that she adopted whatever posture she sensed would ingratiate herself with him. Although she would cease making an effort to synchronize her responses with his before the wedding ring even had a chance to get warm on her finger, prior to the announcement of their engagement she did make a supreme effort to convince him that they were on the same wavelength. "Diana is very sensitive, psychic even," says one of her closest friends. "She is also very intuitive. She can zero right into people and situations. She's very sympathetic. If she wants to, she can give anyone the feeling that she is in tune with them, that she understands what they're going through, that she's right there with them, feeling what they're feeling. It's a very appealing quality."

The Prince of Wales was drawn to that quality. "He fell in love with her gradually," I was told in those exact words by several different sources, including a relation, a courtier, and a friend. The royal relation continued, "What he found appealing about Diana was how much they had in common. She was very *sympathique*. He loves fishing. When they were at Balmoral together, she was happy to spend hours by the riverbank with him in companionable, undemanding, harmonious silence. He has a real need to be in touch with the elements, with nature, and he seemed to think she felt the same way. Of course, we now know differently. Diana's idea of a nightmare is to be torn away from London for more than a day. But, like many women

111

who are trying to hook a man, she was careful to keep her distaste for his interests to herself."

Diana is a real urbanite. She finds the country boring. Although she will occasionally make a concession and join in rural pursuits such as "beating" on a shoot, or following the guns, she is much happier shopping in Harrods and Harvey Nichols in Knightsbridge, lunching in San Lorenzo on smart Beauchamp Place or L'Incontro on Pimlico Road. Her idea of what constitutes non-urban pleasure is tanning herself on a beach in the Caribbean or riding around a Mediterranean cove on a jetski before heading back to the comfort of a luxurious, oceanfaring yacht. She is a true creature of the late twentieth century, a sybarite whose idea of fun is working out on her exercises or dance lessons and not on some Godforsaken Scottish mountain. She does not need nature, not even for her favourite sports, tennis and swimming. She is just as happy swimming in a pool as in the sea, and could not care less whether her tennis balls fly over nets at London's Vanderbilt Racquet Club or an outdoor court somewhere else. She loves the buzz of people, the solidity of concrete. Even dancing, which is the activity she likes best of all, requires music, and is better done in the human environment of a studio. Diana, in short, feeds off external stimulation and all that the wealth of a city has to offer, while Prince Charles is the exact opposite. More than merely disliking cities, Charles has a spiritual hunger for what the country has to offer. "There is no more wonderful place on earth than Balmoral," he has said, in more or less the same words, to many different people to whom I spoke. He needs peace and quiet, the space, sweep and solitude that are the rewards of a rural environment.

"At this point in time, he was not in love with Diana," says a former member of the Royal Household, who knows him well. "But he was getting there. He is a complete idealist, sensitive and rather protective of his feelings actually, and what convinced him that he could allow himself to fall in love with Diana was his judgement that they were so compatible. Everything he liked, she seemed to. Everything he felt, she understood or appreciated. He was used

112

to women who fitted in with his scheme of things, and it looked as if she was prepared to. Why, she even got along with Dale Tryon and Camilla Parker Bowles."

Charles expected to continue his relationships with his confidantes, no matter whom he married. They were a large part of his life and his past, and he would never, I was assured, have contemplated marriage to anyone who did not share this view. Diana allowed him to believe she did, and their romance continued to gather pace.

In August that year, he had bought Highgrove in Gloucestershire, a nine-bedroomed Georgian house with four principal reception rooms and six bathrooms, from Viscount Macmillan of Ovenden. Lady Macmillan put paid to the myth, recounted over the years in various publications, that Diana had a hand in the house's purchase, or that Charles took her to look at the house on a variety of occasions. "The extraordinary thing was, he came and saw it one day and literally bought it on the next. Before he was married."

Having bought the house, Charles now had a discreet meeting place where he could conduct his burgeoning romance with Diana away from the prying eyes of the public and the Palace. Although the house was virtually bare, that did not prevent the lovers from using it. Stephen Barry, the Prince's valet, often drove Diana there. She would arrive for supper, which they often had camping out in a style akin to any other young couple whose house has no furniture. Afterwards, they were left to their own devices. These interludes usually lasted until just before dawn, at which time Diana was escorted out of the house and either driven back to London by Barry, or drove herself if she had arrived under her own steam.

"No one except Stephen Barry was privy to those meetings, and he was of the opinion that they did what any other normal couple would have done," a friend of his told me. "He said Diana used to leave glowing, and her hair was always freshly brushed. Why would she brush it if they'd only been talking?"

"How anyone in their right mind can believe that a passionate Scorpio like The Prince of Wales and a sensuous creature like Diana did nothing but talk for hours on end is beyond me," says the aristocratic sister-in-law of the senior courtier. "Of course they did what every other normal, healthy young couple in love did. You only needed to see them together to know what was going on. Their body language would have given them away even if nothing else did. But they weren't creeping around like two thieves in the night. They were simply being discreet. They were behaving the way any other unmarried couple in the public eye behaved."

There was, however, a real problem with privacy. Ever since Harry Arnold had informed the world of Lady Diana Spencer's existence, the press interest had been overwhelming. With no other girlfriend had it been as sustained or as excessive. Every day an army of pressmen and photographers were camped outside Coleherne Court. For Diana the journey, from the door of the building to wherever her car was parked, was fraught, with the ladies and gentlemen of the press grilling her. She knew, from her sister Sarah's experience, that all it needed was one slip for her to ruin her chances with Charles. "At first, she was nervous," says a friend. "But in a very short space of time —like a week, a fortnight tops—she saw how helpful a good press could be in landing Prince Charles."

Diana had already perceived that she could exert pressure on the prevaricating Prince by getting the press and public to view her as a serious candidate for his hand. "It was obvious to her that he was reluctant to commit himself," says another friend. "She knew it would help if the press were on her side and made her out to be an ideal candidate. Which is exactly what happened, of course."

"Diana is very shrewd. She used to say that she had to court them [the press], make them like her, make them her friends. She may have been only nineteen, but she certainly wasn't naïve. Far from it. She knew exactly how to twist them around her little finger. And she did," says yet another friend.

Within weeks, Diana had established cordial and defined relationships with many of the regulars. Chief among these was James Whitaker, the then *Daily Star*'s royal correspondent, whose importance in the development of the romance cannot be exaggerated. The journalists all liked her. They found her natural, down to earth, unaffected—a sweet, charming girl. She treated them with courtesy, dignifying them in a way that few celebrities, most of whom are very suspicious of the press, ever do.

Diana, of course, is an aristocrat. She has the exquisite manners that are a hallmark of her background. She also has the innate reserve, the dignity that allows one to be natural without being unbecomingly pally. It did not occur to any of the many reporters present that she would actually want the publicity they were there to give her: in their experience, nobs and royals never sought publicity, so they never became suspicious of her motives. Had they done so, it would have been a short step from there to contempt, for the press have an unfailing reflex: they despise anyone who wants publicity. No matter what the reason is—it could be charity, war or famine, they care not a jot—unless the idea emanates from them, or it is in their interest to run a story, they look down upon the subject with withering scorn.

Because the reporters assigned to cover Lady Diana Spencer functioned under the understanding that aristocrats, especially aristocrats being dated by The Prince of Wales, always want to avoid the press and never willingly speak to the representatives of the Fourth Estate, Diana had a tremendous advantage in putting herself across. This she did skilfully, speaking to them as if they were just other human beings on a par with her. She took the time and trouble to wish them good morning, to learn their names, to enquire how they were, to sympathize with the rigours of having to linger outside in all sorts of weather, to answer their questions courteously and considerately. To the press, Diana's behaviour could only mean one thing: she was wonderful.

One feature, especially, helped to divert suspicion away from her motives in so assiduously cultivating the regard of the reporters: her age was on her side. This led the press corps to conclude that her supreme guile was actually youthful lack of guile. Had she been older, they would most certainly have been more suspicious of her willingness to treat them so well. But, because she was young, they marked it down to something it was not. And when her inexperience and the pressure did get the better of her, as happened occasionally, the journalists accorded her a sympathy which others, despite being similarly inexperienced and pressurized by questing journalists, seldom receive but equally deserve.

As September gave way to October, and October to November, Diana became increasingly obsessed with her quest of getting a marital commitment out of The Prince of Wales. Even though she was attracting all the press coverage she needed, and was now generally acknowledged by one and all to be his girlfriend—to such an extent that she was invited to Princess Margaret's party at Claridge's early in November—Charles was still no nearer to committing himself. The reasons for this were twofold. Although he was drawn to her, Charles did not love Diana. He also did not want to get married. This he told more than one friend, including the King of Spain, who repeated it to some friends of mine at a dinner party.

In November, The Prince of Wales was due to depart on a tour of India. "As the date of his departure approached, she became more and more agitated," says a friend. "He was still fighting shy of a commitment, while she had long since been positive of what she wanted from him. It was a very frustrating position to be in. Potentially humiliating too, if he didn't come up trumps. She's a very thoughtful person: thoughtful of others as well as of herself. She fully appreciated the predicament she was in. Can you imagine how she would've felt if he'd not married her after all the palaver? She's very proud and would've died of mortification. Not only failing to get the man she wanted, but having the whole world know: it would've been too awful."

Luck, however, was once more on Diana's side. The *Sunday Mirror* published a front-page story stating that she had visited Charles on the royal train, which was parked in sidings in Wiltshire while he was there on official duties, on the evenings of 5 and 6 November. The inference was clear.

The press, of course, had been trailing Diana ever since the news of the romance broke. With resourcefulness and caution, she and Charles had so far managed to give the trailing bloodhounds the slip while they romanced deep into the night. Although some of these reporters had strong suspicions that Charles and Diana were human beings with red blood flowing through their veins, none of them had so far been able to catch them out in a compromising situation. They knew nothing of the secret rendezvous, the meetings at Highgrove, the switched cars, Stephen Barry driving Diana half-way round the country for private assignations that ended at dawn.

Then a zealous reporter spotted a blonde answering Diana's description come and go from the royal train while it was parked at the sidings. It now looked as if Charles and Diana had been caught out. Although her denials, "confided" to James Whitaker, were splashed over the front pages of the *Daily Star,* and the press took the line that there was nothing wrong with Diana spending a few private hours with her boyfriend, warning bells rang at the Palace. These would prove helpful to Diana.

The most immediate benefit of the publicity was that it put further pressure on to Prince Charles. As with the original story that broke the news of their romance, it catapulted the relationship on to a new level. Charles's decency as a human being and Diana's reputation were now inextricably linked.

This new scenario presented difficulties for Diana, however, and her family set about limiting the damage as best they could. Up to that point the belief at the Palace was that any bride of a Prince of Wales had to have a spotless reputation. Whether she was a virgin or not, they would have to be in a position to present the putative bride to the public as being one. For that reason alone it would have been injudicious to let the story pass. Moreover The Prince of Wales had never given Diana or anyone else any indication that he wished to marry her, and, like any other concerned family, Diana's did not wish her reputation to be called into question without hopping to her defence.

"They knew that he had a long history of love 'em and

117

leave 'em. Why, half the pretty girls who had worked at Buck House had, at one time or the other, been girlfriends of his. Some had lasted little more than the time it takes to blink your eye. But he left all of them with a lasting memory of how potently masculine he is and they weren't going to have Charles love and leave Diana.

"So The Queen, caught up in the frenzy of outraged principle surrounding her, took the unprecedented step of demanding a retraction from the editor of the paper. I can guarantee, had Diana been anyone but Ruth Fermoy's granddaughter and Robert Fellowes's sister-in-law, that story would have come and gone with as much notice as royal stories, whether true or false, customarily receive. Which is none—zero—nought."

The Queen, by coming out batting so firmly for her assistant private secretary's sister-in-law's honour, duly enhanced Lady Diana's stature and endowed her heir's romance with a seriousness it did not yet possess. From his point of view, "Charles was finding it more and more difficult to treat Diana with anything but the seriousness everyone else was. Pressure was making it impossible for him to prevaricate, as was his wont, or to view her with the levity with which he had entered into the romance. Where his heart did not lead, other people's actions were dragging him. He was sufficiently fond of her to want to continue the relationship," says a well-known connection of the Royal Family. "Just not so fond that he was prepared to deliver the goods that he was being railroaded into handing over."

But that was not quite the end of the matter. Bob Edwards, the editor of the *Sunday Mirror,* stood by every word printed in the story and refused to retract. He had no doubt it was true. Moreover, he could not see what the fuss was all about. To him, it merely illustrated how much in love Charles and Diana were, and that they were normal human beings. If only he had known how the aristocracy, the courtiers, and the Royal Family function, he might have had a deeper comprehension of how and why The Queen had entered the fray.

CHAPTER NINE

Hooking the Fish

Charles's departure for India left Diana alone and ostensibly unprotected in London. She still had to run the daily gauntlet with the ladies and gentlemen of Fleet Street. She was still pursued from Earl's Court to Pimlico, still asked whether she and Charles had spoken about marriage, whether she wanted to marry him, whether she felt she would marry him. The journalists covering the Charles and Diana saga had long since made up their minds that she would make an ideal Princess of Wales, and she took great pains not to dissuade them from the belief which she had instilled in the first place. She remained charm and sweetness itself, even during the apparent débâcle of the Love in the Sidings episode. "She played them the way she was playing Charles. Like a real pro. The only thing was, they were a lot easier to handle," says a schoolmate.

By this time, Diana had developed clearly defined relationships with several of the reporters. They were on such cordial terms that one might have been tempted to call them friends, but for the gulf of rank and interest separating them. James Whitaker among others often advised her on what she should and should not say. If, despite this, she did say something compromising, the journalist in question simply did not use it. There was a real camaraderie between Diana and the corps, which continues to this day. They wanted her to marry Charles and, knowing the full extent of their influence, and how easy it would be to scupper her chances, they avoided printing anything that might jeopardize her. Little did they know, but she had got them to join her in achieving her goal.

Popular journalists, of course, are popular journalists. Their every instinct is directed towards the production of a good story. Even when they are well-intentioned, they can no more resist good copy than a lion can avoid pouncing on its prey. And so it came about that the ever cooperative Lady Diana Spencer was placed against the light when she agreed to pose for some shots in the gardens of St. George's Square, with her little charges tugging at each hand. It was one of the few instances when W.C. Fields' warning about children and animals being scene-stealers proved to be unfounded. Diana's legs beneath the transparent voile skirt hogged everyone's attention, including an admiring Prince Charles, who was amused by the whole episode. "Like most men, he's chuffed when people admire his woman," says a former girlfriend.

The next good story, however, which was intended to be equally harmless and as helpful as every other one had been to date, threatened Diana. On 28 November, a pensive Diana admitted to Roger Tavener of the highly respected Press Association News Agency, "I'd like to marry soon. What woman doesn't want to marry eventually? Next year? Why not? I don't think nineteen is too young. It depends on the person." He asked her if Charles had proposed, to which a blushing Diana giggled before cannily replying, "I can't say yes or no to that. I can't confirm or deny it."

When Mr. Tavener filed his story and it was picked up by the papers, all hell broke loose. The first eruptions took place in the confines of Diana's ambitious family. "Once more, they saw the danger immediately," the courtier's aristocratic sister-in-law says. "They're very wily and it took no great genius to figure out the Pandora's Box of horrors which Diana's comments had unleashed. First of all, she committed Sarah's unforgivable cardinal sin. Thou shalt not speak to the press, otherwise thou shalt be cast forth from the Majestic presence. She also rather shamelessly showed her hand. It simply did not do for young ladies, no matter how well-connected they were, to seem so over-eager to get married to anyone, and most decidedly not to a member of the Royal Family."

Something had to be done. Unless it was the very real prospect existed that Diana would have blown her chances with The Prince of Wales for all time. She therefore denied the story. But there was still a problem. Remember, it was the word of a nineteen year old, with a lot to lose if she had said what she was alleged to have said, versus a respected journalist. It would have been extremely surprising if Diana's family had failed to give her counsel and support at such a crucial time. Not being uncaring they quite naturally did so.

The question now arose over who was the most suitable member of her family to come to her rescue as it was patently obvious that she, on her own, could not dig herself out of the hole in which she now found herself. Despite the authority which Ruth, Lady Fermoy, and Robert Fellowes possessed by virtue of being members of the Royal Household, their very links prevented them from stepping publicly into such a controversial breach. So her mother, Frances Shand Kydd came to the rescue.

She wrote a letter to *The Times,* which she sent with dispatch, mindful of the necessity for allaying royal suspicions of her daughter's suitability before those misgivings solidified into permanent ostracism. She wrote an indignant statement of Diana's innocence, with subtle reference to her suitability as a royal bride, while mounting a scathing attack on Mr. Tavener's report.

The assumption of a high moral tone certainly worked for Diana. Frances had made a heartrending and outraged declaration, and it was one which everyone at court, where the defence was aimed, chose to accept. Diana was innocent; the press guilty. Far from freezing her out, the Royal Family, who understand the concept of the dastardly press hounding victims by putting words into their mouths, rallied around Diana. No one blamed her for those indiscreet and over-eager admissions—indeed, no one doubted that she had never uttered one word of those or any other of the many remarks with which she was daily credited by her allies, the ladies and gentlemen of the press.

It was also obvious, to those who knew Frances and Diana, that the world had unwittingly glimpsed how alike were mother and daughter. Diana had inherited Frances's perspicacity along with her looks, dress sense, style, taste and charm. Barbara Cartland commented on Frances's uncanny knack of fomenting "wonderful press" and said, "She is very clever." The same was true of Diana, who did not miss a beat with the press. She still needed them if she were to achieve her objective and become The Princess of Wales. So, cool as ever, every day, as she left her flat at Coleherne Court and got into her car, she remained the same sweet and thoughtful innocent she had always projected herself as being.

It took considerable gumption to face, with openness and friendliness, people who had been helping you, deleting your ill-advised comments, and generally furthering your case, when you had, by inference, recently called them liars to and through your mother. But, as Jacqueline, Lady Killearn noted, "She's tough. Very like her mother. You only need to look at that chin to see it."

As Diana bit her lip, flashed her smile, lowered her eyes, and convinced the supposed liars of the press that she was a shy and guileless innocent, the noble sister-in-law of the courtier was coming to the conclusion that "it was just as well the role of Princess of Wales requires acting skills. Diana is a performer to put all but the great divas in the shade."

Even in late November and early December 1980, The Prince of Wales was not in love with Lady Diana Spencer. There is a considerable amount of doubt amongst his friends, as well as hers, that he was ever in love with her at all, but, whatever his subsequent feelings, everyone I spoke to was sure that he did not approach the state of being in love until well after their engagement.

These conclusions are borne out by his conduct. With his official visit to India at an end, he did not rush back home, as any man in the throes of love would have done. Instead, he sauntered off to Nepal, where he indulged his innate curiosity and taste for the exotic. From there, he set off on a three-day trek up the Himalayas, returning refreshed from the solitude and his communion with nature. This was not the behaviour of a man in love, and later, after the marriage, when dreamland had been replaced by the rocky terrain of reality, Diana would say to a friend, "He was never in love with me. I didn't know it when I married him, but I can see it now."

Charles returned to London, to a frenzy of speculation about his future plans. His presence fed the interest raging throughout Fleet Street as much as his absence did, and this did not abate until well after the wedding, though no one could predict such a phenomenon at the time.

"If ever the hacks pounding out the daily diet of romantic fantasy had known how unromantic the Charles and Diana affair was," says one of his closest associates at the Palace, "their fingers would have seized up into claws in mid-air above their typewriters." As it was, by being so out of touch with how arduously the most exciting romance in the world was progressing, they glamorized Diana and created a romantic ambience that was in large part responsible for its fruition into marriage.

A cousin of the Prince's agrees about the crucial role played by the press. "If it hadn't been for the press, The Prince of Wales would never have married Diana. They turned a perfectly ordinary, though attractive girl, with a pleasing but quite unexceptional personality, into a media superstar. To give her her due, she rose to the occasion magnificently. But it was the press which glamorized her. They presented her as an object of great desire. They have a penchant for hyperbole, and they couldn't resist portraying her as being more desirable than she was. This, in turn, only made her more desirable. The image wasn't her creation. It was the press's. And it's what finally hooked The Prince of Wales."

The hooking, however, was not a straightforward affair. Upon his return from India, Charles was filled with misgivings about continuing a relationship whose pace had long since been taken out of his hands. "He was very undecided about what to do. He was in a difficult position. On the one hand, he did not want to be forced into a marriage with someone he was not in love with," says a former member of his household. "Sure, he liked her a lot, and recognized how suitable she was in many respects. But he wasn't sure that what there was between them could ever develop into something that justified a radical and irreversible commitment. You must remember, the more he saw of her, the more difficult it became for him to extricate himself if he concluded that this [the relationship] wasn't right. On the other hand, he's always put duty above everything else. He's always been very concerned about what people think, of fulfilling their expectations, doing the right thing, that sort of thing. He knew what practically everyone wanted of him. He could see both sides of the question, which made it awkward for him. He really didn't know what to do. He wanted to be fair to everybody—possibly too much so."

So he did not get in touch with Diana upon his return. "Diana was furious. She told me that she took the phone off the hook so that when he tried to reach her, he could not. 'I did it to teach him a lesson,' she said. 'Let him chase me a little.' It was a clever move. It rattled him. Threw him off balance. Put him on his toes. Made him keener."

"They were like two swimmers who are propelled down a fast-moving river by a strong current. Even though they had started swimming on opposite shores, there was an inevitability about them linking up," says a European royal.

The pressure upon Charles was acute. Overwhelmed by the press, he was mindful that many millions of his future subjects were now rooting for a union with Diana. Everyone in Britain, except The Queen, seemed to be in favour of marriage. But that was a huge step. Long ago he had said that, if you were The Prince of Wales, you had to let your head rule your heart when the question of matrimony arose. Whomever he married, he expected to be stuck with her for the rest of his life. There would be neither private nor public escape if he made a mistake. That in itself was an awesome prospect, for the consequences of getting it wrong would devolve not only upon Charles the man personally, but also upon Charles the Prince, the nation, and possibly the monarchy too. "He had to be convinced that she had a character he liked, admired, could live with. She had to have a personality he found compatible. He wanted to be able to feel that whomever he married today, he would like, love and respect more in five years, and even more in ten. And that she would be up to the job of being Princess of Wales and maybe, one day, Queen," says a foreign royal cousin of Charles.

Here the dilemma presented itself. Charles could not get to know Diana better unless he saw more of her. And he could not see more of her without feeding the public's expectations as well as Diana's. But his life had been full of one paradox after another, so, putting his reservations to one side, and hoping that a positive attitude would produce what everyone seemed to want, he resumed his courtship of Diana.

Whenever he telephoned her flat, if one of the flatmates answered, he coyly gave his name as Renfrew. Baron Renfrew is one of his titles. He did not, however, ever identify himself as Mister anything, as some of the newspapers subsequently alleged. A gentleman never prefixes his surname with a title, whether it be mister, baron, prince or anything in between. To do so is the height of vulgarity, and whatever else he is, The Prince of Wales is not vulgar.

The problem of where to conduct the romance was still as pressing as ever. Charles wanted time to be with Diana, to get to know her better. "Even though he was hoping to be in a position to fulfil everyone's expectations, he was not so self-abnegating as to get himself embroiled in a marriage he did not want," a cousin said. Peace and privacy were what he needed, not another snatched night at Highgrove or the use of his cousin Lord Romsey's house, Broadlands in Hampshire. Queen Elizabeth The Queen Mother, giving voice to her sentiments about a union between her grandson and her lady-in-waiting's grand-daughter, offered the lovers the use of Birkhall, her house in the Scottish Highlands near Balmoral. There they spent blissful days together, growing closer than they had ever been.

Charles returned to London somewhat more convinced

that Diana might be the right girl for him. "She was completely in love with him. Devotedly besotted. Which man can resist a lovely young woman who's so desperately in love with him? She made it plain what she wanted, or, as he put it, what she had in her mind. By the time they went to stay with Andrew and Camilla Parker Bowles at Bolehyde Manor, what she sought from the relationship was already under discussion," says a close friend of his. "It was there, in the cabbage patch, that they had that famous talk about marriage. He didn't propose. He didn't make a declaration of intent. What he did was feel his way to where she stood. She was very frank and forthright. She's much more strong-minded than him. She set the pace. Yes, it's fair to say she's bewitching. And she bewitched him."

Weighed down with the decision of whether Diana Spencer was the right girl for him or not, Charles joined the other members of the Royal Family at Windsor for Christmas. Diana was not invited. This sacrosanct time, the only occasion throughout the year when all the members of the family gather together, is never diluted by outsiders, not even by the royal in-laws, with the result that anyone who marries into the family never again spends Christmas with their blood relations.

"The Duke of Edinburgh didn't miss an opportunity to rib and rile The Prince of Wales," a courtier says. "It's no secret that they can't stand each other. Prince Philip positively relished Prince Charles's discomfiture. He kept on taunting him about getting married, telling him he'd better get on with it before he was so old he couldn't get a girl of child-bearing age, that sort of thing. The Duke can be a real pig when he wants to be, but he also has a wonderfully practical side, and when he wasn't taunting The Prince of Wales, he made some pretty incisive points. Like, you can't prevaricate and drag this out forever. You're dealing with a young lady of good family. You have to treat her with respect. You have to consider her feelings, and the feelings of her family. You must make up your mind as soon as possible, for the good of all concerned.

"The romance remained *the* topic of conversation. Even

The Queen got in on the act. She seconded the Duke on the question of The Prince of Wales making up his mind at the very earliest opportunity. But she did not pressurize him to stay in or get out of the relationship. She had strong reservations about Diana. She felt that she didn't have the right sort of character for the job. She was concerned that Diana had never stuck to anything she had undertaken. She also felt that they did not have anything in common, that once the thrill of their newfound passion wore off, they would have a problem. Not even she envisaged just how big a problem it would become, but she was the only person who spotted the weakness. You must remember, she's spent her whole life dealing with all different sorts of people. She's known every world leader of any consequence, and has had to work her way through many a snakepit. It's made her an exceedingly good judge of character.

"The Duke of Edinburgh, on the other hand, was enthusiastic about Diana. You know he's always had an eye for a pretty girl, and Diana buttered him up every opportunity she got. But it went deeper than that. In some ways, they're similar personality types. Both very aware of their sexuality. Both flirtatious. Both raunchy and witty. They still get along like a house on fire, which is more than we can say for The Queen or The Prince of Wales."

From Windsor Castle, the court moved to Sandringham, taking to that sleepy Norfolk outpost all the hustle and bustle that had so illuminated Diana's youth. Diana, who had spent Christmas with her family, now joined Charles. So too did the popular press. Intent on capturing the latest developments in the royal romance, they swooped down like avaricious vultures circling the fatted calf, and used the many public rights of way crisscrossing the estate to gain access to the Royal Family. Only if you have had the experience of a pack of hungry journalists, intent on devouring your flesh in the quest for a juicy story, can you fully appreciate the arrant animalism implicit in such a scenario. Unless you want the publicity, you really do learn what it is like to be a hounded animal before the kill.

As such hounding was in clear breach of the tradition

that the press leave the Royal Family to enjoy their holidays in peace, The Queen, who takes everything about her station in life seriously, shouted at the assembled journalists and photographers, in an uncharacteristic display of temper, to leave them alone. "It's insupportable," she was later overheard saying to The Prince of Wales. "I cannot have this [continue] much longer."

The only other person, aside from The Queen, who was not enamoured of Diana was The Prince of Wales's private secretary, the Hon. Edward Adeane. Despite what some writers have alleged, I was informed by a member of the Royal Household that he was not in favour of a prospective marriage. "He didn't think about liking or not liking her. He thought about suitability. She was too young. She'd never finished anything in her life. She wouldn't be a stayer. He preferred Anna Wallace. She was a determined horsewoman. That showed she had the character and determination needed by a Princess of Wales. And she was the right age. There was the matter of her racy past, but one only needs to think of Fergie to see how unimportant that was. Diana didn't have a history, at least none that was generally known or could be proven, and that was a plus for her, but what else does she have, he asked himself? He was wrong, of course. They all were. She does have staying power."

Nevertheless, Edward Adeane and The Queen were partly right. Taken as a whole, Diana was not suited to the rigours, pressures and sacrifices that the role of Princess of Wales demands of its occupants. Brilliant as she would prove to be in executing its starry and sympathetic aspects, behind the scenes she has not been an unqualified success. The full spectrum of her personality reveals that while she does possess astonishing tenacity for the things she seeks or values, she has also a reckless disregard for aspects of the Monarchy that do not personally matter to her, and for the consequences of her actions. "She is astonishingly self-centred," a courtier says, "and doesn't give a stuff what havoc she wreaks if anything is standing in the way of what she wants. She really doesn't care who she hurts or what she damages, as long as she gets her own way. What Diana

128

wants, Diana must get. She possesses dogged determination and definitely has staying power. She only lacks it when she can't get what she wants. Then she's apt to throw in the towel."

Despite the pressure from practically every source to marry the demure and suitable Lady Diana Spencer, the heir to the throne was still not ready to succumb. Throughout January 1981, he refused to commit himself, although he did turn the question over and over with his closest friends. "It was what everyone wanted, and she seemed tailor-made for the life," says the former member of the Royal Household. "Even Camilla Parker Bowles and Dale Tryon were in favour of the Prince marrying the youthful Diana, cloaked as she was in an aura of unworldliness. Charles himself was also under the impression that she would fit in with his scheme of things."

Diana had been careful to project precisely the image to achieve the prize she sought. Despite Charles's dithering, she now began to scent that achievement of her goal was only a matter of time. "The longer it went on, the more confident she became. Though he was still holding back, it became more and more impossible for him to back out," says a friend. Moreover, the romance was going well. This too encouraged Diana's optimism. "He's very sensitive, like a little boy almost, about his feelings. He was opening up more and more. A woman senses that a man is crossing over that invisible line, the one that marks the divide between retaining his independence and throwing in the towel. He was moving closer and closer to her, helped in no small way by the powerful physical attraction they now shared."

Charles had long preached about the dangers of infatuation blinding a man to the realities of an unsuitable mate. "When the shoe was on his foot, he didn't see it," says a royal cousin by marriage. "He was very aware of the dangers of physical desire leading him up the wrong path, but that's exactly what happened. That and Diana obfuscating him completely with her 'butter couldn't melt in my mouth' routine, when we all know now she only needs to bite hard to reduce granite to dust."

There had been a possibility that Diana would join Charles on his annual skiing holiday at Klosters, Switzerland, at the end of January. But they decided that they would have to forego the pleasures binding them ever closer, if the Prince's skiing holiday were not to be entirely ruined by the pursuing press. So he flew off on his own, leaving his girlfriend to prepare for her own forthcoming vacation.

The perennially shrewd Diana and her ever-helpful family had come up with yet another tried-and-true method of hooking the slippery Prince. Since adoration and the pressure from the press had not landed him yet, the time had come for elusiveness. But, as it was not feasible to start taking the telephone off the hook once more, the Raine Spencer/William Lewisham technique for catching reluctant bridegrooms was implemented. Diana removed herself from the royal presence by flying off to Australia, for her first visit to her stepfather's remote ranch.

It emerged that the well-laid plans were not needed. In Switzerland, flying down the virgin slopes of piste, Charles finally made up his mind about Diana. He returned to London on 2 February. Promptly getting in touch with her this time on his return, he arranged a proper dinner *à deux*, instead of their usual suppers consumed off trays, to be served in his sitting room at Buckingham Palace. It was there, in suitably romantic surroundings, with a recognizable sense of occasion marking this momentous event, that he proposed.

The Prince of Wales explained, "I chose the moment so that she would have plenty of time to think about it, to decide if it was all going to be too awful." To Diana, however, being asked to sit at the majestic table after months of plotting and scheming with her nose pressed against the grindstone was not her idea of horror. Without a moment's pause, she did as her mother had done. She accepted the proposal. The die was cast.

CHAPTER TEN

An Engagement is Announced

*R*oyal families absorb people. No matter what your capacity, inclination, function or position, if you are too close to the royal orbit, you quickly find yourself being sucked in, with an inevitable loss of independence and individuality. It matters not a jot whether the family in question is the British, the Swedish, Norwegian, Belgian, Japanese or Kuwaiti.

"Royalties," a turn-of-the-century aristocrat said, "are astonishingly self-centred. They don't mean to be. They simply are." That is as true today as it was a century ago. I have never encountered a member of a reigning royal family who did not function as if the world revolved around him or her. Whether they are warm or cold, nice or nasty, young or old, they all share that trait. Their way is the only way, their desires the only desires, their convenience the only one worth considering. From early childhood until the grave, they are surrounded by people who defer to them, put them first, step aside for them, lie, cheat, pander, and sacrifice to be with them.

It is not their fault. If, all your life, people lead you to the conclusion that you should come first, you will naturally believe that that is your right. It is hardly surprising therefore that royalty develops an exaggerated sense of its own importance, and the consequence of such an opinion is that everyone who joins the orbit ends up playing the royal game, irrespective of what they started out playing.

To Diana, swapping a mundane but free existence for an extraordinary one without freedom was a price well worth paying. She had been brought up to marry a secondary prince; now she was betrothed to the premier one.

But she was only nineteen. She did not realize just how exacting an exchange the gilded cage would prove. "Had she been able to peer into a crystal ball and see how miserable she would often be in the future," a school chum said, "she'd have done the same. She's like Isak Dinesen. If you remember, she got syphilis from her husband, Baron Blixen, and spent the last fifty years of her life in unbelievable agony. But she felt that the prestige of being a Baroness made the pain worth enduring. Diana feels the same way about being Princess of Wales, though she hates having to pay the price she does. It enrages her. She can't see why she shouldn't have the freedom to do exactly as she pleases when she wants, without the restraints that bind The Queen and the other members of the Royal Family. Yes, I suppose it is fair to say she wants all the perks of royalty without the restrictions."

Charles had asked Diana to think over his proposal while she was in Australia. This she did not do: her mind was already made up. Instead, she enjoyed her last days of freedom as a non-royal individual. Good Hope Farm is an average Australian farmstead with a typical, rough and basic house. The furniture is functional rather than decorative, but Diana did not care about the absence of luxury. She had finally achieved what she set out to achieve, and she was with her mother, who had not only helped her to win the prize, but was also someone whom she cherished.

Throughout her Australian stay, Diana enjoyed absolute privacy. Frances and Peter Shand Kydd issued categorical denials that Diana was with them, and the press left them alone. According to Frances, "I was determined to have what my daughter and I knew would be our last holiday together. We had a private holiday in our house on the beach. A normal family holiday, swimming and surfing. Of course we talked about Diana's future life."

132

Frances also said how much she wanted her daughters to marry men they loved. This, however, did not invariably ensure her approval and even introduced an apparent contradiction when put to the test. When the nineteen-year-old Diana wanted to marry a man twelve years her senior, her mother approved, although according to Sarah, when she at a similar age wanted to marry a man with a similar age difference, her mother had advised against the union. Her counsel then had been that Sarah was too young and the age gap too big, and that such marriages, as Frances knew to her personal cost, usually failed.

Diana returned to London as sure of what she wanted as she had ever been. Ever a stickler for correct form, Charles formally asked her father for her hand in marriage. In a glimpse of the humour that had so appealed to the late King George VI and to his many friends, Lord Spencer mischievously observed, "I wonder what he would have done if I had refused?"

There were details to be attended to prior to the announcement of the engagement. One was rather less pleasant than the others. A well-known connection of the Royal Family says, "Diana was given a thorough physical examination, to ensure that she was in good health. Had there been any glaring reasons why she could not reproduce and fulfil what was, after all, the primary purpose of the marriage, these would have shown up. The purpose of the examination was not, as might be supposed, to determine whether she was a virgin. There was no need for that. No one expected her to be a virgin. That was an invention of the press."

Prince Charles's conduct with some of his previous girlfriends certainly substantiates this royal relation's assertion. Anna Wallace had definitely not sported a hymen, yet this had not sullied her chances or stood in the way of Charles proposing marriage. Indeed, it could be fairly said that, while a spotless reputation was a desirable feature for any future Princess of Wales, the odd blemish did not rule out a prospective candidate. For instance, while Charles was friendly with Anna Wallace, there was a strong rumour in fashionable circles that her temper was not the only part of her prone to eruption. Many a dinner party was enlivened with speculation as to whether Charles would soon be sporting cold sores, and if so, where. *Private Eye,* the satirical magazine, added fuel to the fire when it ran a story stating that Anna had the most fashionable venereal disease of the day: herpes. The Whiplash confounded her detractors and admirers by not suing. She did not even ask for a retraction, forcing everyone to the conclusion that she did indeed have gifts that might not bear examination in a court of law.

Although Anna Wallace's more intriguing facets did not deter Prince Charles from viewing her as an eventual consort on the throne of England, the prevailing belief amongst the courtiers was that Diana had to have a pure image. This was proving to be an uphill struggle.

First, there had been the intimations arising from the Love in the Sidings stories. Not even Diana's assertions in print that she "did not have a past," had never had "boyfriends," and that, as she was "only nineteen" she had not had the time to have "lovers," entirely convinced everyone. Journalists are by nature curious, and while those assigned to cover Lady Diana Spencer were rooting for her, there were others, further behind the scenes, who were quietly ferreting away trying to find out the truth behind the innocent façade. They wanted answers to questions, as they did not believe nineteen was too young to have a boyfriend or a lover—it was old enough for many girls to be mothers. Moreover, they were not confident that Diana Spencer was the only attractive nineteen year old to have been entirely untouched by the values, attitudes, and codes of behaviour of the late twentieth century.

Upon digging deeper, journalists discovered that one name kept on cropping up regularly. In the year before she started going out with Prince Charles, Diana's perpetual escort had been the Hon. George Plumptre. They had done all the ordinary things that any other dating couple do: they had been to the cinema, to dinner, to friends' dinner parties, to parties. They had even been away repeatedly on weekends in the country together. Even though the attractive Mr. Plumptre was uncooperative and would not make any compromising comments about his former girl-friend, the very tone of their relationship spoke for itself. The time had come to shed some light on just how sheltered was a nineteen year old living away from her parents' home in a flat of her own in the centre of the metropolis.

Journalists, however, are not free agents. They may publish only what their editors wish them to. At any given time, there are countless subjects which are taboo. The truth, contrary to what the idealistic may believe, is not the deciding factor. Boosting circulation, and flattering the people the paper's proprietor wishes to impress, are the criteria which eventually determine what is or is not printed.

The editors of Fleet Street collectively decided at the end of 1980 that they would lay off digging into Diana's past. By doing so, they were effectively buying the image of Lady Diana that she herself, the Palace, and the Fermoy family were selling. Why they did so bears some examination. Diana, Frances Shand Kydd, The Queen, and the chairman of the Press Council all had made it clear in their different ways that they wished her privacy to be protected in an unprecedented manner. Above all, however, the editors did not wish to offend The Queen. The public did have a right to know the facts, and the public interest did dictate that these be placed before a newspaper's readership; not, though, when the price was royal ostracism or flying in the face of the overwhelming evidence that the newspaper's readership wanted Lady Diana to be pure as the freshly driven snow, as she tobogganed down the slopes on her way to a royal marriage.

Journalists wishing to probe into Diana's past now found themselves out in the cold. Always, in the past, whenever their editors did not wish to run a story they knew to be true, they had turned to the satirical magazine *Private Eye*. Now they once more took their stories to *Private Eye*, which the family feared would ask questions about the past that Diana had asserted she did not have.

The timing could not have been more impeccable. Plans had been laid for the announcement of Diana's engagement to Charles on 24 February. And the rumblings were starting. "Were the family worried? What would you call nail-bitingly horrendously out-of-their-skull frantic?" says the aristocratic sister-in-law of the top-ranking courtier. "Until she was married to The Prince of Wales, the marriage could be called off. The prospect of opening up the next issue of *Private Eye* and reading that Diana was not a virgin filled them with dread. You must remember that leading courtiers are the first to advise the royals to distance themselves from anyone who is involved in any controversy at all. I cannot think of one instance when they have put loyalty before public opinion. If Diana had become embroiled in a scandal, Robert Fellowes's and Ruth Fermoy's voices would have ceased to carry weight. After all, they were related to Diana, and they were a lot less senior than the top chaps. Remember, Ruth Fermoy was only a lady-in-waiting to Queen Elizabeth [The Queen Mother], and Robert Fellowes was merely The Queen's Assistant Private Secretary. Outranking him were the Private Secretary and the Deputy Private Secretary, both of whose advice counted for far more."

The family were not prepared to permit the rumblings of a minor publication to ruin their joy, however, and neither were the happy couple. Having made up his mind to commit himself to Diana, The Prince of Wales now threw himself into the romance with all the intensity at his command. "Diana was very kittenish with him," says a cousin of the Prince's, "and he soaked it up. She was always on his lap, stroking him and generally making a fuss of him. No one had ever been quite so effusive about him. He loved it."

Sarah-Jane Gaselee, whose father Nick trained the Prince's horses, met Diana around this time, when she was eleven. She says, "I remember clearly when I first met Lady Diana, as she then was." Diana was also adept then at engineering what she wanted, as Sarah-Jane recalled. "She'd give me a little Indian bracelet and make me go up to Prince Charles and say, 'Look what Lady Diana has given me.' It was to make him feel guilty about presents."

Notoriously parsimonious, The Prince of Wales was no more generous with Diana than he had been with any of his previous girlfriends. "The only thing he gave us," says one, "was huge doses of himself." So it would prove with Diana, who would eventually have to put aside her dreams of the beautiful presents that a Cartland-style Prince Charming should provide. "Mr. Generosity he is not," the Princess would later snap to a friend in a moment of frustration.

Although Diana's manoeuvrings with Sarah-Jane Gaselee did not produce the mythical diamond bracelet or any of the other jewels she hoped for, Charles did have to loosen the purse strings somewhat when it came to the engagement ring. He asked Garrards, the crown jewellers, to send round a selection of rings from which Diana could choose. At the top of the range of eight was a £28,500 diamond and sapphire ring. It was set in eighteen-carat white gold and had a large central sapphire surrounded by eighteen diamonds, but was hardly the stuff of a gold-digger's dreams. The women I know would be most put out if their fiancés had been able to afford a truly decent ring and had had the gall to fob them off with such an inexpensive trinket. After all, £28,500 might sound like a lot of money, but to the seriously rich it is a paltry sum. Diana quite sensibly chose this ring because, according to her, "It was the biggest."

There were preparations to make before Diana became officially betrothed. Frances Shand Kydd came down from Scotland to be with her youngest daughter. They went shopping together; in Harrods, Diana bought a royal blue two-piece suit, with a blue and white dotted blouse. The manufacturer was Cojana, a firm owned by Neil Kinnock's erstwhile good friend, the Labour Party benefactor, financier and millionaire fugitive, Harry Costas. That outfit would unleash a welter of unforeseen and hitherto unrevealed consequences, but neither Frances nor Diana envisaged anything adverse when they selected it.

At eleven o'clock on the morning of 24 February 1981, the Lord Chamberlain, the late Lord MacLean, interrupted an investiture to make an announcement. To the astonishment of the assembled throng, he glanced down at a piece of paper from which he proceeded to read, while The Queen beamed from ear to ear: "It is with the greatest

137

pleasure that The Queen and The Duke of Edinburgh announce the betrothal of their beloved son The Prince of Wales to the Lady Diana Spencer, daughter of the Earl Spencer and the Honourable Mrs. Shand Kydd." At that same moment the engagement was being officially announced to the media. After a plethora of false alarms by the press, including marrying Charles off, against the Act of Settlement, to the Roman Catholic Princess Marie Astrid of Luxembourg, only one newspaper managed to scoop the Palace. *The Times,* rather than one of the popular papers, carried the news of the engagement in its morning edition, much to the fury of The Prince of Wales, who wanted to know whence the leak had sprung. He was never to find out.

As soon as the announcement was made, The Prince of Wales's office rang Victoria Wilson, the Principal of the Young England Kindergarten, and informed her that Diana would not be returning to resume her duties. At midday, a happy Prince of Wales and an ecstatic Lady Diana Spencer took their places on the garden steps of Buckingham Palace for their first press conference. They recounted the development of their romance and answered questions about their feelings for each other. "Are you in love?" "Of course," Diana replied, while Charles said, "Yes—whatever that may mean." In that and other exchanges, Diana came across as being more certain than Charles. Their answers revealed, to those who had an insider's knowledge of the relationship, just who set the pace. But the significance of what the lovers were saying was lost on the listening journalists, who could not imagine that a demure nineteen year old would actually be the driving force in a relationship with any older and more experienced man, much less one as eminent and as chauvinistic as The Prince of Wales.

There was much jubilation at the Palace. Everywhere there was a party atmosphere, and in The Prince of Wales's office, Edward Adeane and the Lady Clerks—Jenny Allen (now the Hon. Mrs. John Denman), Pauline Pears, Claire Potts, Julia "Lulu" Malcolm, Philippa Tingey, and Sonia Palmer (now a BBC TV producer)—toasted the happy couple in pink champagne. The Queen also toasted her son and future daughter-in-law and got so involved in the great excitement that she avidly followed the television interview from behind a curtain on the first floor.

Afterwards, Charles and Diana watched themselves on television with The Queen. That is when the problems began. "Diana," according to a member of the Royal Household, "was horrified when she saw herself." What, for her, should have been a purely joyous occasion, was ruined by the way she looked. Worse, however, was to come. When Diana saw the newspaper photographs, which made her look even more squat and pudgy than she did on television —quite an accomplishment for someone who was nearly six feet tall—she flipped. She had managed to convince herself that the television shots were an aberration, but when she was confronted by more of the same in print, she developed a sudden and abiding loathing of her image.

"Alan Fisher [the Wales's former butler] told me that Diana definitely had a real problem with food," continues the courtier. "She's fanatical about what she eats. She's obsessed with her weight. Sometimes she eats practically nothing. And she binges. Alan told me how she polished off a whole chocolate cake once. And another time she ate practically a whole leg of lamb on her own in one of her midnight raids on the fridge.

"The problem began as soon as she saw her engagement photos. Many famous people become obsessed with how they look when they see unflattering images of themselves. I've seen it happen time and again. It happened with Diana, and it happened with Fergie. Diana was appalled by how chubby and dumpy and matronly she looked. She set about curing the problem immediately. She wanted to look her best as a bride. And since then she's wanted to look her best, full stop. She wants to come across as tall and slim and beautiful and have everyone think she's beautiful. She likes pleasing people and she knows they like her looking good."

The courtier goes on to contradict the accounts that Diana's bulimia has been caused by her unhappy marriage. "She developed it before she was even married. I was there at the time and I vividly remember what happened.

139

It all started when she saw the engagement pictures and decided she had to lose weight. She herself told me, 'I've discovered a great way of dieting. You eat all you want, then . . . .' and she finished off the sentence by opening her mouth wide, pointing to it with her finger, and mimicking vomiting."

The weight, however, did not fall off quickly enough, so she then tried skipping meals. "The problem with her is she has a voracious appetite. She had always been a binge eater, but now that she wasn't eating regularly, it was as if she saved up all her hunger, then satisfied it at one huge meal. She was quite open about it in those days. The hiding away and gorging herself on a whole turkey, as she did once, didn't start until later on, after she was married, by which time The Prince of Wales was going out of his mind with worry about the problem. It was at that point that she began concealing what she ate, not because she was ashamed, but because it was her way of proving that she did not have a problem. He wanted her to admit that she did. He tried to get medical help for her. But she was like an alcoholic or drug addict who doesn't want to give up what they're taking. She was implacable in her refusal to admit there was anything wrong with her. It really is unfair of her to now try to blame him for a problem that developed purely because of her vanity. He did his best to help her. She was the one who did not want help."

This, however, is not an uncommon occurrence with sufferers of eating disorders. Diana's sister Sarah, who suffered from the related condition of anorexia nervosa, proved to be as difficult a patient as the Princess, although she was cured much more quickly. The fact that two members of one family could have manifested similar disorders is a clear indication that their personality problems stemmed from childhood and were the inevitable effects of the Spencer heritage.

Diana's bulimia proved to have a devastating effect upon her marriage. As The Queen says, "Her bulimia caused the problems in the marriage. The problems did not cause her illness."

This is a view shared by everyone who knows the couple

well and is one that all responsible doctors would share. As the noted psychologist Dr. Gloria Litman said, "Bulimia nervosa causes depression, anxiety and severe mood swings. Repeated vomiting deprives your body of vital minerals such as potassium and zinc which in turn induces a state of chronic lassitude. It reduces the sex drive and makes the sufferer hypersensitive and highly emotional." Living with someone in the throes of such an illness is like living with a drinking alcoholic or an active drug addict. The bulimic is unreasonable, has no sense of proportion, and is often subject to fits of violent rage. She blames everyone but herself for her problems, and indeed denies, as Diana did for several years, that she has a problem. She is also excessively demanding of everyone with whom she is emotionally involved, especially her spouse, and ultimately destructive not only of her own health and well-being but also of the health and well-being of those closest to her. "The Prince of Wales certainly agrees with that description, and so do I," one of his relations says.

As one problem was about to begin, another came to an end. The Fermoy family, recognizing the *Private Eye* threat for what it was, swung into action yet again. With all their years of courtly experience behind them, they had the knowledge and the confidence to do whatever it took to kill off the press's further delving into Diana's private life. But they knew they had to do it soon, before some muckraker turned up to throw a spanner in the whole works. "Diana's uncle told me that they [the family] were very worried about *Private Eye*," says a family friend, with one of the most eminent titles in the land. "They had heard that Nigel Dempster was getting ready to do the business on Diana—incorrectly, as it turned out. They had endless conferences about the best way of dealing with the problem. If they allowed that rag to ferret around, it might have published something which could have ruined the whole marriage.

"It was decided that the most effective method of silencing *Private Eye* was for someone in the immediate family to pit themselves against the gossips: the family's word against the magazine's. The difficulty was who to use. It had to be someone close enough to Diana to be credible, but distant enough so that she wouldn't be affected if the operation boomeranged. Her mother and grandmother were too close to her. Furthermore, her mother had only recently gone into battle on her behalf. To do so again would have seemed like overkill, like a hysterical and over-ambitious woman perpetually anxious to further the cause of her offspring. The grandmother was no good either. Aside from being too close, she would not have jeopardized her own position within the Palace hierarchy, not even for her grand-daughter's advancement.

"Frances Shand Kydd's brother Edmund Fermoy emerged as the most suitable spokesman. As Diana's uncle, he was close enough to be credible. He was a lord, with a history of public service, all of which went to increase the respect the press had for him. The problem was fixed very cleverly. There was a reporter called James Whitaker who rather fancied himself as having helped Diana nab The Prince of Wales. The family decided that he should be Mercury, the messenger who would disseminate the story they wanted put about. Yes, he was a sitting duck. They used him, but it was a case of their hand scratching his back and vice versa, as he was given the story exclusively.

"The story? Edmund Fermoy declared that Diana was a virgin, that she had never had a lover."

It may not seem like much of a story now, but in 1981 Lord Fermoy's exclusive to James Whitaker created a sensation. Never before had an uncle of any prospective bride of any well-known person, and certainly not a member of the Royal Family, privately or publicly commented on the intactness of his niece's hymen. His comments made the front pages of just about every popular paper in every country of the free world.

"We all know the Royal Family have stronger stomachs than they're given credit for," says the eminent family friend of the Fermoys. "They didn't bat an eyelid. Nor did their advisers. But that was hardly surprising considering the interconnection.

"Edmund Fermoy's behaviour and quite extraordinary comments were unprecedented. Did I approve? No. I thought it was appalling. I don't care what was at stake. A gentleman simply does not speak about his niece's private parts to a tabloid reporter. Not even to a *Times* reporter. Not even to safeguard her marriage to The Prince of Wales. It was inexcusable."

Whatever the rights and wrongs of such conduct, Lord Fermoy's statement did have the desired effect. It silenced *Private Eye* and any other prospective organs which sought to question what Diana had got up to prior to her trip down the aisle. Diana, who constantly left The Prince of Wales at dawn, was now solidly enshrined as a virgin in the eyes of the public. Unless the press could furnish a photograph to the contrary, or produce a lover who had sworn an incontrovertible affidavit—never a serious prospect amongst men who were as honourable and discreet as Diana's beaux—further speculation about her past would seem like muck-raking.

Thereafter, the press did not ask questions, not even valid ones. The query remained, however, as to whether an uncle is in a position to give an authoritative declaration about the state of his niece's hymen—especially a girl who had got about as a woman of the world for two years, and still persisted in doing so? Moreover, had Edmund Fermoy ever been so close to Diana that he could speak on her behalf, unless he was put up to the job in a cynical public-relations exercise? The answers were all resoundingly negative. But Lord Fermoy succeeded in his objective. Diana's reputation was unsullied and the family's acquisition of royal and allied status no longer threatened. To Edmund Fermoy, a crown was well worth a few comments that were rather too close to the bone for your old-fashioned gentleman or lady.

Once the announcement of the engagement was made, Diana's world changed dramatically. Superficially, it now appeared as if she had the resources and the opportunity to indulge all her heart's desires. But the truth was somewhat different. In more ways than one, she was about to begin a starvation diet in the midst of plenty. The price of being a

Princess, she was due to discover, was rather higher than she had reckoned.

Diana was immediately taken under the Royal Family's umbrella. In its shade she was leaving the sunshine of freedom behind her, though she did not yet realize this, nor the terrible effect upon her in the years to come of being hemmed in so totally. She was assigned her own detective, Chief Detective Paul Officer, a forty-year-old public school alumnus, who would thereafter follow her wherever she went. It was only a matter of time before she began to feel that he was a prison warden, not a buffer against potential hostilities, and, after five months of antipathy, he became the first of a long stream of employees to depart in less than happy circumstances.

Diana was also instructed that she had to vacate Coleherne Court. Saying goodbye to Carolyn Pride, Ann Bolton and Virginia Pitman, Diana moved into Clarence House for two nights. The press and public were deceived into thinking that the young and innocent Lady Diana Spencer was safely tucked under the righteous wing of Queen Elizabeth The Queen Mother and her own grandmother, the upright Ruth, Lady Fermoy. However, after she dined with them on the first evening, they thereafter saw next to nothing of her. Diana moved into Buckingham Palace, into the nursery, near The Prince of Wales. They both wanted easy access to each other, to come and go as they pleased. The nocturnal visits which had given them so much pleasure, and which seldom ended before dawn, could continue unimpaired by the inconvenience of subterfuge or the threat of discovery and subsequent speculation.

With the move to royal quarters, Diana became inaccessible to all who had known her beforehand. Kitty Waite Walker from the Young England Kindergarten complained that after the engagement "It became very difficult because her friends couldn't get to see her. It was very hard to see her alone, and if you were with other people [after the wedding] you had to call her Your Royal Highness. I think they [the Palace advisers] meant to cut off all her old friends so that she didn't know what she was missing."

Not everyone agreed with that assessment of Diana's

sudden inaccessibility. "She chose to avoid her old friends," I was told by a member of the Royal Household, who had a lot to do with Diana at the time. "She had new fish to fry, a new identity to work on, a whole new way of life to adjust to. She didn't want too many reminders of her old life bogging her down."

Chief amongst Diana's new preoccupations was a desire to be svelte and trim for her wedding in July. "She told me that she was going to lose her puppy fat if it killed her," says the same person. With that in mind, Diana went on a rigid diet. This was relieved only occasionally, when she was so overwhelmed by hunger that she had to go on one of the binges to which she had been prone, even as a schoolgirl.

Losing the weight was not enough. As it fell off, Diana, who had thrived on the joys of exercise since early childhood, tightened and toned her muscles. She asked her music and dance teachers from West Heath, Lily Snipp and Wendy Vickers, to come to the Palace and give her ballet lessons. Twice a week, she put on a black leotard and repaired to the throne room, where they put her through her paces. Dancing was more than just a supplement to dieting. "She lived for ballet," Miss Snipp said, explaining that the "lessons helped her get away from the pressures of being a member of the Royal Family."

Nor did Diana limit herself to dancing only when she had a lesson. She often put on her tapes, working out on her tap and jazz routines on her own. Strenuous exercise floods the bloodstream with endorphins, the body's natural equivalent to morphine, creating a feeling of well-being, a natural high that all athletes come to love.

Diana indubitably needed as much release as she could get. For much of the time, she was like a prisoner in a gilded cage. "She was desperately lonely," a friend says. "She was shut away in that vast mausoleum. She couldn't come and go as she pleased any more. She hated Paul Officer [her detective] trailing her everywhere, as if she were an imbecile or criminal. Her friends no longer had easy access to her, and when you were at the Palace, there was always someone hovering in the background. If you're not used to that level of surveillance, it's freaky."

Once, Diana wanted to pop out to do a bit of shopping. She hopped into her red Metro, which was parked in the quadrangle at the Palace with the other family cars, and started up the engine. Before she could even release the handbrake, Paul Officer had opened the passenger door and was in the seat. "Where are you going?" he asked.

"Out," Diana replied.

"Not without me, I'm afraid," he informed her. Diana was not amused.

"It didn't help that her move to Buckingham Palace made no dent at all in The Prince of Wales's schedule," says the member of the Royal Household, who had a lot of contact with her in those days. "He still had all his official duties, planned months before, to honour. And he made no concession to her presence whenever he had time off. He still came and went as if he were a man on his own. If he wanted to play polo, visit friends, or fly to the moon, she had to fit in with his plans. It wasn't easy for her."

The Queen was concerned that her future daughter-in-law might not have the personal resources to meet the challenges and restrictions facing her in her new life. "She was worried by Diana's dismal track record of chopping and changing, or starting things without ever seeing them through," says the former member of the Royal Household who is close to the Waleses. "She instructed Lady Susan Hussey [a lady-in-waiting, wife of the BBC Chairman Marmaduke Hussey, and sister of Tory minister William Waldegrave] and Edward Adeane [The Prince of Wales's Private Secretary] to do everything in their power to ease her in gently. She was afraid she'd get frightened by all that was expected of her, and bolt."

Several steps were taken to assist Diana. "Her mother came into The Prince of Wales's office for a few days to help. There was a flood of congratulatory letters. These had to be replied to. Diana did not know how to word the letters or even how to sign her name properly. And there were a thousand things to attend to before the wedding. There was her wardrobe, the guest list, the bridal register.

It was beyond the scope of any nineteen year old, no matter how clued up she was."

Frances was "magnificent. She is wonderful with people —warm and charming and so capable and elegant. It was a pleasure having her around." Lady Susan Hussey was also an invaluable help. "The Queen has the utmost respect for her. The fact that she was delegated to pave the way for Diana shows just how concerned The Queen was. It was her responsibility to keep an eye on Diana while giving her a crash course in being royal. You and I know how nebulous the royal persona is. Well, she had somehow to convey it all to Diana. Making a royal out of her was a bit of an uphill struggle. She was terribly eager to please though. To her credit, she's a listener, someone who will absorb a lesson even when she doesn't want to. In that respect, she's an easy pupil, not that she is an easy pupil. She's very self-willed and she was wildly over-excited by the whole business."

Another member of the Royal Household told me, "If you could ever have seen Lady Susan Hussey teaching Diana how to wave, you'd have died of laughter. She was like Marilyn Monroe and Princess Michael of Kent rolled into one and multiplied by six. You've never seen anyone so over the top in your life. Talk about excited about being centre-stage. It was hysterical. She wiggled and waggled and oohed and aahed—and the way she smiled. She never stopped flashing those molars. You'd have thought she was competing with Farah Fawcett for the Colgate ad."

Diana also had to be taught how to walk, how to enter a room, how to exit from a car, how to hold herself while she was being spoken to, how to pose for photographers without appearing to do so, how to look at them so that her gaze was directed at them and not away from the camera, ruining their pictures. In short, she had to learn how to become the glorious cover girl she now is, while maintaining the decorum required of a royal.

Lady Susan, however, was not the only person responsible for making Diana over. Before the engagement was announced, The Prince of Wales took steps to ensure that Diana's transition would be as smooth as possible. Oliver

Everett, a career diplomat at the Foreign Office, had been seconded to Buckingham Palace, as was the custom, for two years in 1978, to act as the Prince's Assistant Private Secretary. When his term of office ended, he was replaced by Francis Cornish. But Charles had not forgotten how easy Oliver Everett was to get along with. He was young, fun, approachable, and married: everything the Hon. Edward Adeane was not. While the two men were almost contemporaries, Adeane was as stolid as Everett was flexible, as intimidating as the kindly Oliver was reassuring. Oliver Everett, the Prince concluded, would be the perfect person to ease Diana into the role of Princess of Wales, the ideal Private Secretary and Comptroller for her.

Royals see more of their private secretaries than of their spouses, and it is absolutely crucial that they get along with the men who control every aspect of their working and public lives, as well as much of their private lives.

The Prince asked Everett to return to work for him. A courtier says, "The difficulty in accepting The Prince of Wales's offer was that the Foreign Office was not prepared to give him an additional secondment, so Oliver would have to resign from the Foreign Office if he wanted to join the Prince's staff again. He was a high-flier, and there was no doubt that he was going straight to the top. So what The Prince of Wales was really asking him to do was give up a promising career to go to work for him. Everyone advised him against doing so. He was giving up a glorious future for a very low-paying and difficult, albeit prestigious, job.

"But Oliver decided to go for it. He liked The Prince of Wales, knew that the job would be interesting, and, while it didn't have the prospects, being The Princess of Wales's Private Secretary had so much kudos that that compensated for the downside. He returned to the Palace on the understanding that he would have a lifelong career. He was designated the Assistant Private Secretary to The Prince of Wales, but in reality he was Diana's Private Secretary, in much the same way that Dickie Arbiter is called The Queen's Assistant Press Secretary but is really The Prince and Princess of Wales's Press Secretary."

At first, Diana and Oliver Everett got along like a house

on fire. "They really were friends," says a member of the household, who witnessed the relationship from inception through degeneration to awful finale. "He was as close to her as it's possible to be. He was very kind and thoughtful to her. He didn't push her, but took the time and trouble to lead her gently through her paces. Everything she learnt, she learnt from him or Lady Susan Hussey. He even taught her how to sign her name, so that her signature would have a suitably regal look. Oliver has a wonderful sense of humour, and they would lark about and giggle like two kids. She was happy enough when he helped her with things like practising walking with a sheet attached to her, in simulation of the big day when she had to walk down the aisle at St. Paul's with a lengthy train and veil. But she wasn't so thrilled about boning up on history, of having to plough through required reading about the Royal Family—various biographies of previous Princesses of Wales and things like that. It was crucial that she learn what the responsibilities and requirements of her new role were, but she said to me, 'I didn't leave school to have to study bloody homework.'"

Nevertheless, Diana did the required reading. At least, she did it at first. Despite being unhappy at all the work that she was now discovering went along with being a star in the royal constellation, she was careful not to rebel until after the wedding ring. She applied herself diligently, relieved her tension with dancing and exercise, and looked forward to her big day. "There were times when she thought she'd go out of her mind with boredom and loneliness. She was used to an active life. In the past, she'd kept herself busy. Whether it was washing shirts for a friend, cooking for a dinner party, charring for someone, or taking care of babies, she was always on the go. That's how she liked being," a relation of hers told me.

Diana tried solving the problem of enforced inactivity the way she had done at Althorp during the brief period between her father's inheritance of the title and Lady Dartmouth taking over and becoming chatelaine. Whenever she was at a loose end, she engaged whatever footman crossed her path in conversation. If none was available, she popped into the kitchen. The Palace, however, was not

Althorp, and Diana soon came a cropper. The servants, mindless of the encroachments and attitudes of the twentieth century, still abided by a hierarchy in which each person knew his place and lived up to, and within, it. The more senior members of the staff did not like Diana's egalitarian approach. They felt that she was threatening the established order and might set a dangerous precedent of familiarity. Their fears were not for her; they were for themselves. If Diana were allowed to get away with speaking to humble footmen and kitchen help as if they were her equal, those same footmen and scullery maids would soon be speaking to their superiors, the valets and butlers and cooks, as if they were *their* equals. This could not be allowed to continue, so Stephen Barry, the Prince's valet, and the Yeoman of the Glass and China both decided to teach her her place. Barry told her footmen friends to back off, and when Diana next ambled down to the kitchens, the Yeoman pointed haughtily to the door and said, "Through there is *your* side of the house. Through here is *my* side of the house," and positioned himself, blocking her way, until she got the message and scurried away like a wounded rabbit.

Diana's attitude towards the domestic staff was, of course, typically aristocratic, but the born royals seldom befriend their servants, or indeed anyone other than fellow royals and relations, with such egalitarian alacrity. For instance, The Prince of Wales suffixes his every command with the pleasing refrain, "If you don't mind," although there is no doubt that what he is saying is anything but a request. He is a kind man, justly revered throughout the nation for his compassionate attitude, but he is no egalitarian. Like all the other members of his family, he will not tolerate anyone speaking to him as if he is their equal. To one and all, he remains Your Royal Highness in the first instance and Sir thereafter. Not even his girlfriends were allowed to call him by his Christian name. Even in bed, at the moment of passion, they were forbidden to shout out his name. It was Sir or goodbye.

Such pomposity did not come naturally to Diana, and it is to her credit that she has not allowed it to warp her concept of how people should relate to one another. At first, she kept her distance, but once she became Princess of Wales and found her footing, she set about chipping away at a mode of behaviour that is as antipathetic to good human relations as it is anachronistic.

In the meantime, however, she had to get herself married. With no one to talk to, she took to rattling about the Palace, a Walkman tightly clenched to her ears, swaying to and fro in the corridors in time to the music and the beat of isolation. On one occasion, The Queen, happening upon her, called out to her, but Diana, oblivious to her surroundings, sailed ahead, unhearing. She even used to roller-skate in the corridors, and this has been confirmed by a relation of her late Aunt Lavinia.

It has become generally accepted as fact that The Queen made no time to receive Diana during this period. "It's not true that she never saw The Queen, and that she never had lunch or dinner with her," says a courtier. "Diana was often present at dinner parties. In fact, she complained to friends that there were too many dinner parties at the Palace for her liking."

Another courtier confirms this. "I distinctly remember her coming from lunch with The Queen. She was very funny about it. She'd worn red tights. She said, 'I was sitting there and the corgis were yapping all around me [Diana does not like animals] when I suddenly realized they were fascinated by my red tights. I thought, My God, what if they think my legs are steak? I had visions of the whole lot of them tearing into me and devouring my legs. I nearly burst out laughing but managed to suppress it. I wish I hadn't worn those wretched tights though. I couldn't wait to get out of there.' "

That courtier also opines, "After the initial thrill of living at Buckingham Palace, the enormity of what she was letting herself in for started to hit Diana. As she adjusted and learnt more and more, she became increasingly nervous. She was a lot more relaxed with The Queen at first than later. Once they actually started to have a relationship, the gulf between them grew and grew. Not that The Queen wasn't kind and thoughtful, for she was. But they're

151

such different personalities that, once they'd got the niceties out of the way, there just wasn't any common ground.

"The same was true of Princess Anne. She didn't dislike
Diana. She simply had no feeling for her. They had absolutely nothing in common. Everything Diana liked, Princess Anne considered a waste of time, and vice versa. Can
you imagine the Princess Royal getting off on shopping in
Harvey Nicks? She regarded Diana as an airhead and a
lightweight, and couldn't understand why her brother was
marrying her.

"Diana had more cordial relations with Prince Andrew
and Prince Edward, but at the time they were both away,
one in the Navy, the other at university, if memory serves
me correctly. I think Diana thought that things would look
up when they returned home, so to speak. She came from a
close family and believed that the royals are close. You can
see how she made that mistake. Up to that time, all her
experience of them had been on holidays. At Sandringham,
at Cowes, at Balmoral, when they're all together. But you
know as well as I do that they're only ever together for set
pieces, and otherwise they see next to nothing of each
other. It was quite a common occurrence for The Queen,
The Prince of Wales, and Princess Anne all to be in the
Palace together, each of them having their dinner off a tray
in their own rooms. The same rule applied when the
Waleses were replaced by the Yorks. They can all go for
weeks, sometimes months, without ever seeing each other.
It would never occur to them to drop in, or to be companionable together."

One other member of the Royal Family with the same
need for human exchange as Diana was Princess Michael
of Kent. "She welcomed Diana with open arms," a friend
of hers tells me. "She asked her round [to her apartment in
Kensington Palace] for lunch and tea. Diana was happy to
go. They became pretty chummy. Marie Christine remembered how difficult her entry into the Royal Family had
been. She'd had a tough time of it, and often complained
that the British Establishment were opposed to her because she was a foreigner, sophisticated, and animated."

Undoubtedly, there is an element of justification in Princess Michael's assertions. Had she been a drab and retiring "gel" from the shires, she would undoubtedly have received more of a helping hand than she did. "She felt misunderstood and isolated, and hoped that she and Diana would become fast friends."

In a way, Princess Michael's actions, with hindsight, were more generous than they might now seem. From the time of her marriage until Diana's, Marie Christine was perceived as being the most glamorous and exotic royal. She was the starry princess, the one member of the family whose presence bestowed style upon any event. To open her heart and her house to a young woman still considered gauche by one and all was a warm and hospitable thing to do. Yet Diana would repay her kindness by distancing herself as soon as she married Charles. "She realized she didn't need Princess Michael for anything. She was more senior in rank."

While Diana was adjusting to the loneliness of her life in the confines of Buckingham Palace, she was also preparing for her wedding. In an impressive show of the familial support without which Diana Spencer could never have achieved such heights, all her family continued swinging into action behind her, employing their expertise and connections as the need arose. Frances and Jane in particular brought their considerable energy to bear, advising and helping with everything from the selection of the wedding lists to the compilation of Diana's trousseau.

Getting Diana kitted out for her future role was an exacting and time-consuming task. Hereafter, she would need a multitude of garments and accessories for a variety of tasks and occasions. She would have to plant trees, attend first nights, be the belle of many a ball. She would have to watch polo matches, visit the dying, celebrate with the living. Each event would require a complete new outfit, reflecting her youthfulness and taste but in keeping with the dignity of her new position.

There had been no Princess of Wales since Princess May of Teck became Queen Consort in 1910. There was therefore no immediate precedent to follow. Certainly there were basic guidelines. But there had been only one youthful princess in recent memory, and no one seriously expected Lady Diana Spencer to emulate Princess Anne. They were too different, and while Diana would also be expected to wear hats and gloves, she was actually free to break new ground.

Mindful of the enormity of the task before them, Frances and Jane roped in Anna Harvey of *Vogue* magazine, who had employed Jane prior to her marriage to Her Majesty's esteemed Assistant Private Secretary. Anna Harvey knew about fashion: she knew all the designers, and could help to equip Diana for her forthcoming role. She could choose the designers, contact them, and have them send around sample garments to Vogue House, where Diana duly went to view them before making her choices, in conference with Anna Harvey and Grace Coddington, the former model and *Vogue*'s *éminence grise*.

One of the first tasks facing Diana's advisory team was dressing her to tackle the hurdle of her first public engagement. Anna Harvey steered her towards the Emanuels, who, up to that time, were known for their romantic and eye-catching creations only in the narrow confines of fashionable London society. "Diana was anxious to start the way she intended to continue," a friend says. "She wanted to make her mark—to make a big splash. To come across as glamorous and sophisticated." She chose a strapless, low-cut, black ballgown with a vast, crinolined skirt, to accompany The Prince of Wales to the famous Gala in aid of the Royal Opera House at Goldsmiths' Hall, at which Princess Grace of Monaco was giving a poetry reading.

The dress created a sensation, "which of course was precisely what Diana intended. She's always been very good at getting herself noticed. Even when she was at school, she would put things together so that they'd grab your attention. She's always been an impact specialist," a schoolmate said, confirming her headmistress Miss Rudge's observation that Diana had an innate aptitude for eye-catching attire.

The Prince of Wales anticipated the response. As he stepped out of the car ahead of Diana, he commented to the assembled press corps, many of whom he had known for years, "Wait till you get an eyeful of this." No sooner were the words out of his mouth than out popped Diana, her ample pre-diet bosom in danger of bursting forth from the low, not quite perfectly fitting *décolletage*. There was a collective gasp, followed by a cheer, as the proud Prince of Wales shared his fiancée's attributes with the admiring throng of pressmen, who captured Diana's curves for the world to behold.

Inside, Princess Grace, looking magnificent in a blue gown with her hair wrapped in pearls, received Diana, who curtsied to her, for Diana was not royal yet, and protocol dictated that she acknowledge the superior rank of the charming and gracious former filmstar. "Diana told me she was very nervous," a friend said, "but Princess Grace told her not to worry, she looked great and she was doing well. That, and The Prince of Wales's obvious delight, calmed her down."

Chuffed as Charles was, there were those amongst the Establishment who were horrified by Diana's non-verbal statement. Several of the guests at the gala thought that her dress was in appalling taste. It was too revealing for a prospective royal, and, as one *grande dame* told me, "anyway, one does not wear a ballgown to a reception where there is no dancing, does one?"

Those sentiments were shared by the powers that be at the Palace. The following morning, Diana was informed that royal women never wear black unless they are in mourning. She could wear dark blue, dark green, dark grey, or dark brown. They could be so dark as to be virtually indistinguishable from black. But they could not be black. "She was mortified by the solecism," says one of the ladies who worked at the Palace at the time. "You notice she's never made the mistake again."

Had that been the end of the matter, Diana might have felt that her first foray into official duties had been a mixed blessing but an overall success. But she fell foul of her future grandmother-in-law. "Queen Elizabeth [The Queen Mother] was not amused," says a relation of hers. "She informed Charles to inform Diana that she must never again wear a dress that revealed the royal jewels. You

155

know how fond Queen Elizabeth is of low-cut dresses, and what a vast bosom she has. But she takes care never to go too far. In fact, when she's dining at Clarence House and one of the footmen comes to serve or clear her, she always covers the royal bosom. Sometimes, she even makes a quip about it once they're out of earshot. But she's adamant that the *hoi polloi* must never get an eyeful."

If the aftermath of her début as a royal embarrassed Diana, she could nevertheless be pleased that she had indeed made her mark. The world had been alerted: a new and glamorous royal was about to join the international stage. And she was no shrinking violet.

Diana now brought the monumental and suppressed force of her personality to bear to secure her hold over the man she loved. "Once they started living under the same roof, the romance really took off," says a member of another royal family. "It was really very touching to behold. The Prince of Wales is very much an artistic personality. He's as much a sentimentalist and idealist as any *fin de siècle* painter starving in his garret. I believe he'd always wanted someone who would love him for himself. I also believe he'd always secretly feared that most people, women included, have difficulty in seeing past the rank to the man with a very fine and sensitive character. I think he became convinced, just before his marriage, that he'd finally stumbled upon someone who genuinely loved him for himself. Diana certainly seemed to be in love with him. I'd go even further and say, it looked as if she worshipped him. There was something so pure and convincing about so much adoration that you couldn't doubt its sincerity. It seduced him, and I believe that once he became convinced that it really wasn't going to disappear, he unwound and gave his more sentimental and romantic side full vent. He reminded me of a character out of Dickens. He was like a little orphan who gets a visitor who turns out to be a fairy godmother bearing all sorts of goodies, which he's secretly wanted but not dared to admit to, not even to himself. It was at that stage that he fell in love with her."

A schoolmate remembers, "Beneath the smiles and pleasing façade Diana is emotionally hungry. She has an insatiable appetite to be loved and needed, to be the centre of attention. Quite what would have become of her if she hadn't made it as Princess of Wales, I don't know. She'd most likely have tormented some poor chap from the shires with her constant and crushing need for attention." Charles, however, was happy to play Romeo to Diana's Juliet, at least until she began alienating him with her demands, and, sensing the shift in power between them, Diana now moved against all the other female influences, save those of his immediate family, in his life.

The subject of the guest list for the wedding was preoccupying everyone. All over the world, there were people who would be grossly insulted if they were not asked. This was going to be the most important wedding of the second half of the twentieth century. Reputations could be made or lost by one's presence at or absence from St. Paul's Cathedral. Diana used the opportunity to reward those who had pleased her, such as her seamstress, to punish those who had not, such as Madame Vacani, and to exclude others for a variety of reasons. Despite being good Spencer family friends, Lord and Lady Freyberg were not extended an invitation that would, under normal circumstances, have been expected. Barbara Cartland suffered a similar and even more ignominious fate. In full view of Michael Colbourne, a member of The Prince of Wales's staff, Diana personally crossed her step-grandmother off the guest list. "I don't intend to have her upstage me," she commented, her competitive spirit surging rather unreasonably to the fore. Not even the intervention of the late Lord Mountbatten's Private Secretary on behalf of Barbara Cartland could change Diana's mind about a woman who had invariably been kind and generous to her. She preferred to subject Miss Cartland to public embarrassment, in the process creating a minor scandal that assured the authoress of far more attention, unwelcome or otherwise, than she would have had if she had been invited, as custom dictated she should be.

After the marriage ceremony, there was to be a wedding breakfast at the Palace for the *crème de la crème*. Once more, Diana availed herself of the opportunity to wield her new-found power. She excluded Camilla Parker Bowles and Dale Tryon from the one event that certified who ranked as indispensable. "She did not want them at her wedding breakfast and made The Prince of Wales know where she stood in no uncertain way. If she'd had her way, they wouldn't have been asked to the wedding at all. But he put his foot down. He said, with a certain amount of justification, that, as she was asking all of her old beaux, he saw no reason why he couldn't have his," says a Spencer relation.

This, however, was just one of Diana's forays into battle against the women whom she regarded as competition for the soul of her husband-to-be. "Diana made it very clear that she did not like Lady Tryon or Mrs. Parker Bowles," says a cousin of the Prince. "She would make these little comments about them, putting them down or making them look ridiculous. No one could've been in any doubt as to how she felt, including The Prince of Wales, who started to distance himself from them.

"It mattered awfully to Prince Charles that his marriage work; he isn't a confrontational sort of person at all. He has a short fuse and will snap at one, but he won't stand up and have a real row. It's not his style. He'll back off and either dig his heels in if he doesn't want to do something, or change what he can if he feels that that's what's called for." Confronted with a fiancée who did not wish to associate with the two women who had been most important to him for the last decade, Charles decided to sacrifice his relationships with Dale and Camilla. He was doing so, to use a favourite phrase of his, "for a peaceful life." Diana was mollified, at least for the moment.

With the confidantes dispatched to the outer reaches, and Charles's doubts dissipating under Diana's ministrations, the lovers settled down to their marital preparations in what was to prove the most untroubled period of their whole relationship. There was a five-week interruption, when The Prince of Wales went off on a tour of Australia, New Zealand and the United States of America. Out of sight, however, did not prove to be out of mind. The idealistic Prince kept in close touch by telephone and their love continued to grow. Not even a public fuss over whether their telephone calls had been tapped disturbed them.

The omens were getting better and better by the day. Even when Charles returned to England, and the strain of the last lap began telling on Diana to such an extent that her dieting spun out of control and she had difficulty in eating anything at all, they grew closer and closer. He became positively protective of her, even before she broke down in tears at a polo match at Tidworth, where he was playing, five days before the wedding. On that occasion, his old—and brief—girlfriend Penelope Eastwood, by then married to his cousin Norton (Lord) Romsey, had been on hand to offer Diana a sympathetic shoulder until her dashing Prince rode off the polo field to offer her the comfort of his arms.

There were other moments when Diana was overcome by emotion, but everyone marked it down to being overwrought, to pre-wedding jitters, to the strain she had been under. She was under severe pressure, but no one realized, as a friend of hers told me, that "she was already haunted by doubts as to whether she hadn't bitten off more than she could chew, and moreover she had begun to manifest the early signs of the extreme emotional disturbance that was tied up with her bulimic condition."

But of one thing Diana was sure. Regardless of the problems she might have in adjusting to the tedious and tiresome ways of being a royal, she was doing the right thing. She wanted her Prince. He wanted her. And it looked as if they would have a happy marriage.

CHAPTER ELEVEN

The Wedding

*T*he marriage of HRH The Prince of Wales to the Lady Diana Spencer, on 29 July 1981, was watched by more people than any other wedding in history. Thanks to television, hundreds of millions of viewers, all over the world, shared a truly joyous day with the couple, their families, and the rejoicing nation.

Much cant is retailed about the Royal Family. Few people can ever speak about them without launching into hyperbole, with the result that anything said about them, to the discerning ear, immediately becomes suspect. As Janet, Marchioness of Milford Haven, whose elder son is the present head of the Mountbatten family and whose late husband David was The Duke of Edinburgh's first cousin and best man, said to me, "It's absolutely true that one must always consider the source whenever one hears anything about any member of the Royal Family."

It is not an exaggeration to state, however, that Prince Charles's wedding was the cause of great national rejoicing and international interest. All over the land and the world, people gravitated towards their television sets, irrespective of the time. No one, it seemed, wanted to miss the early morning preparations or the arrival of the many distinguished guests at St. Paul's Cathedral. Everyone of consequence to the Royal Family, or of national interest to the government, trooped in at some point. From Nancy Reagan and Princess Grace of Monaco, to the deposed monarchs of Eastern Europe and the Household staff at

Buckingham Palace, they all took their seats in Wren's historic edifice, to be joined, later on, by the immediate members of Diana's family. Her mother and grandmother, I was intrigued to notice, sat as far apart as it was possible to be, and remained so throughout the rest of the day. Nor was the Lord Chamberlain, whose responsibility the arrangements were, daunted by the anomalies of an extended family. Blood proved to be thicker than a marriage certificate, resulting in Raine Spencer's and Peter Shand Kydd's banishment to the general congregation. There was room too for only one formidable granny, so Queen Elizabeth The Queen Mother took her seat in the royal pews, facing those of the bride's family, without the distracting and detracting presence of the other *grande dame* with a penchant for pearls, hats and fussy costumes: Barbara Cartland played hostess to the St. John's Ambulance Brigade while the spotlight shone brightly on her humiliation at not being asked to the wedding, resulting in Diana achieving the very opposite of what she had set out to avoid. But the royals did not mind the redoubtable author's absence. "They think she's frightfully vulgar and a real publicity-seeker," says another royal.

The celebrations began the evening before. In Hyde Park, Prince Charles lit the first in a chain of 102 bonfires, following which there was a vast fireworks display illuminating London's skyline for nearly an hour. There were half a million onlookers in Hyde Park alone, and traffic came to a standstill, but no one minded. The air rang with good-natured celebration, presaging the mood of all. I was but one of the many residents of Belgravia, which flanks both Hyde Park and Buckingham Palace, who commented on how everyone seemed to become involved, treating the fireworks display, and, the next morning, the wedding, as if they were one gigantic party, and everyone, invited or otherwise, was a guest.

One person who remained out of view during that last evening was Diana herself. She was safely tucked up in bed, at Clarence House, to which she had moved for her last night as a commoner. "Yes, the move was a deliberate attempt to deceive the public as to where she spent the period of her engagement," a courtier admits. "The Palace [that all-encompassing word which can mean The Queen, her royal relations, or her advisers] did not want the public to know that Charles and Diana had spent the previous months living under the same roof. I don't know whether I'd use the word cynical to describe the deception. I think I'd sooner say it was a decorous way of maintaining standards. But, yes, it was undoubtedly a deception—a calculated deception."

Decorous or hypocritical, Diana went to her solitary bed early, to rest up for her big day, which had a 6:30 am start. After an enormous breakfast, "to stop my tummy rumbling in St. Paul's," she received Kevin Shanley, the hairdresser from Headlines, to whom she would faithfully cling until he later baulked at giving her a new hairstyle for the State Opening of Parliament. She would then dispense with his services as peremptorily as if they had never known one another, but for now all was sweetness and light, and he, with his wife Claire in attendance as an assistant, abided by her wishes. These were for a light, simple and unfussy variation of her normal hairstyle, crowned with the Spencer tiara and veil. The result was something of a flop, in the literal and the figurative sense. As the day wore on, her hair looked more and more droopy, for it had needed far more setting lotion and spray than Diana would allow Shanley to use to maintain its shape.

Better was the result of Barbara Daly's endeavours. She too was at Clarence House early that morning, making up Diana with the consummate professionalism and tastefulness for which she is known. She remained on hand throughout the day, as did Shanley, to touch up Diana's appearance.

No amount of glossing over, however, could hide the somewhat patchy result of the wedding dress. Designed by David and Elizabeth Emanuel, in evocation of a dress worn by a Spencer ancestor in a painting hanging on the walls at Althorp, it was made from English silk, from the only silk farm in the country, at Lullingstone. Sewn single-handed by a 58-year-old Greek seamstress, Nina Missetzis, whose reward was an unexpected seat in St. Paul's, the fabric creased badly, far more than silk ought to. Nor did the bodice fit as well as it could have, thanks mainly to the many alterations made to it as Diana lost more and more weight. It even had to be taken in by a quarter of an inch on each side the day before the wedding. It could be fairly said that too much of a good thing proved to be the undoing of Diana's dress in more ways than one, for many arbiters of taste viewed the design as overblown, fussy, and excessive, and to the extent that she chose her wedding dress, she must share responsibility with the Emanuels for a stunning fiasco. The frilled neckline overlaid with lace, the massive sleeves fussily decorated with unnecessary bows and yet more lace, were in themselves a testament to the dictum that simplicity will always win out over ostentation. As if that were not enough, there was also the bodice, with yet more embroidered lace, and the vast crumpled skirt glittering with even more tiny pearls and sequins, looking as if it had been dropped in glue and sprinkled with glitter. Piling it on, the dress also sported a matching twenty-five-foot train—the longest in royal history—edged in yet more glistening lace and overlaid by a veil of the same length.

For all its faults, the dress did have an air of romance. The colour, ivory, also suited the bride's skin tones, even if it was not white and did not therefore reaffirm her publicly declared virginity. The overall effect was stunning, to such an extent that The Duke of Edinburgh's great-niece Princess Katarina of Yugoslavia was able to reminisce recently, "One of the things I particularly remember is how stunningly beautiful Diana looked. She really was an absolutely gorgeous bride."

When Diana's glass coach, pulled by Kestrel and Lady Penelope, two bays from the Royal Mews, pulled out from Clarence House into the Mall, she did indeed look beautiful. Smiling radiantly, waving as she had been taught by Lady Susan Hussey, she was a veritable picture of loveliness beside her father. From that moment until the coach pulled up at the steps of St. Paul's Cathedral, Diana presented a perfect façade, and while this was shattered somewhat when she stepped out of the coach, revealing the full

163

extent of her wedding dress's shortcomings, it took only as long as the journey into the cathedral for her dress to be straightened out and Diana, her beauty and joy diminishing all else, to be restored in all her pre-eminence as the reigning queen of romance.

The Prince of Wales presented a complementary picture of romance in his admiral's uniform, and as Diana began the three-and-a-half-minute walk down the aisle on her father's arm, a treat was in store for the world. A great idealist and a perfectionist, Charles had taken pains over the service. A lover of music as well as architecture, he had chosen St. Paul's as the setting because it could house a full orchestra and also had a world-famous boys' choir. In consultation with Sir David Willcocks, Director of the Royal College of Music, he selected a programme that was both joyous and moving, and included works by Purcell, Handel and Jeremiah Clarke. These were performed by three orchestras, the Bach Choir, and the soprano Kiri Te Kanawa, who was made a Dame shortly afterwards by The Queen, upon the recommendation of her native New Zealand government.

Charles was greatly moved by the whole event. He told a cousin, "There were several times when I was perilously close to crying from the sheer joy of it all. It was tremendous to learn that one was so appreciated, to feel that everyone cared so much, that people were there with one. It was magical."

Diana mirrored Charles's feelings. She told a friend, "It was heaven, amazing, wonderful, though I was so nervous when I was walking up the aisle that I swore my knees would knock and make a noise."

The crowd outside played their part. Princess Katarina of Yugoslavia told me, "When Diana said 'I do'—or was it 'I will'?—the crowd let out a huge roar which washed over us like a great wave. It felt as if there were no walls separating us from them. It really was the most extraordinary thing, and very affecting. Everyone was moved by the wonderful feeling of oneness which we all felt."

After the marriage, Charles and Diana returned, amidst wild cheering, to Buckingham Palace. There they, their families, and the other members of the reigning European royal families posed for photographs by Patrick (the Earl of) Lichfield, after which they joined the 118 guests for a wedding breakfast of quenelles of brill with lobster sauce, *Suprême de volaille,* strawberries and Cornish cream, washed down with German wines and champagne.

Diana was now a royal, the highest-ranking Princess in the land, possessor of the second most eminent royal title in the world. She was the first English commoner to become a princess since Lady Anne Hyde, the daughter of the Earl of Clarendon, had married The Duke of York, later King James II, in 1660. Her new status was forcibly brought home to her when she arrived back at the Palace and the members of the Royal Household bowed and curtsied, calling her Your Royal Highness and Ma'am. Did it feel strange? "Not a bit."

Barbara Cartland and Frances Shand Kydd had done their work well. Diana certainly had no problems with either her imagination or her self-esteem. But, more to the point, she was embarking on an exciting and unusual course for any human being: she was living her dream. And her family had realized theirs. One of them had finally made it into the charmed inner sanctum. One of them was royal.

The honeymoon was conceived as romantically as the wedding service. It was meant to combine beauty, majesty, privacy, and satisfaction. It was a blend of luxury and simplicity, tradition and adventure. The first two days were spent at Broadlands, the Hampshire home of the Prince's honorary grandfather and actual great-uncle, Earl Mountbatten of Burma, where The Queen and Prince Philip had also spent their honeymoon.

Mountbatten's grandson Norton Knatchbull, now Lord Romsey, resided there with his wife Penelope, who had fleetingly been one of Prince Charles's girlfriends while she worked in The Duke of Edinburgh's office. The former Miss Eastwood, according to a member of the Royal Household, "was nothing but a fling. I thought he treated her like dirt. She was almost, though not quite, common.

Her father was a businessman who had done well for himself, and while she was a nice girl, she wasn't grand enough to marry The Prince of Wales. But, like most of those Palace girls, she was ambitious and had her head well screwed on, so she settled for Norton Knatchbull without batting an eyelash. But she definitely wasn't Royal Family material."

Whatever her calibre, Penny vacated Broadlands with her husband, leaving her cousins by marriage, The Prince and Princess of Wales, alone—but for the servants—to break matrimonial ground in peace.

After two days of rustic simplicity, during which Charles fished on the River Test while Diana rested, the Prince and his new Princess flew to Gibraltar to board the royal yacht *Britannia,* which was berthed there. This had caused a row between Spain, which lays claim to the territory, and Britain, preventing King Juan Carlos and Queen Sofia from attending the wedding. It is indicative of how the Royal Family functions that Prince Charles's convenience was put before his two cousins' positions, despite the relative unimportance of the one and the national significance of the other. Although it would have been a simple enough matter to board *Britannia* anywhere else in the Mediterranean, thereby averting a diplomatic incident and showing a modicum of respect and consideration for another country and its monarch and consort—friends, indeed, of the British Royal Family—this was not done.

Despite the rumpus, Charles and Diana set off on an idyllic cruise of the Mediterranean and the Aegean. There were only two women on board, Diana and her dresser Evelyn Dagley, and when her husband was resting or doing his exercises, Diana happily drifted about the ship, chatting to the ratings and once even barging in on them after they had been showering. Seeing the men sitting around with only towels covering their nakedness, she laughed coquettishly and said, "It's all right. I'm a married woman now, aren't I?"

Sauciness had always been one of Diana's virtues, though the public had so far been denied a glimpse of it. The crew of the royal yacht, however, were another matter, and throughout the honeymoon there were occasions when

The Prince of Wales with his first love, Lucia Santa Cruz, and Nicholas Soames. *(Alpha)*

Above: Charles and the girl who already had a title, Lady Jane Wellesley. *(Anwar Hussein)*
Left: Diplomat's daughter Georgiana Russell, now Lady Boothby: pretty, sweet, with a penchant for sexy clothing.

The Prince of Wales with Lady Diana Spencer's eldest sister, Sarah, at the height of their romance. *(Alpha)*

Above: Sabrina Guinness turns the charm, that so beguiled Mick Jagger and Ryan O'Neal, on to Prince Charles. *(Anwar Hussein)*
Right: Sheila Ferguson of The Three Degrees, in whom the Prince had a long standing interest. *(Alpha)*

Left: Charles's love before Diana: the exciting and passionate *Whiplash,* Scots landowner's daughter, Anna Wallace. *(Alpha)*

Above: Charles and the girl on whom tragedy left its mark, Davina Sheffield. *(Anwar Hussein)*

The Prince of Wales with two former fancies, actress Susan George, and his Kanga, Lady Tryon, at a fundraising polo match for SANE, a charity for which the latter was Co-Chairman with Sir Ralph Halpern. *(Alpha)*

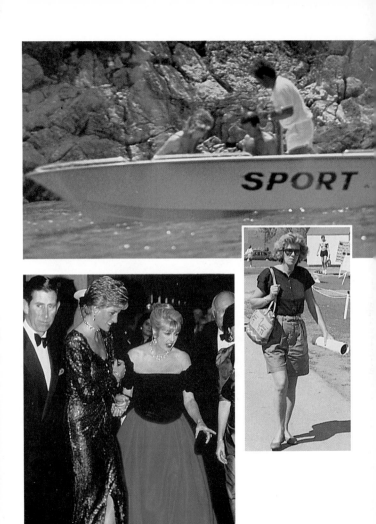

Top: The Prince of Wales sporting with Camilla Parker Bowles recently. *(Rex Features)* **Right:** Camilla, descendant of a Royal mistress, and The Prince of Wales's closest friend. *(Alpha)* **Left:** Charles and Diana with Dale Tryon, whose reputation the Princess has sought to enhance. *(Alpha)*

Top: Charles and Diana, putting paid to rumours of disapproval, at the Soames' wedding, with her good friend, Philip Dunne, immediately beside her. *(Alpha)* **Above Left:** Diana and The King of Spain, enjoying one of their happy times together. *(Alpha)* **Right:** The ill-fated Sergeant Barry Mannakee, with Diana and Prince Andrew, before his fatal accident. *(Alpha)*

Athletic Gulf hero, Captain James Hewitt, displaying his prowess. *(Alpha)*

Earl Spencer and his adored, but controversial Countess, Raine.
(Alpha)

Left: Diana's formidable granny, Ruth, Lady Fermoy, whose actions played such a part in the children's early lives. *(Alpha)*

Below: Diana with her charming, popular, but equally formidable mother, Frances Shand Kydd. *(Alpha)*

Left: Sisters Sarah (in Diana's hand-me-downs), and Jane, whose cast of mind has long been the admiration of her friends. *(Alpha)*

Far Left: Sir Robert Fellowes, The Queen's influential Private Secretary and husband of Diana's elder sister, Jane. *(Photographers International)*

Right: Diana and
Charles were never
happier than at the time
of her first public
engagement, with
Princess Grace of
Monaco. *(Alpha)*

Right: A jubilant
Princess of Wales
shows off the regal
skills, taught on The
Queen's instructions,
en route from St. Paul's
Cathedral to Buckingham
Palace, watched by her
proud and solicitous
Prince. *(Alpha)*

Above: In June 1984, a
still-solicitous Charles
with Diana, at polo.
(Anwar Hussein)

Above: The Prince and Princess of Wales show their public and polite faces to the world in Canada, in October 1991. *(Photographers International)*

Left: In Derbyshire, March 1990, Charles and Diana show the strain and distance their less than ideal marriage has placed upon them. *(Alpha)*

Above: Diana's greatest friend, in the early days, was her Private Secretary and Comptroller, Oliver Everett, seen here carrying her shopping bag when she was pregnant with Prince William. *(Rex Features)* **Below:** The Prince of Wales's Private Secretary, intellectual traditionalist, the Hon. Edward Adeane. *(Photographers International)* **Right:** The man who knew all Charles's secrets: his valet, the louche Stephen Barry. *(Alpha)*

Left: Over the years Diana has perfected her look until it is slick, stylish and unfussy. However, she has never forgotten the period of Press criticism, and always tries to present a businesslike image for her daily engagements. *(Photographers International)*

Above: In the evening, Diana can give full rein to her luxurious taste. Even her simplest gowns are the finest money can buy. *(Photographers International)*

Above: Her wings clipped, Diana, flanked by Carolyn Bartholomew (formerly Pride), attends the marriage service of former flatmate, Virginia Pitman to Henry Clarke in September 1991. *(Photographers International)*

Left: A passionately devoted mother, Diana enjoys a day out, at Niagara Falls, with Prince William and Prince Harry, during the Royal Tour of Canada in October 1991. *(Photographers International)*

Above: Israel Zohar, the Russian artist, was so affected by the force of Diana's personality, that the finished portrait bore no resemblance to the original conception. *(Israel Zohar Collection)*

Left: Astrologer Penny Thornton held the keys that unlocked significant doors for a distraught Diana.

Top Left: Diana tours a CRUSAID ward at the Middlesex Hospital in July 1991 and touches yet another soul. *(Alpha)* **Middle Left:** An animated Diana with King Constantine of the Hellenes, as she is never seen by the public, at the private luncheon prior to the King Constantine Cup. *(Lady Colin Campbell Collection)* **Top Right:** International socialite Kari Lai, meets Diana at *A Royal Gala Evening* in Washington, October 1990: an occasion rescued by the Princess's deft handling. *(Lady Colin Campbell Collection)* **Bottom:** Impresario Alan Sievewright had good reason to sing Diana's praises at a *Serenade to a Princess,* in 1991. *(Alan Sievewright Collection)*

the fashion-conscious Diana dispensed with the top of her bikini rather than develop unsightly tan marks. One red-faced sailor was embarrassed to get a glimpse of the royal bosom when he inadvertently stumbled upon her. Had the old-fashioned Queen Elizabeth The Queen Mother known to what extent her dictates were being ignored, she would have blown a fuse.

Sunbathing was something Diana, and unusually for him, Charles, spent a lot of time doing. When they were not on deck soaking up the sun, or swimming, scuba-diving, snorkelling, windsurfing, and having barbecues on white sand beaches, they were in their stateroom. This had a brand new queen-sized bed, specially bought after Princess Anne tipped them off about how she and Mark Phillips had had to lash two twin beds together. "They were ecstatically happy," reports someone who saw them. "They were obviously completely besotted with each other. All over each other. He couldn't take his hands off her, and she was forever in his lap kissing him or pressing her body close to his."

The honeymooners saw many exotic places, including the Algerian coast, Tunisia, Sicily, Santorini, Crete and other Greek islands. They headed for the Red Sea by way of the Suez Canal, stopping off in Port Said, where they entertained President Anwar Sadat and his wife Jehan to dinner on board. In Egypt, Diana discovered the discomfiting side of her new life. "When she met the Sadats, she was stuck for something to say," a courtier recounts. "She kept on saying, over and over and over again, 'Oh, I do like mangoes.' It was desperately embarrassing, but, of course, the Sadats were kind and pretended not to notice."

In fairness to Diana, most twenty year olds, saddled with a middle-aged couple from so different a background, would have difficulty in achieving common ground. But she did make an effort to be charming, and when the Sadats were walking down the gangplank, an ebullient Diana, quite forgetting Lady Susan's lessons in regal restraint, blew them kisses and waved like a baby.

Despite being touched by his child-bride's effusiveness, The Prince of Wales realized that something had to be done. "One could not allow The Princess of Wales to jibber and jabber and flutter like a mindless bit of fluff, for, no matter how cute she might be, she had to possess solidity if she were to maintain the dignity of her position," says a member of the Royal Household.

Charles, however, was not prepared to rock his marital boat by taking Diana to task. Aside from the fact that he loathes confrontation and goes out of his way to avoid it, the royal way has never been to bark, not when you have so many dogs to do it for you. So, after the Sadats saw them off in an RAF VC10 at a military airfield at Hurghada, and they touched down in Scotland, Charles asked Diana's Private Secretary to begin the process of amplifying her conversational skills by deepening her knowledge. The marriage had hit its first rock.

"The Princess of Wales hated anything that smacked of academia. She loathed reading anything but Barbara Cartland, Barbara Taylor Bradford and Danielle Steele with a passion," says a courtier who was privy to the inner workings of the Waleses's marriage. "When they came back from their honeymoon, the Prince had a word with Oliver [Everett]. He asked him to take steps to improve her mind. There was a several-fold purpose in this. There was the fact that she had made such a fool of herself with the Sadats, but more importantly, he wanted her mind improved for himself. The Prince of Wales, you must remember, is a thinker, a very deep thinker. He is well informed on a variety of subjects, and has many, many interests, some very profound. He'd already realized that they'd never have a meeting of minds—which, to him, is the most important aspect of any relationship—unless she had something in her mind. But all she thought about was romantic nonsense à la Barbara Cartland, clothes, and the childish antics of her Sloaney friends. If he was going to have something to speak to her about, aside from how much he loved her and how much she loved him, if he wasn't going to expire from boredom before the end of the honeymoon, something had to be done, and quickly."

"The honeymoon period," says a connection of the

Royal Family and possessor of one of the greatest titles in the land, "did not last past the honeymoon."

Before the intellectual issue became a real problem, however, Charles and Diana struck another rock: in fact, another two rocks. The first was her loathing of country life. "Christ, you have no idea how much the country bores me," she told a friend. "Balmoral," she said to someone else, "is as deadly as a graveyard."

After the Mediterranean cruise, which did appeal to her sybaritic late-twentieth-century taste, Diana and Charles went straight to the "graveyard" in the Highlands. Balmoral has long been Prince Charles's favourite place. "He has complete privacy there," says a well-known banker. "It's the only place on earth he can let his hair down." In Charles's opinion, it is also "one of the most heavenly places on earth. It is where my heart is."

A famous beauty who is connected to the Royal Family, and who likes both Charles and Diana, said, "He loves the drama and majesty of the Highlands. He needs their remoteness and peacefulness. He is a man whose whole life has been geared towards people, towards fulfilling their expectations, irrespective of his natural inclinations. He's never been allowed to indulge himself the way you or I or Diana have. His every natural tendency has been bent towards fulfilling his duty, a large part of which revolves around other people, their needs and expectations. He needs the tranquillity and undemandingness of nature. But Diana needs the feedback of humanity."

Because Diana had given every indication throughout their courtship of loving country life in general and Balmoral in particular, Charles confidently expected their honeymoon to continue in the pleasing mould it had done to date. "He believed that Diana would be happy to relax at the castle, doing needlepoint, going for long walks, talking to the other ladies, and doing all the other things the women had always done, while he fished and shot and did all the things he'd always done. She'd led him to this belief, so you can't blame him for it," says a well-known connection of his.

Yet, to Charles's consternation, no sooner were they in

residence than the dramas started. In one scene, he was observed departing from the castle in one of the royal Range Rovers with an irate Diana running alongside shouting, "Yes, dump me like garbage. Leave me on my own again. Run off and have lunch with your precious Mummy." In another, she was overheard screaming at him sarcastically, "What am I supposed to do all day while you're off enjoying yourself? Die of boredom? You call yourself a husband. Some husband you are."

These rows were a harbinger of what was to come. They were the bedrock on which the marriage was built, so it is worth looking at their relationship at this early stage to see precisely what the dynamics were. "They are both very strong-willed people," says a member of the Royal Household, who was closely involved with them during the early days of their marriage. "Both are very intense and easily wounded. But where she will create scenes, he runs from them. Her big mistake—and it is one which she has persisted in—is trying to browbeat him into toeing her line. From the very start, if she wanted him to do something and he didn't want to do it, she would try to impose her will on him. Her initial tactic was to be plaintive, which, of course, makes most men bristle. To them, it smacks of emotional blackmail, and makes them feel they're being manipulated. This in turn only brings out the rebel in them, and makes them more intent on doing whatever it was they planned to do in the first place. Diana has never been able to see that, though, and rather than backing down, she'd get hurt and angry and insistent because he didn't want to please her. She's very determined and has quite a temper, and didn't hesitate to use it when she wasn't getting her way. She'd rant and rave, hoping that argument would win out where inducement had failed. It never did, of course, and before the honeymoon was over she'd already managed to push him away."

Diana, of course, could not see this. To her, it was eminently reasonable that Charles would want to spend as much time as he could with her. "If he loved me, he would," became her refrain. She simply did not understand that few mature and busy men have it in them to be romantic all day, every day. Her concept of love required constant devotion and attention, but this was real life, not a novel by her step-grandmother, and while Charles was undoubtedly selfish, her expectations were unreasonable. In fairness to her, however, most twenty year olds in love would react as Diana did. At that age, young couples are more absorbed in each other than older couples. That is what young love is all about. But Charles was not your typical man, much less a young man. From early childhood, his upbringing had been such that his emotions were pushed to one side, and while he was undoubtedly sensitive, idealistic, and intense, it was in a more independent and contained way. He was an individual who had been forced, through circumstance and training, to stand on his own. Diana was not. She wanted someone to complete her identity, to live out her romantic fantasies with her, to pay constant attention to her, to share every waking hour with her, in never-ending bliss. Aside from the fact that any woman past twenty-five knows that such paragons of masculinity just do not exist, Diana had chosen a man who was constitutionally incapable of such absorption in another human being. "Nice and kind and concerned though he is, The Prince of Wales is as selfish a person as I have ever met," says a courtier. "He does exactly what he wants, when he wants, with never a thought for the effect it will have upon anyone else. To show you what I mean, I remember once he flew in from a trip across the Atlantic. Upon landing he decided to change his plans and drive straight to Highgrove. It didn't even cross his mind that the people who had to accompany him had also flown across the Atlantic, and, aside from being tired and grubby, wanted to see their families. He was very nice about it, asking everyone if they didn't mind. But the bottom line was, he knew they'd have to say yes. And he had no right to ask. It was astonishingly selfish and inconsiderate. But he does things like that all the time."

Although some of her railing was against this ingrained attitude of the Prince's, Diana could not accept that her histrionic behaviour and her stubbornness were alienating her husband and making him less, rather than more, willing to spend time with her. For his part, Charles could not understand why Diana was behaving as she was. He had always behaved as he was doing. Not only had no other woman objected, with the exception of Anna Wallace, but Diana had not done so either, not until the wedding ring was on her finger. "He felt that she was stifling him. It made him feel as if she were a gaoler. He didn't like it."

Princess Katarina of Yugoslavia said that, at the wedding, "The whole family was delighted that Charles married Diana. Everyone welcomed her with open arms." But in the space of a few short weeks, that story had changed.

"The Queen never thought that Diana was the right girl for The Prince of Wales, and now her misgivings were coming to life before her eyes," says the aristocratic sister-in-law of the senior courtier. "She feared that Diana was a bolter, so she was really anxious to keep her happy. The possibility of having The Princess of Wales leave the heir to the throne filled The Queen with unspeakable horror. It took years for her to get over that fear. What did it was Diana's tenacity and public success in the face of all the behind-the-scenes dramas and difficulties in the marriage."

Most of those difficulties were still to come, however, and as Diana tussled with Charles over who was in control of their life together, he resisted only up to a point. "She felt that the role of wife gave her the right to have a say in every area of his life," says the courtier. "There was nothing that escaped her attention. While he bucked her attempts to get him to play coochie-coo all day, and refused to allow her to interfere with his sporting activities—left up to her, he would have had to give up polo just so she could be spared the task of watching him play—he did let her wield influence in other areas.

"She said he looked too fuddy-duddy. She was embarrassed by the way he dressed. She thought he looked like a stiff, and saw no reason why he shouldn't be as smart and as contemporary as her friends. She set about changing the way he dressed and combed his hair as soon as they were married. She didn't even pause to draw breath, to wait until their relationship had matured and time had given her a natural amount of influence. She insisted he have

172

Kevin Shanley cut his hair instead of his barber, and made him change his tailor from Johnson & Pegg in Clifford Street to Anderson & Sheppard in Savile Row.

"One effect of taking over The Prince of Wales's wardrobe was that Diana started choosing what he would wear. That cut into Stephen Barry's job, whose duties included selecting what the Prince would wear each day and laying it out for him. I know as a fact she did it deliberately. She resented Stephen's influence and felt uncomfortable with him. He'd seen too much. She hated knowing that when he looked at her, he also saw the legion of other girls who had gone before her. She wanted to sever all Charles's links with the past, and knew she could never do that as long as Stephen Barry remained his valet."

CHAPTER TWELVE

Creating the Setting

*T*he construction of a married life is always fraught with difficulties for any newlyweds, and in this regard The Prince and Princess of Wales were no different from the millions of subjects over whom they would one day reign. They did have rather more raw material to work with, however, and from the very outset Diana and Charles dedicated a fair amount of their attention to the basic structure of their life together.

Their chief preoccupation was doing up their homes. The Duchy of Cornwall had bought Highgrove House in August 1980 for £800,000. Set in 350 acres, it was Georgian, with four main reception rooms, nine bedrooms and six bathrooms. "I fell in love with the garden. That's why I bought it," Charles told a friend, describing the mature trees that had taken several human lifetimes to reach fruition.

It might, however, have been more accurate to say he fell in love with the potential of the garden. "It had lots of very beautiful trees which the previous owners, a hundred years ago, had planted," Katharine, Viscountess Macmillan of Ovenden said. "But I wasn't a great gardener. It did have a few flowerbeds and the lawn in our day, but he's laid down most of the flowerbeds and really made the garden what it now is."

One feature to which the Prince turned his immediate attention was the walled garden, which has become his "refuge." He also happily set to work developing the rest of the garden, planting a variety of fruit trees which were given as a wedding present from the Fruiterers' Company, as well as the herb garden given by the Sussex branch of the Women's Institute. He called upon his friend Miriam Rothschild, a renowned expert on fleas, butterflies and wild flowers, to help him with the planning and seeding of the wild-flower garden that now flanks the driveway leading up to the house. He also sought advice from the Marchioness of Salisbury, a well-known gardener and friend of the Queen Mother.

One person whom Charles did not involve in his horticultural pursuits was Diana. "Yuk," she said to a friend. "Gardening reminds me of Miss Rudge and all that weeding I had to do at West Heath," when she was punished for disciplinary offences.

While Charles's attention was directed outside the house, Diana's was focused entirely on the interior. The Prince gave her full rein to indulge her taste, which is exquisite, even before it had been put to the test. To help her was her mother's interior designer, Dudley Poplak, a South African whose speciality is putting together the classic, aristocratic, country-house look that the smart set all have, whether in the country or in town.

Although money was no object, Dudley Poplak's hands were tied rather more tightly than they would have been for other less celebrated but nevertheless illustrious clients. "The Prince of Wales is notoriously tight-fisted," says the senior courtier's aristocratic sister-in-law. "His houses were furnished almost entirely with wedding presents. From the kitchen to the bed linen, everything was bought by someone else. He lives the Beluga life on a baloney budget. He gets away with it because there are always people who are happy to pick up his bills. For years one friend after another has bankrolled his polo-playing, and Armand Hammer was always most generous with the use of his private plane. It's a case of 'you give me things and I give you the prestige of my friendship,' though, of course, in the case of the wedding presents, it was a more acceptable exchange."

Diana and Dudley Poplak were in complete agreement

175

about what needed to be done at Highgrove. They chose soft and bright pastel colours such as peach for the walls, colourful chintz for the sofas and chairs. By the time the carpets were laid and the pictures hung in their gilt frames, the effect was cheerful and elegant, even though the finishing touches had not yet been added.

This was in marked contrast to many of the rooms at Sandringham, Balmoral, Buckingham Palace and Windsor Castle. The Duke of Edinburgh's study at Buckingham Palace, for instance, has all the cachet of a film set for a styleless *petit bourgeois* professional from the 1950s. And Princess Michael of Kent antagonzied The Queen shortly after her marriage by complaining that her bedroom at Windsor Castle must be a mistake, so tackily appointed was it. There is a reason for this sad lack of elegance. "It's because the royal residences are furnished almost entirely with hand-me-downs," says the aristocratic sister-in-law of the courtier. "The good hand-me-downs are the finest antiques in the world, but the modern [twentieth-century] furniture is enough to induce nightmares. Often, there is a frightening juxtaposition of elegance and junk within one room, while an adjacent room will be superbly furnished in the finest antiques. But this gem will lead to yet another room that is stuffed to the hilt with furniture that can only be described as real junk."

Refusing to be fobbed off with eyesores, Diana bought what she was not given. "The Prince never saw the bills because they were sent directly to his office," says a courtier. "If he'd ever seen them, he would've burst a blood vessel. Not that she was extravagant, for she was not. But she did demand the very best and you know how things pile up. They spent over a million pounds doing up the place."

The expenditure on furnishings was trivial compared with the cost of improving security. Because The Prince and Princess of Wales are prime targets for assassination, an elaborate security system had to be installed. Closed-circuit automatic television cameras scan every centimetre of the property. The nerve-centre for surveillance is what was once a charming farmhand's cottage. There are computerized monitors in the attic of the main house, which are watched around the clock by two police officers, irrespective of whether the Prince and Princess are in residence. In case there is a full-scale assault on the property, an impregnable twenty-foot-square steel room has been constructed on the first floor of the house. This is a house within a house, and is designed to fall to the ground intact should the rest of the house be destroyed. It has sufficient long-life food and drink for months, a plethora of medical supplies, a well-stocked armoury, the latest communications equipment, air purifiers and lavatories.

Added to the cost of the security equipment was the need to build a staircase linking the attic with the back of the house. "Diana was already having problems coming to terms with the constant surveillance," says a royal relation. "Anyone who's led a carefree life would chafe at being watched twenty-four hours a day. She couldn't adjust to the knowledge that she could not even go to the loo without the policeman watching her seeing exactly how long she'd spent there. On the basis that out of sight is out of mind, the decision was taken to keep the duty officers out of view as much as possible. Hence the finesse of a staircase for them to come and go undetected."

With Dudley Poplak's help, Diana succeeded in making Highgrove a charming and elegant country house. It is comfortable and unpretentious, aristocratic rather than royal in feeling and appearance, though the same cannot be said for the way it is run. In these days of democratization, when not even the richest and grandest aristocrats have an army of servants, it is maintained to an unusually high standard. This strikes you as soon as you set foot in the house and notice the Wellingtons lined up against the wall, glistening like diamonds. Nothing is ever faintly dull or out of place, for Diana has never outgrown her mania for cleanliness and tidiness. But not even she has any control over The Prince of Wales's study. His desk is a glorious jumble reflecting the artistic nature of its owner. Beneath that apparent chaos lies an order known only to him, and on it he has placed a prominent notice warning everyone, including Diana, "Do not move anything on this desk."

Despite the successful refurbishment, Diana has never liked Highgrove House. "It's too small for her taste," says a relation of hers. "Even though she doesn't like being at Althorp, it's her sort of house: large, grand, and imposing. There's nothing grand or imposing about Highgrove. The only people who think that Highgrove is big are those who don't know what a big house is."

That, indeed, is true. The aristocracy have a different scale for measuring houses. Diana cannot be faulted for this. I vividly remember the first time I saw Inveraray Castle. My husband was inordinately proud of his ancestral home, which is one of the leading stately homes in the land. It is also every child's idea of a fairytale castle brought to life, and has one of the finest collections of eighteenth-century French furniture in existence. Yet I was flabbergasted by its relatively small size, although Inverary has some 100 rooms. Nor was I alone. My step-brother-in-law, Brian Sweeny, told me recently that he was at Inverary, where "I hadn't been since Mummy [Margaret, Duchess of Argyll] was married to Big Ian [the 11th Duke]. Compared to Belvoir [Castle, the home of his sister Frances and her husband, the Duke of Rutland] it's *tiny*."

Aside from its modesty, Highgrove had other drawbacks for Diana. "Practically everything that The Prince of Wales viewed as an advantage, The Princess of Wales regarded as a disadvantage," says a famous beauty connected to the Royal Family. "For instance, its location appealed strongly to him. From his point of view, it was in the middle of everything. Cirencester polo ground was only a short drive away. Windsor was reasonably accessible. So too were the Quorn, the Beaufort and the Belvoir [with which the Prince hunts]. It was smart. Princess Anne lived nearby at Gatcombe Park, and, because of this, the police in the area already knew the score [with regard to protecting the royals], and that made settling in that much easier. And we mustn't forget another big plus in favour of the location. Camilla Parker Bowles and Dale Tryon lived in spitting distance, in Wiltshire. That, in itself, would have been enough to make Diana loathe the area. She *never* wanted to see the Parker Bowleses or the Tryons. He, *naturelle-*

ment, was forever angling to see as much of them as he could."

Diana preferred her other marital home, at Kensington Palace. KP, as it is known to everyone in royal circles, is not one palace, but a series of grace-and-favour residences situated in a compact village on the south-western side of Hyde Park, known as Kensington Palace Gardens. Some of the residences are houses, others flats, and all are in the gift of The Queen, who allocates them to relations, courtiers and friends in consultation with her Private Secretary and the Master of the Royal Household. No one has a right to the property under occupation. One does not pay rent, and if The Queen asks one to leave, one must do so promptly. The Department of the Environment is responsible for the upkeep of the William and Mary buildings, which are Grade I listed, and the only expenses the occupants had prior to the introduction of the community charge were gas, electricity, water, heating and the rates, which were considerable. Princess Margaret alone paid over £10,000 per annum, though with the change in local taxation, she now pays the same as any other resident of Kensington and Chelsea.

The Queen gave her heir two apartments. Together, Numbers 8 and 9 Kensington Palace comprise one large, L-shaped, three-storey house, with twenty-five principal rooms and many subsidiary ones. But it was not the largest apartment—that was inhabited by Charles's architect cousin Richard, Duke of Gloucester, who lives in splendour in thirty-five principal rooms and innumerable smaller ones, with his Danish wife Birgitte, his heir the Earl of Ulster, his daughters Lady Davina and Lady Rose Windsor, and his octogenarian mother, Princess Alice, Duchess of Gloucester.

Prince and Princess Michael of Kent are the Waleses' nearest neighbours. They occupy apartment Number 10 and share a courtyard, where the royal cousins all park their cars. This apartment had been Princess Margaret's, until she complained to her sister that she could not entertain properly in a place that was no larger than a "doll's house." With ten principal rooms and several of less signif-

179

icant dimension, it was vast by most people's standards, but Princess Margaret is not an average person, and her standards are even more exacting than any aristocrat's. She was therefore moved to apartment Number 1a, which is only half of Princess Louise, Duchess of Argyll's vast old apartment, Number 1, but is nevertheless sumptuous and regal. It has a quantity of spacious rooms and more than enough space to entertain Ned Ryan, Anouska Hempel, Roddy and Tania Llewellyn, and her other close friends.

Also in KP's favour was that Diana's closer sister, Jane, lived there, in a cottage called the Old Barracks, with her Assistant Private Secretary husband, Robert Fellowes. They could pop in and out of each other's houses as they pleased. This they did often, especially in the early days, when Diana was having trouble adjusting to married life.

"KP is definitely more Diana's speed than that pokey little house in the country," says a fellow royal. "From her point of view, there was hardly any sense in becoming a member of the Royal Family if she ended up living less grandly than her friends and relations." A friend confirmed this. "Highgrove was embarrassingly modest, but KP was just the ticket. It was grand. It had prestige. It was in the middle of everything. And she would be the envy of her friends and acquaintances."

The principal rooms in Kensington Palace are large and bright, with massive windows about six feet wide running from a few inches below the ceiling to a few above the floor. Diana and Dudley Poplak brought their talents to bear in this most elegantly proportioned of houses, even though they were stuck with some pretty garish acquisitions. One was the ghastly green and grey carpeting in the spacious entrance hall on the ground floor. Its motif is The Prince of Wales's feathers, and the effect is reminiscent of the worst excesses of boastfulness combined with the insufferable taste that one sometimes sees in third-rate hotel lobbies. Nothing can minimize the awfulness, and countless people, including Bob Geldof, have commented upon the carpet to The Prince and Princess of Wales. It remains laid, however, "because it would cost money to replace it," observes the aristocratic sister-in-law of the top-ranking courtier.

A glorious Georgian staircase lined with a variety of old and valuable paintings leads up to the first floor, where the drawing room is located. It is an elegant and comfortable room, with silken wall-coverings of deep, rich yellow, down-filled sofas of pale, crisp salmon, and yet more beautiful paintings in elaborate gilt frames. There is also a Broadwood grand piano which Diana and many other illustrious guests such as Vladimir Horowitz and Elton John have played, though the Princess does not have her grandmother's talent and could never have made her living as a pianist.

Diana conceived the drawing room as a place for entertaining. It was specifically furnished so that she and Charles could receive their guests there. There was space left for liveried footmen to serve vintage champagne to a maximum of seventy guests.

Situated nearby on the same floor is the dining room. This boasts a circular mahogany table, "so that no one can be disgruntled about being placed beneath the salt," Charles, ever conscious of the comfort of his guests and the effect his position has upon many, commented to a friend. Once more, Diana and Dudley Poplak chose a cheerful and elegant colour scheme. The walls are peach, the woodwork white, the curtains and chair coverings an elegant ripe plum. A massive landscape dominates one wall, and between the two large windows is a charming portrait of an eighteenth-century beauty, framed once more in gilt.

The gilt frames also go some way towards adding warmth and elegance to Diana's sitting room. These hold antique oil paintings, and a circular eighteenth-century mirror over the fireplace, which is painted white and provides a tall and elegant focus to a well-proportioned, rectangular room. The colour scheme is pink, blue, and white. On either side of the fireplace is a pair of matching sofas, covered in rose pink. Behind one is a circular table covered in blue floor-length silk, and nearby is a side table with a quantity of photographs of Diana's loved ones in silver frames. The paintwork for the skirting, doors and windows is once more white, and the walls pick up the predominant colours in the room. They are covered in specially woven silk, designed by Dudley Poplak, with The Prince of Wales's feathers as a motif. It goes to show what a bit of taste can do, for the design is subtle, and the effect, which is finished off with blue trimming, pleasing.

When Diana was doing up Kensington Palace, her marriage was in considerably better shape than it has been since. This was especially reflected in the main bedroom, where the passionate newlyweds confidently expected to be spending most of their nights. Also on the first floor, along with the other major rooms, it is large by anyone's standards. Measuring forty-five feet square, its main feature is the Prince's favourite four-poster bed. This is made of mahogany and is seven and a half feet wide. When they moved from Buckingham Palace, the bed followed them. On it is a mountain of cushions, and once more, the effect of the room is attractive.

Off the bedroom, on either side, are "his and hers" bathrooms, and beyond The Prince of Wales's, there is another bedroom which was originally intended to be his dressing room. "But he now uses it as his bedroom," says a connection of the Royal Family. "Now that he and Diana don't sleep together any more."

How Kensington Palace and its decorations strike an onlooker without a privileged background is described by Israel Zohar, the Russian-born artist who exhibits at the prestigious Roy Miles Gallery in Bruton Street, Mayfair. He was commissioned by The Royal Hussars to execute a portrait of The Princess of Wales. He says, "When I went for our first meeting, at Kensington Palace, before we met, I was given a tour to show me the environment, how she lives. Not being English, it was exciting for me to see the connection between the British and the Royal Family. To be in the Palace and see the central pole, the post of English history, indeed of Europe. As you enter, the furniture, every item, has some historical linkage to British history, to world history. In a way, it's like seeing the chain of what makes the culture of a nation, of humanity grow and develop through art, through furniture. It was fascinating to see the chairs, the art, all the visible symbols of culture."

CHAPTER THIRTEEN

A Rift in the Lute

While the houses were being decorated, and while she was still on her honeymoon in Scotland, Diana became pregnant. "She did it on purpose, to avoid the pressure they were heaping upon her about her official duties," says a member of the Royal Household, who saw a lot of Diana at the time. "Oliver Everett and The Prince of Wales had big plans for her. But she didn't want any of it. She told me so. She said she didn't see why she had to be subjected to so much pressure at her age. So she became pregnant. It was a big shock for The Prince of Wales. My understanding was that she wasn't going to get pregnant for the first three years. He wanted to give the marriage time to settle down, to give them a chance to build up a strong relationship between them. He also wanted her to become acclimatized to the royal way of life before embarking on motherhood. But she opted out. She used her pregnancy to avoid tasks and responsibilities which were odious to her."

Even before the marriage, plans were afoot to launch Diana in an official capacity. "The Prince, Edward Adeane and Michael Colbourne all thought she should start off in Wales," says a member of Charles's staff. So they worked towards the date chosen, October 1981, when the honeymoon was at an end.

Being a member of a reigning royal family meant that Diana now had her own show. While The Prince of Wales had a fully operational staff, which could absorb much of the initial work, Diana needed her own as well, to get, and keep, the show on the road. The prime position, Private Secretary, had already been satisfied by Oliver Everett. The next most important, a lady-in-waiting, needed to be filled.

This was rather easier said than done, for the lady in question would have to be a paragon of virtue, with the constitution of an ox, the sensitivity of a gazelle, the hide of a rhinoceros, the eyes of an owl, the nose of a spaniel, the adaptability of a chameleon, and the looks of a breed that would not upstage the competitive Princess. Moreover, she had to be young enough to get along with the youthful Diana, but old enough to possess the twin virtues of responsibility and discretion.

All the senior members of the Royal Family and their advisers were pressed into action. Several "gels" of around thirty were considered, but the choice fell upon the one person who was truly ideal. Anne Beckwith-Smith was the daughter of Major Peter Beckwith-Smith, Clerk of the Course at Epsom and, as such, a chum of the racing-mad Queen Mother. She came from a devout Anglican family, and her brother James is a well-known and well-liked figure in ecclesiastical as well as social circles.

It was The Queen Mother, in conjunction with Diana's grandmother Ruth, Lady Fermoy, who championed Anne's selection, and what good judgement that turned out to be. Anne was nice, bright, charming, good-humoured, flexible, adaptable, dignified and unstuffy. Eight years older than Diana, she was pleasant-looking but definitely not competition for the newly svelte and image-conscious Princess. Like Diana, she was an alumna of West Heath, and, like Diana's grandmother Ruth, she had an erudite background, having studied art in Florence and Paris. She spoke good Italian and French; she had worked for the Arts Council of Great Britain organizing exhibitions, before taking off for six months to travel extensively around India and the Far East, and had returned to London to work in the British Pictures Department at Sotheby's for four years, whence she was poached by the Palace.

In September 1981, Anne Beckwith-Smith was appointed lady-in-waiting to The Princess of Wales. Thereafter, she would perform as social secretary, public and private prop, and friend. When she and Diana were on public duties, she would hover nearby in the background, ready to intervene at the first sign of trouble, or if the Princess were being bogged down by people or her own enthusiasm (public events have a timetable which cannot be ignored entirely). She would write thank-you letters to Diana's hosts, answer much of Diana's correspondence, and do all the other duties, such as holding flowers for the Princess, that ladies-in-waiting generally do.

The month after Anne's appointment, Diana's first official engagement took place. This was the carefully planned three-day tour of the Principality of Wales. Prince Charles presented her to the people of Wales from the balcony of Caenarvon Castle, where his Investiture as Prince had been held twelve years previously. Sensitive as ever to the feelings of those she wished to win over, Diana embarked upon a course she has since adopted, and dressed in red and green, the national colours of the country. This was a clever move, and won her the immediate acclaim of the crowds, who were touched that she had cared enough for their sensitivities to make such a small but significant gesture.

Diana, however, had only started. As she and Prince Charles went walk-about, it soon became apparent that everyone wanted to see her. "It was the most frightening thing I've ever done," she said. "I was terrified. But they made it so much easier for me, they were so welcoming." Diana plunged right in, heading especially for the children and the older folk, with whom she was comfortable from her years visiting the needy when she was a student at West Heath.

Diana is genuinely thoughtful, has the faculty of sympathy, and cannot help touching strangers when she wishes to establish contact. This is not a voluntary response, but an innate action over which she has no control. It is a trait which has endeared her to literally tens of thousands of people whose paths she has crossed, and, as she began her first official engagement, touching first the sleeve of an old lady, then the hand of a little girl, before squeezing the fingers of someone else who was holding out a hand to her, Diana was inadvertently but naturally laying the ground for the phenomenal success she has since enjoyed. Nor was she either calculating or insincere in the performance she was giving. When the rain was pouring down and she refused an umbrella, she did so out of innate good manners and a desire to put herself on a par with those around her by putting herself in the shoes of others, which is one of her more endearing qualities. To those who had been waiting for hours in the wind, cold, and rain, she made such comments as, "Poor you. I feel cold myself. My hands are freezing, and yours must be much worse. Thank you for waiting for us," and, "You're soaked to the bone. You must be freezing. I am. Thanks for coming to see us."

This overtly humane approach was not entirely novel, for The Prince of Wales often behaved like that. But Diana did not have his grimacing reserve, so she came across as being more egalitarian and empathetic than he. This, combined with her looks, her eagerness to please, her apparent openness and her glamour, won everyone over. People were touched that she would bother to dress up, then not mind having the torrential rain ruin her clothes, her hair, her hat, and her make-up, as she happily pressed flesh without the benefit of an umbrella.

The tour was not without its problems. There had been terrorist warnings even at the planning stage, giving Diana her first taste of the rigours and dangers of royal life. She was serenely unworried by the prospect of assassination, although she was somewhat more rattled when she was subjected to placards and chants of "Go Home, Diana" accompanying "Go Home, English Prince" by the Welsh Nationalists. Paint was sprayed on her car, students at Bangor demonstrated with stink bombs, chants, and scuffles, and the police waded in, making arrests.

Despite the problems, Diana, taking her cue from Prince Charles, resolutely kept the smile on her face. From the Rhondda Valley through the mountains of Wales to the seaside resorts in the north, she set out to charm, and charm she did. She even upstaged The Prince of Wales, who, up to this time, was the unrivalled royal superstar. But Charles, a loving and benevolent husband, did not mind. He even joked about it, and would continue to do so for some time yet, until he began to question the motives behind Diana's conduct. At that point, the marriage would hit yet another rock, and a very large and injurious one indeed, but these difficulties were yet to come.

In the meantime, the tour was coming to an end, and when it did, Diana was presented with the Freedom of the City of Cardiff. She was only the second woman to be honoured thus, the first being The Queen, and when she came to reply, in what became her first public speech, she took yet another leaf out of her husband's book. She used some Welsh. Appreciative of her efforts, the people went wild. Diana was launched on her phenomenal road to public adoration.

The key to Diana's success has always been her exceptional personality. Most people, when they meet her, have reasonably uniform impressions of her, and I have taken a cross-section of these to demonstrate what her effect is.

Lady Teresa Manners, who has known Diana since they were both little girls (their parents are family friends), also has the advantage of knowing Prince Charles as well. She says, "I like Diana. She's lovely. Very nice and natural. She's made a great success of her life and I admire her for that."

A generation older is the Dowager Empress of the British charity world, Princess Helena Moutafian. President of the Ladies' Committee of Help The Aged, one of Diana's favourite charities, as well as being a Vice-President of the charity itself, she comes into regular contact with the Princess. "She's charming and diplomatic. Always well groomed, and well briefed and advised. She's nice. You can tell about people by looking into their eyes. She's got warm, sparkling, nice eyes. She has a vivacity, she is pleasing to people. People like people who vibrate, who carry something in themselves that reflects on to other people. That's why she attracts masses, not just individuals. It's a quality great stars have. They attract people like magnets."

Dame Barbara Cartland concurs. "All the Spencers have strong personalities. Diana has magnetism. Wherever she goes people find that irresistible attraction which makes them want to know her, and where women are concerned, copy her. There is only one other lady in Britain who has this compelling appeal for everyone she meets, and that is Queen Elizabeth The Queen Mother. When the Queen Mother is talking to someone, they always feel they are the only person who matters and that she is vitally interested in them as a person. It is this quality which The Princess of Wales has, and which leaves people laughing and smiling long after she has left them. They cherish everything she says and does and they will remember it all their lives."

Israel Zohar, who painted her, provides the artist's impression. "I must say, you prepare yourself for a certain person. The feeling is, the Princess is not a regular human being like you or me. Then I meet her and a total human being comes into the room, so open, so friendly, so warm, so human. She's treating everybody with such friendliness. So direct, so much to the person, all the feeling of formality you imagine in advance isn't there at all. Immediately she creates a feeling of lightness and friendliness and easiness, an atmosphere. She doesn't give you a feeling that you're lower or less than she is—quite the opposite. She treats everyone with a lot of respect. I liked her. She had an enormous effect on the painting. The Royal Hussars wanted something classical which will fit in with the other paintings at the Headquarters, where the paintings are mainly from the nineteenth and eighteenth century. Obviously I thought I'd do something very formal, to make her bigger than life, to glorify her. After meeting her, I changed my whole opinion. I decided to look for something more human, simple, soft, as was my feeling about her. In the picture, she makes contact with the viewer, a sharp and open look in her eyes looking directly at the viewer. I wanted to emphasize that. I realized when she's very relaxed her lower lip opens a bit, which indicates an openness, a softness. I chose that way of portraying her though it's difficult for an artist to capture."

To her credit, Diana does not reserve her charm only for

the grand, the charitable, or the artistic. Terry Dixon, the porter at the flats where I live along with many other titled people and members of the Royal Household, often acts as a butler for them and for connections of the Royal Family. As a result, he has served Diana as well as most of the other members of the Royal Family on several occasions. He says, "She's lovely. So warm and natural and bright and bubbly. She never forgets to say please and thank you, and always makes you know that she appreciates whatever you do for her. She is a real lady. Just wonderful."

It was this appealing personality which the Welsh people sensed, and which made her first tour such a success, despite the political turmoil surrounding it. As it was, the timing prevented her from enjoying it to the full. On the one hand, "she was very insecure," says a member of the Royal Household. And on the other, having become pregnant in a desire to escape the pressures of official life, she now had to endure a serious case of morning sickness. This began as soon as she was pregnant, and she complained to a friend, "I cannot tell you how bloody awful it is. They call it morning sickness. But I feel sick all the time." It persisted for much of her pregnancy, making it a purgatory. Ironically enough, having become pregnant in an attempt to avoid unwanted chores, she ended up with the worst of both worlds: failing to avoid all the pressure, she felt sick throughout most of the pregnancy.

But those were not the only problems Diana was having as she settled down to married life. The courtiers and staff were driving her to distraction, and the smoothness, efficiency and completeness with which The Prince of Wales's life was run were making her feel redundant. "I married to be a wife and mother," she said, but she was discovering that the first role left her scope only for the things she did not want, while the second was making her feel like the living dead. The one positive effect was that she abandoned her diet and succumbed to the urge to gorge herself. Christmas Day was now every day; breakfast at West Heath every meal.

According to Barbara Cartland, "From the very beginning the Princess understood that what she ate, how she felt and behaved would affect her unborn child." An ardent non-smoker like Prince Charles, she did not have to give up that habit, and Barbara Cartland could not imagine Diana "eating or drinking anything that might have affected her children. She is too vividly conscious that prenatal behaviour is very important where a child's life is concerned." With that in mind, Diana eliminated everything potentially harmful from her diet, limiting herself to white meat, pasta, salads, vegetables, and lots of fruit. Gradually she managed to wean Charles off his public schoolboy diet of red meat and stodge, until nowadays the Waleses keep such a politically correct dietary household that even their dinner guests are served previously disdained dishes like pasta and chicken. The only deviation from absolute healthiness is Diana's voracious consumption of sweets, which has remained constant throughout her life. Her bulimia ceased for the first time since her engagement, and while her mood swings took time to lessen, even they began to do so.

Intent on producing as healthy a baby as possible, Diana also went to the *éminence grise* of pregnancy. Betty Parsons was the expert co-opted by every grand or fashionable prospective mother with a desire to give birth healthily and naturally. She had taught The Queen exercises when she was pregnant with Prince Edward, and it was she, not Prince Philip, who stayed with The Queen throughout her youngest child's birth, telling her how to practise the myriad methods she had taught her to ensure a natural and healthy birth. Once more, Mrs. Parsons was invited to return to the Palace, this time to instruct Diana, and also Charles, who took an active interest in his wife's pregnancy and wanted to participate each step of the way.

Despite Diana's attempts to approach her pregnancy with as little stress as possible, she was not living a stress-free life. To begin with, she and Charles were still "camping" at Buckingham Palace, waiting for Highgrove and KP to be ready. While this was hardly pressure, compared to the strain on a poverty-stricken wife with a husband out of work, it was nevertheless far from ideal. From Charles's point of view, however, it did have one convenient aspect.

His office was handily situated a few yards away from their bedroom.

That was a definite disadvantage to Diana. Being so accessible meant she could never avoid the very pressure which she had sought to escape. Although her pregnancy curtailed her official duties once it was officially announced on 5 November 1981, it did not eliminate them entirely. She still fulfilled obligations like turning on the Christmas lights at Regent Street and going for the odd charity visit, but she was not subjected to a strenuous round of engagements.

Despite this, a courtier said, Diana's attitude towards her work was creating problems. "She really hated doing her homework, and she refused to see that she had to do it, otherwise she wasn't doing her job properly. She thought she could sail through engagements without being properly prepared. You know, faking it with a lot of charm and smiles.

"The form was the same for all the royals. Before an engagement, they were presented with background material. If it was something to do with a charity, for instance, they would be properly briefed on the organization, its aims, accomplishments, how it was run, that sort of thing. Then they'd receive details about the people they were meeting, so that they'd know who they were, what their function was, so that they could speak to them in an informed way. Remember, royalty must always initiate conversations, so it was important that they were adequately briefed. If they weren't, they couldn't speak intelligently to the people they met.

"That was the problem with Diana. She stubbornly refused to read her background material, so she could only ooh and aah and giggle when she turned up for an engagement. Oliver [Everett, her Private Secretary] tried everything to get her to improve her attitude. The whole office was used to The Prince of Wales, who is a voracious reader and happily ploughs through piles and piles of stuff. It was difficult to know quite how to cope with Diana's wilful refusal to do what was a valid part of her job. Oliver settled on a combination of cajoling and cutting the material down, down, down. Eventually he distilled it so that it was practically no more than cue card comments. That's what she now reads, though at first it took some doing to get her to look at even that.

"I remember once, I was in her bedroom with her. Oliver was trying to reach her on the squawk box, which connected the office to the bedroom. He was chasing her up about some reports which she was meant to be reading. By then he knew she wouldn't even look at them if he didn't keep on at her. If he did, she'd at least give them a cursory glance. That was better than nothing. Anyway, to cut a long story short, as soon as he came on to the squawk box, she took some pillows off the bed and buried it to block out the sound. She had a determined look on her face. Her jaw was set, her eyes spitting daggers.

"Her attitude was, 'The public already think I'm marvellous, so why should I waste my time boning up on boring subjects.' She was firmly convinced she could sail by with coy smiles, and that she didn't need to do anything more than smile and say, in those honeyed tones of hers, 'How marvellous,' or 'How awful,' or 'How brave.' She had no intention of developing her mind or her conversational skills, and when it became apparent—as it quickly did—that she was lost around everyone but children and old people, she decreed that all her official engagements must somehow revolve around them. That's how she came to choose the fields she is now involved with. They've brought her a lot of admiration, and she has done some excellent work for the young and old. But she arrived at her choice by default.

"Of course, it was never possible for her to limit herself to only those two segments of the population. Royalty has to mix with a variety of people. She has to be Colonel-in-Chief of regiments. She has to mix with the armed forces. There are official banquets, when she's seated beside world leaders, other royals, captains of industry, scientists, philosophers, famous writers. The whole spectrum of society's contributors, people who have something to say and want to hear what she has to say as well.

"Well, of course, Diana was just hopeless with all of

them. Reports began flooding back to the Palace about how she never had anything to say to anyone at anything official, except pop and TV and movie stars, whom she was obsessed with. Then she could chatter for hours on end. Otherwise, things were rather glum. It would have been so easy for her to bone up on, say, Portugal if she was going to be sitting beside the Portuguese Ambassador, or learn enough about British Aerospace and the aeronautical industry if she was going to be the chairman's dinner companion. But she resolutely refused to do her homework."

This refusal created problems on several levels. "She made Oliver's job very difficult, though he was always very kind and gentle and understanding. He had the patience of Job with her." The Prince of Wales was fully aware of the problems Oliver Everett was having with Diana. In part, he had been responsible for the initiation of the process, having isolated the need when he witnessed Diana's conversations with President and Madame Sadat. Not even he, however, could budge Diana.

She had always been stubborn and wilful. From early childhood these two characteristics had been most pronounced. They were double-edged swords, responsible for the determination and tenacity which had enticed The Prince of Wales against the odds. Without them, she would never have become Princess of Wales, but now that she was, they were undermining her relationship with her husband. Ultimately, they would help destroy the love, affection, regard, and intimacy which Charles felt for Diana, wounding her immeasurably in the process.

"She simply refused to accept that she needed to grow in any way. As far as she was concerned," says the member of the Royal Household, who was closely involved with the Waleses at the time, "she was fine just as she was. She was the world's darling. If The Prince of Wales wasn't satisfied with her as she was, it was his failing, not hers. She could not accept that a man might want a real companion instead of a glamorous mirage whom everyone who did not know her thought was wonderful. Chuffed though he was by the admiration of the readers of the *Sun* and the *Mirror* for his wife, he nevertheless felt that that was hardly an acceptable substitute for the substance he required from a wife. He couldn't get over the fact that she never ever read anything, and if she did, it was a magazine like *Tatler* and *Harper's & Queen* or some crummy romantic novel. 'I don't understand it,' he used to say to me, 'she doesn't read. Can't you get her to read?' "

Intent on doing all he could to keep his marriage as happy as possible, the idealistic Prince tried to please Diana in every way. When she baulked at going away on a skiing holiday early in 1982, saying that she did not wish to endanger the baby, he willingly got in touch with his cousins the Brabournes (the film producer Lord Brabourne and his wife Patricia, the Countess Mountbatten of Burma) and arranged to borrow their house on the Bahamian island of Eleuthera. "He willingly sacrificed one of his greatest pleasures for her," says a royal relation. "Of course she was right to be careful with the baby. She did have a point. It isn't safe to ski when you're five months pregnant. But the truth is, Diana prefers holidays in the sun to skiing, even though she is an excellent skier, contrary to popular opinion."

Despite showing willingness, The Prince of Wales was not blind to the way his marriage was developing. "Before Prince William was born, things had degenerated to the stage where he never wanted to be in the same room as her unless someone was there with him," says a member of the Royal Household. "We all used to try to get him to go and talk to her when she was alone, but he'd say, 'I don't have anything to say to her.' The reality was, he wanted intelligent exchange from the relationship. She wanted love-talk."

"Diana," according to the aristocratic sister-in-law of the top-ranking courtier, "undermined her marriage by believing her own publicity. She's not the first celebrity and she won't be the last who's fallen into that trap. If she'd been sensible, instead of just clever, she'd have realized that you can't keep the interest of a highly intellectual man without maintaining an intellectual rapport."

Blind to the danger of the course on which she was setting herself, Diana looked around for reasons why her fairytale marriage was unravelling into unseemly reality. She began questioning Charles's feelings for her. Never once did it occur to her that an equally valid variation on her point of view was, "If I really loved him, I would want to please him, and not simply expect him to please me." For someone who was so sympathetic to anyone in distress, it was puzzling that she could have been so out of tune with the man she loved. But it is important to remember that Diana was very young, and with immaturity, by definition, goes a lack of insight and wisdom.

With the folly of youth, Diana appears to have allowed the security of marriage to steer her down a path she should never have taken. "Having won the prize of marriage, Diana was no longer so obliging as she had been. It was quite a switch. Prior to the wedding," says the same source, "she could not do enough to ingratiate herself in his eyes, to convince him that she was the right girl for him. Once the wedding ring was on her finger, she pulled the rug from under his feet. She became extraordinarily demanding. She made it very clear that any changes that were going to be made were going to be made by him. I can't think of many men who would put up with a wife with an attitude like that. It disappointed him. It also antagonized him. But he's a peacemaker and, being royal, well used to making the best of a situation he'd much rather not be in. He didn't stand his ground and fight; he withdrew. He was still nice and kind and solicitous towards her when he was around her. He simply made sure he was around her as little as possible."

But the strong Spencer personality which Barbara Cartland described, allied as it was to Diana's overwhelming stubbornness, had only begun to do its dastardly work. "Diana was anti-polo, anti-hunting, anti-everything he liked," says a lifelong friend of hers. "No one could understand her objections. She was used to hunting, in the family she comes from. Sarah's hunting-mad and Diana's even joined her on hunts at Belvoir. How could she expect her marriage to be good when she became anti-everything he was for? I like Diana, and she's made a great success of her life. Pity she couldn't do the same with her marriage. But she's too dominant, that's her problem."

Certainly Diana's role models had never exhibited a worthwhile example in their marital relationships. Her parents' marriage had hardly been something anyone in their right mind would wish to emulate. Nor had their subsequent marriages been recipes for success. "Peter and Frances Shand Kydd's relationship was not my idea of what a good marriage should be," says a friend. "He was not particularly warm with her and the children, and she seemed to vacillate between filling a void with the force of her personality, and almost buttering him up. Yes, I suppose it was a case of one partner being in the ascendant, followed by the other partner becoming the top dog for a while."

Several sources confirmed that Raine and Johnnie Spencer also had a relationship based on dominance, and my observations of them in social contexts bore this out, a friend said at the time. "There is no doubt that Raine utterly dominates Johnnie, and that he loves it."

But The Prince of Wales was not used to dominant women. "The Queen has always allowed Prince Philip to be the master of their household," says a fellow royal. "There has never been any question of who the man in that relationship is. It is definitely The Duke of Edinburgh."

Nor was Prince Charles used to people expecting him to dance attendance on them. All his adult life, it was they who had done so on him. "He was absolutely stunned by Diana and her behaviour," says the senior courtier's sister-in-law. "He thought he was marrying a docile, compliant, sweet-natured, adoring girl. He woke up to a dominant, determined woman who did not hesitate to rant and rave if she wasn't getting her own way. It was like buying a succulent peach because it's soft. You take it home, bite into it without looking, and break a tooth, because the fruitmonger switched the fruit on you. Was he disenchanted? His feelings went way beyond disenchantment. He was married to a woman he hadn't chosen—would never have chosen. He was stuck with someone he did not want: stuck for life. He began to resent her bitterly."

His feelings of resentment were also borne out by one of Diana's closest friends, who said, "She believes he never loved her and resents her because he's stuck with her for life. She told me so quite categorically." In fact, all the evidence indicates that he did love her. Princess Katarina of Yugoslavia attested to the obvious love he had for Diana at the time of the marriage, and another relation said, "He's a great romantic and very idealistic. He always wanted a close and loving marriage based on love, respect and companionship."

Over the years, in private and in public, The Prince of Wales has voiced the same sentiments about what he wanted from marriage. A variety of sources, including friends, relations, courtiers, all said that the difficulties in his marriage had been a source of great regret and disappointment to him, and that he had been tremendously perturbed by the turn taken by events. No one enjoys seeing a marriage go wrong, and certainly not an isolated figure who had high hopes for a marriage which seemed to promise companionship and compatibility.

The same was true of Diana, of course. She had also gone into the marriage with high hopes. She expected that her husband, being the nice, kind, sensitive man he was, would be flexible enough to change in the ways she wanted him to. She did not yet understand that her marriage was already in worse shape than she thought, or that you cannot change people fundamentally, but when the penny dropped, the suffering she endured was terrible.

Although a close friend of Diana said she already sensed that Prince Charles was closing her out even at that early stage, she was nevertheless still protected from the full extent of his disappointment by the way he behaved towards her. He was very aware that his marriage had to succeed, at least well enough for Diana to be kept reasonably happy. He understood that if she became too dissatisfied, or if things should degenerate to the point of bitter unhappiness, she just might leave him, thereby undermining his position as Heir to the Throne. From the royal point of view, that would be an unmitigated disaster which just might rock the monarchy to its foundations. "The Queen was *very* concerned," says a member of the Royal Household, who was in a position to know what was going on with all the parties. "She told Lady Susan Hussey to keep an eye on the situation and make sure that Diana was kept as happy as possible."

Keeping Diana happy became the order of the day. The perpetual press attention, which had not died down since the wedding, began to perturb the pregnant and highly emotional Princess, who no longer had any need of the publicity that had helped entice Charles; she now became tired of it. "Diana started to loathe the press," says a royal relation.

"The fuss about the press was a red herring," a friend says. "What was really disturbing her was the way her marriage was going, and being pregnant didn't help." Nevertheless, The Queen was very anxious and, taking the problem at face value, embarked upon yet another unprecedented course of action on behalf of her highly strung daughter-in-law. She called in all the editors of the Fleet Street newspapers to Buckingham Palace. Only the editor of the *Sun* declined the opportunity to hear Her Majesty plead for a curtailment of the constant coverage. His response could hardly have been more surprising than that of the editor of the *News of the World,* however, who informed a confounded Monarch that Diana could not expect liberty of movement without attendant attention. To Elizabeth's consternation, he advised that Diana desist from shopping and send a servant out whenever she wanted to buy winegums.

The Queen's approaches had the desired effect. Publicly, the newspapers resisted the temptation to pursue Diana relentlessly. And privately, the pressure was eased off her. Yet, beneath the calm surface, there were still forces and currents pulling to and fro, propelling Diana towards misery and the marriage towards emotional stagnation. Charles's and The Queen's method of coping with the real problem, which was the direction the marriage was taking, was counter-productive. In their attempt to cushion her from the realities within her life, they were effectively though unintentionally depriving her of an opportunity to deal with the problem before it became permanent and insoluble.

This would have a profound effect in the future, but it also had an immediate effect. Because Prince Charles had married Diana believing that she wanted to please him, and would develop along compatible lines, so, as she persisted in her wilful refusal to acknowledge any of his needs or desires that did not meet with her approval, his alienation from her worsened perceptibly. "He is not the sort of man a woman can bend or break," says a royal relation. "He is no Prince Michael of Kent. A domineering woman does not win with him. Her approach was all wrong. He would gladly have sacrificed anything for her, if she'd gone about things the way she did before the marriage. But she didn't."

The aristocratic sister-in-law of the senior courtier concurs. "I doubt that she realizes, even now, what pushed him away. It is interesting to speculate if she'd have behaved differently if she'd known. Possibly she would have. She was madly in love with The Prince of Wales. She might have been able to make the adjustment, though I personally doubt it. Bulimia nervosa or no bulimia nervosa, emotional disturbance or no emotional disturbance, she's a very dominant personality. It's difficult to go from that to being someone who relates to a man on a more equal footing. She might have, though. You never know. She was certainly young enough to be able to make the transition. And she's made so many other transitions, like from being work-shy to enjoying her work, that she just might have been able to make this, the most crucial one of all."

Blind to what was really happening and its effects, Diana believed her assertive tactics were working. This naturally only drove her on to greater heights of assertiveness, with increasingly disastrous but till then undetected results. Yet she cannot be blamed. The main body of the evidence before her suggested that she was getting the marriage and the life she wanted, even though, as she told a friend, "I always had my doubts about how he really felt. There was never anything concrete for me to grab a hold of, but I did have these feelings about things, that things weren't quite right."

CHAPTER FOURTEEN

A Prince is Born

*U*sing the influence she had, Diana now proceeded to shape her life in ways that would afford her the freedom and self-expression she desired. From her advent in the Prince's life, she had resented the way the courtiers and staff surrounding him built a shield around him, protecting him not only from the world, but also from her influence. She set about breaking down that structure with a vengeance, complaining, "It was as if Charles was married to them, not me."

Diana's first target was Stephen Barry, whom she had long resented and against whom her list of complaints was legion. Her dislike had been triggered by the valet preventing her from seeing Charles, when he was otherwise engaged, prior to their marriage. But there were other, more substantial reasons. "Stephen had shared the whole of the Prince's adult life," says a former member of the Wales household. "They had memories of incidents, places, and people to which Diana would never be privy. She felt excluded, and it galled her to think that a man she disliked knew more about her husband than she did. Moreover, Stephen had had a lot of influence with him before Diana came along, and she felt she had to compete for the premier position with him." This made Diana's hackles rise. "She was always jealous and competitive, even when she was a little girl at school," says a schoolmate of hers.

Far more to Diana's taste was Ken Stronach, Barry's assistant, who had been valet to Earl Mountbatten of

Burma until his assassination in 1979, after which John Barratt, Lord Mountbatten's Private Secretary, had arranged for him to go to work for Charles. Stronach was affable, approachable, malleable. He also knew his place, which was a necessity for working peaceably with someone as dominant as Diana. "Although not pompous, she did insist upon subservience," a courtier says. "But Stephen Barry had never been subservient, not even with The Prince of Wales. He'd always allowed him a great deal of latitude."

Determined to supplant Barry with Stronach, Diana set about making the reigning valet's life uncomfortable, hoping that in doing so she would force him out. "She made it impossible for him to do his job," says another member of The Prince of Wales's staff. "She quite deliberately made it her business to take over every aspect of his job, except that of tending to The Prince of Wales's uniforms and maintaining his clothes. Stephen had always chosen the Prince's clothes. Every day he'd choose a shirt, tie, suit, shoes, handkerchief—the whole works. He'd lay them out for His Royal Highness first thing. The Princess started doing that. There's no denying she was more interested in her husband's appearance than your average wife, but it was more than wifely concern. She wanted to usurp Stephen's role, to make him superfluous, to leave him nothing to do.

"But she didn't stop at making him superfluous. She made him feel it too. She froze him out, the way she freezes out anyone who displeases her. The atmosphere was hardly conducive to cordiality, and in the end he told me he was going to chuck in the towel. He said he couldn't stand it any more. They didn't have a row though, and he definitely wasn't fired. He resigned. And he remained on good terms with The Prince of Wales, even after he'd written his books. He'd never signed the Official Secrets Act, you see."

There has long been the suspicion that homophobia was behind Diana's actions. That was not so. "The Palace has more homosexuals than an anthill has ants," says the noblewoman whose brother-in-law is a top-ranking courtier.

"You need only cite her rather excessive friendship with Adrian Ward-Jackson to kill any doubt about her feelings on that score." The issue was purely one of control.

But Stephen Barry was not the first employee whom she forced out. That distinction belonged to Chief Detective Paul Officer. Diana could not abide this six-foot, ex-public schoolboy, who had long been a favourite of her husband. He had saved Charles's life, when a rating on a Royal Navy training exercise at Poole, Dorset, had run amok and tried to crack the Prince's skull with a chair. Intervening without a thought for his own safety, Officer had foiled the attempt, thereby earning the Prince's undying gratitude. Charles had sacrificed this most excellent of detectives so that Diana could have the finest in royal protection, but there were several clashes of personality between the punctilious Chief Detective and his wilful charge. Diana resented the way she was made to feel by his presence. Unused as she was to the constant invasion of privacy that protection inevitably brought in its wake, she made him the focus of her hostility, and proceeded to make him as uncomfortable as she later made Stephen Barry. Officer was transferred from duty with Diana at the time of her wedding.

Had Barry and Officer been the only members of staff to resign, Diana might not have received the subsequent unfavourable press. But she was responsible for several other departures. According to a friend of Diana, the socialite ex-wife of a famous financier, "I understand she's extremely pernickety. Very difficult to work for. Everything has to be done exactly as she wants it. How? Well, if her dress isn't pressed exactly as she wants it to be, she returns it. And evidently not nicely either. She'll throw it down or issue a sharp rebuke."

On the other hand, if her employees do perform to the required standard, she is a warm, kind, generous and loyal employer. Some of her staff have been with her since her marriage, and everyone who has remained with her sings her praises.

When news of the constant flow of staff from the Wales household hit the press, it caused Diana's brother Charles to hop to her defence. Rather unfairly, he dismissed people who had given the Prince many years of loyal service as being "hangers-on" whom Diana "weeded out." He described Diana's methods as being "subtle," though there is no doubt that Stephen Barry, Paul Officer and the other departing staff would have chosen different adjectives. In the process, he once more showed the world how masterly the Fermoy/Spencer clan was at employing the methods of the courtier class to defend one of their own, and to perpetuate Diana's image as a soft and gentle soul.

In fashionable circles, though, the secret had long since been out. As Jacqueline, Lady Killearn observed, "She's tough." Many people, myself included, admire that trait in Diana. It shows she has character, that she is a moulder of circumstance, who shapes the clay of her life into a form she finds pleasing. No one could argue with her desire to be surrounded by employees she finds compatible, and a member of the Royal Household sums the situation up by saying, "Which woman doesn't want to have some say in how her life is run? I didn't blame Diana one bit. She was totally right to grab the reins out of other people's hands. Left up to The Prince of Wales, life would have continued exactly as it had been, with only one minor change, namely the acquisition of a quiet and malleable wife. But Diana wasn't having that. She's got mettle, that one, and I admire her for that. His life was already so well organized that she could easily have stepped into it without ever making a change, and everything would still have run like clockwork. But she wanted to make her mark, and that strikes me as perfectly natural."

The birth of a child often papers over the cracks in a marriage, and so it proved with the Waleses when a happy and proud Diana was delivered, two weeks early, of a 7 lb 10 oz boy at 9:03 on the evening of Monday, 21 June 1982.

Three adjacent rooms had been cleared of patients on the top floor of the Lindo Wing of St. Mary's Hospital in unfashionable Paddington, and a screen put up by her room for the duration of her stay, so that The Princess of Wales could have privacy and shuttle across the corridor from her 12×14 ft room to the two bathrooms and two separate lavatories.

Diana and Charles had arrived at the hospital at five o'clock that morning, entering through a side door. After taking the lift twelve storeys up to Diana's room on the top floor, the couple settled down for what promised to be a typical delivery. George Pinker, the most fashionable obstetrician of the day, was in attendance.

No birth, however, is ever painless. Irrespective of Betty Parson's lessons and Prince Charles's aid, Diana was not able to endure the arduousness of childbirth once the pain hit her. Like many a woman before and since, she threw all desire for natural childbirth out of the window and opted for the blessed relief of an epidural.

Prince Charles was as rapturous over his son as Diana was. She told Barbara Cartland, "having a child is a miracle," while he told the assembled journalists, "I'm overwhelmed by it all," and called the experience "marvellous." Privately, he described the event to a cousin as "the most wonderful thing that's ever happened to me."

The infant was tagged Baby Wales and breastfed by his mother, who was adamant that he should not be circumcized like his father. Charles seemed as reluctant to be separated from his son as Diana, and arrived bright and early the following morning to a room flooded with the roses he had arranged to send. There were also a wealth of other flowers from friends and relations.

At nine o'clock, Charles, Diana and Baby Wales were joined by Frances Shand Kydd and Jane Fellowes. To the delight of the assembled newsmen, waiting outside the hospital, the constant stream of visitors did not dry up. At eleven the baby's other grandmother arrived to inspect him: The Queen turned up in her favourite car, a moss green Rover behind whose wheel the residents of Belgravia could sometimes glimpse her as she drove herself to or from her "real" home, Windsor Castle. Earl Spencer also turned up to inspect the child, who had finally, after two hundred and fifty years, ensured that the blood of the Spencers would flow legitimately in the veins of a King of Great Britain. Before departing in his Rolls-Royce, the ebullient grandfather of the future king commented upon his comeliness to the press corps.

It was a proud day all round. The Queen returned to the Palace to toast the heir in line to her throne. Frances Shand Kydd treated the passengers and crew on her return flight to Scotland to a celebratory glass of champagne with which to toast her grandson, the future monarch, although when the moment for settling the bill came, the airline graciously waived the charge. Charles and Diana also toasted the baby, and she rang up several friends and relations on the private telephone line beside her bed.

Hospitals, however, are a bore for anyone who does not feel sick, and the healthy Diana was anxious to get back to the comfort of home. She asked Mr. Pinker to release her that same day, and, confident that she had all the back-up any new mother needs, he did. At six o'clock, The Prince of Wales took his wife and son home.

Home was no longer "bunking" at Buckingham Palace. The family had moved a few weeks before into their apartment at Kensington Palace, which was as elegant as it was comfortable, with every modern household convenience. Nor had Diana and Dudley Poplak neglected to create a charming nursery for the baby and his nanny on the second floor.

Baby Wales's space was hardly cramped. There was a day nursery or playroom, as well as a night nursery of baby's bedroom and bathroom, plus a bedroom and bathroom for the nanny, and several other bedrooms and bathrooms for any future arrivals and their staff. Nor was this Baby Wales's only province. At Highgrove he also had a spacious suite of rooms, stuffed as solidly as his London home with colourful, cuddly toys.

Waiting to take care of the baby was someone whom Charles's Aunt Margot, Princess Margaret, had found for her nephew and niece. Barbara Barnes was no ordinary nanny. She was virtually a member of the family of the Hon. Colin Tennant (now Lord Glenconner) and his wife, the former Lady Anne Coke, to whom Diana's father had been unofficially engaged and whom he had left when passion, in the shape of Frances Burke Roche, had struck him so many years beforehand.

Princess Margaret was also on very cordial terms with Barbara Barnes. For fifteen years the refreshingly unsnobbish, bohemian PM, as all Princess Margaret's friends call her, had watched her raise the Tennants' twin daughters. They shared holidays *en famille* in Scotland and Mustique and everyday life in London, for Lady Anne Tennant was a lady-in-waiting as well as a close friend. Through her, PM knew that Barbara Barnes no longer had any real work to do, and, having a high opinion of this most excellent of nannies, she recommended her to Charles and Diana.

The public reaction to such an apparently unconventional nanny for the heir in line to the throne was instantaneous. The speculation about how The Prince and Princess of Wales could employ a ground-breaker, who neither wore a uniform nor answered to her surname, revealed to what extent the press were ignorant of the changing values and mores of the aristocracy and the Royal Family. Barbara Barnes was not a precedent, nor was she an anachronism. She was a normal example of a contemporary nanny, for, unbeknown to the press, aristocratic nannies no longer wore uniforms. Nor did they answer to their surnames, and the very prospect of categorizing them as servants was old-fashioned. Indeed, no one, except the ignorant, ever spoke of anyone as servants anymore. Even The Queen referred to hers as "staff." The world had changed. Only the press did not yet know that the changes had actually permeated the upper reaches of society.

The baby's birth heralded a happy time for Charles and Diana and a welcome respite for the nation. As anyone who lost a loved one in the Falklands Campaign knows, 1982 was the year of the war with Argentina. Indeed, Prince Andrew was posted in the South Atlantic at the time, and had to be informed of his nephew's birth and his subsequent reduction in rank while on helicopter duty.

The Prince of Wales marked the momentous occasion by buying Diana a diamond necklace with a heart as a centrepiece. It was not a lavish present, but a touching, romantic gesture. It was also, and this Diana knew, a very unprepossessing piece of jewellery as diamond necklaces go. A man of Charles's worth could have afforded something more important, as the truly expensive, sumptuous items are referred to in the trade. But the parsimonious Prince was not capable of opening his purse widely, even at the moment of his greatest happiness. Diana, who loves jewellery, therefore had to continue relying upon the few decent pieces that her in-laws had given her, such as the copy of Zenaide, Princess Youssoupoff's tiara (a present from The Queen), and the huge sapphire and diamond brooch (a present from Queen Elizabeth The Queen Mother) that she converted into a choker. She also had a stunning suite of diamonds and sapphires from the Crown Prince of Saudi Arabia, and would later receive other important pieces from other Middle Eastern potentates, such as the Sultan of Oman, obviating the need quite so frequently for her to supplement her dearth of jewels with fakes from Butler & Wilson.

Pleased with the thought, if not with the size, of her diamond necklace, Diana threw a party at Kensington Palace to celebrate the baby's birth. It was a scrambled eggs and champagne lunch, attended by Princess Michael of Kent, Lady Sarah Armstrong-Jones, her sisters, and various friends.

But the real celebration was reserved for the christening, which was deliberately held on Queen Elizabeth The Queen Mother's eighty-second birthday. Wednesday 4 August 1982 was a warm, sunny summer's day. The Archbishop of Canterbury, Dr. Robert (now Lord) Runcie, who had married Charles and Diana thirteen short months before, officiated. Present were various members of the Royal Family, George Pinker, the four nurses from the Lindo Wing who had been involved in the delivery, and the godparents.

The baby was christened William Arthur Philip Louis, names chosen according to the royal custom of giving a royal child only names held by previous royals. In a touching tribute to Oliver Everett, to whom the Princess was extremely close despite the difficulties she placed in his path, the baby's first name was that of the Everetts' little boy William. This choice neatly dovetailed the private and public, for four Kings of England had borne that name, including the conquering Norman, the Prince of Orange, and the Hanoverian uncle of Queen Victoria. Arthur was a purely royal name, last held by Prince Arthur of Connaught. Philip was self-evident, and Louis was Prince Charles's accolade to his adored great-uncle, the late Earl Mountbatten of Burma.

The godparents were also chosen by the royal dictum that suitability must reign supreme. There were six in all: the exiled King Constantine (Tino) of the Hellenes, head of the former Prince Philip of Greece's family and a close friend of Prince Charles; Lord Romsey, another friend and cousin, through his grandfather, Lord Mountbatten, to whose title he was heir; Sir Laurens van der Post, the South African philosopher and writer; Princess Alexandra, Charles's cousin "Pud," a great friend, as well as everyone's idea of the perfect princess; Lady Susan Hussey, The Queen's lady-in-waiting, by now a close friend of Diana; and the Duchess of Westminster.

So hidebound with protocol was the Palace that Charles and Diana were both stymied in their original choices for godparents. "The Prince of Wales wanted Armand Hammer," says a member of the Royal Household. "He'd been wonderful to him. He'd given him a great deal of money for United World Colleges, which the Prince took over from Lord Mountbatten and regarded as a sacred trust. He used to lend him his private plane. The Prince cannot use The Queen's Flight except for official business, and by that time he had got rather used to avoiding commercial flights, with all the attendant hassle. So Armand Hammer was a great friend as well as a useful connection. The Prince had the greatest respect for his accomplishments. He was a great philanthropist, had a wonderful art collection, and was one of the most successful entrepreneurs of the twentieth century. He had been a friend of every American President and every Soviet leader since Lenin. But Edward Adeane [the Private Secretary] would not allow it. He said that Armand Hammer was too controversial a figure to have as a godfather for Prince William. Faced with Edward's implacable opposition, The Prince of Wales dropped the idea and chose Sir Laurens van der Post instead. But he was definitely not his first choice. Maybe he did choose Sir Laurens because he's a good story-teller, as he afterwards explained, but the old man was absolutely not his first choice."

Diana also encountered the limits placed upon her freedom of choice. As with the wedding, when she had been thwarted in her desire to have her flatmates as bridesmaids, she was not permitted to choose personal friends whose rank was not sufficiently illustrious. There was no question of the future King of Great Britain having Miss Carolyn Pride as a godmother. Faced with those constraints, Diana hit upon "Tally" Westminster, the wife of Britain's richest man. She possessed an exalted enough rank and a suitable background. Her maternal grandmother, Lady Zia Wernher, had been the daughter of the Grand Duke Michael of Russia and one of The Queen's closest friends. Her father, Harold "Bunnie" Phillips, had also been the lover of Lady Louis Mountbatten for many years, and that, in a curious way, was also a recommendation. The propitious meeting between Tally's father and the highly eligible Gina (Georgina) Wernher had prevented a break-up of the Mountbatten marriage, had kept The Duke of Edinburgh's uncle and aunt free of scandal, and had permitted all the sides of the triangle to pursue uninterrupted good relations in public.

Although Tally Westminster was not one of Diana's closest friends, they were close enough. The former Natalia Phillips was two years older than Diana, they were both Betty Parsons devotees, they both had young children and immensely rich older husbands, and they were both coming to terms with lives whose obligations involved an exacting amount of public service. Moreover, Diana had stood as godmother to the Westminsters' second daughter, Lady Edwina Grosvenor, five months previously.

They also had another thing in common. According to the late James Dorset, a renowned genealogist, Diana and Tally both possessed "coloured blood." Diana's came from Eliza Kewark, the dark-skinned woman whose mother was indubitably Indian. Dating back to the last century there had been the myth that this ancestor of Diana's had an Armenian father, but James Dorset could find no proof that the illegitimate Miss Kewark did actually have a father of those origins. Not even her surname was Armenian, and he therefore dismissed the family's claims to Armenian blood as being an attempt to pass her off as white, or at the very least, of possessing more Caucasian blood than she did; in so doing, the family had completely ignored the racial antecedents of Eliza's mother. This was not simple snobbery. In a day and age when the progeny of interracial unions were considered unfit for marriage with whites, none of Eliza Kewark's descendants would have been deemed "suitable" by any of the many families into which they subsequently married.

The fiction of Miss Kewark being white worked well enough for her descendants Ruth, Frances and Diana to make good marriages, but in the case of Tally Westminster's ancestor, it was not possible to retreat behind such a convenient smokescreen. She was descended from a famous Negro slave, Hannibal, who, upon being freed, rose to become a general in the Russian Army. He was also the grandfather of Alexander Pushkin, the great Russian writer. Despite such illustrious achievements and connections, Hannibal's descendants were, of course, of mixed race. When one of them fell in love with the Tsar's cousin, he forbade the marriage on the grounds that a Negress was not a suitable wife for a member of the Imperial Family. But Grand Duke Michael loved Countess Torby, and rather than abandon her, he abandoned his country. They married morganatically, were exiled from Russia, and, by a curious twist of fate, were spared the consequences of the Revolution because of their love for each other. They came to live in England, where they were received by everyone of any consequence, their secret safe from public knowledge. One daughter, Nadeja (Nada), married The Duke of Edinburgh's uncle, Lord Mountbatten's brother George, second Marquis of Milford Haven. She was a famous lesbian but a warm and affectionate second mother to the young Prince Philip of Greece and to her son David, who became head of the Mountbatten family upon his father's death. The second daughter Zia married the immensely rich baronet, Sir Harold Wernher.

In this day and age, when British society has become so mixed, with a diversity of races and cultures forming a new hegemony, it should be reassuring for the ethnic minorities to know that their blood also flows in the veins of some of the grandest families in the land. The future king is part Indian and his godmother part Negro, as is his and her mutual cousin, the head of the House of Mountbatten.

Charles and Diana, however, were not at all concerned with the exotic ancestry of their own child or anyone else, as they allowed themselves to be swept up in the joy Prince William of Wales brought to their life together. "If it is possible, he was even more besotted with the baby than she was," says a friend of theirs. "He's always loved children. He was marvellous with Dale's and Camilla's, and with Prince Andrew and Prince Edward when they were young. Remember, he even wrote that book, *The Old Man of Lochnagar*, as a result of the stories he made up to keep his younger brothers entertained. Where children are concerned, he's very much a late-twentieth-century man. Thoughtful, sensitive, sympathetic."

Gone were the days of awkwardness, when his staff had to push him to see the wife to whom he had nothing to say. Now they had a constant channel for conversation. Charles and Diana never tired of speaking to the baby, of speaking about him to each other, of speaking about him to anyone who would listen, and of playing with him.

Determined not to miss out on these precious, irreplaceable early days in his son's life, The Prince of Wales cut down on his public engagements. This earned him the heartfelt disapproval of his Private Secretary, who was only too aware of the criticism that would, and did, ensue, especially as Diana was also going to be out of the public eye for several months.

Diana's position was directly affected by her husband's precedent-breaking behaviour. When her turn came to challenge the received wisdom of the Old Guard, as it soon did, she had his conduct to refer to as justification for the freedom she demanded. It is therefore useful, at this juncture, to look at Charles's relationship with his Private Secretary to see how he broke the mould for the functioning of royal Private Secretaries. As neither he nor Diana has ever looked back, since that time, to the stultifying days when Private Secretaries were more like headmasters to errant schoolchildren than a means of implementing their employers' policies, his conduct was momentous, and it precipitated changes that have affected both their lives for the better.

The Hon. Edward Adeane, the Private Secretary, was a creature of the "old school," a barrister by training, an intellectual by inclination; his father, firstly Sir Michael Adeane and latterly Lord Adeane, had been The Queen's Private Secretary until his retirement. His great-grandfather Lord Stamfordham had also been Private Secretary to Queen Victoria and King George V. "Edward was a traditionalist who had been steeped in Palace ways all his life, and he was absolutely wonderful at his job," says a fellow member of the Prince's Staff. "His manner was remote but he had a good sense of humour. He indubitably knew what the job was all about. But he and The Prince of Wales didn't see eye to eye. They had different ideas about what sort of role was fitting for a Prince of Wales.

"The Prince felt entitled to break new ground, to seek out areas that he regarded as being 'relevant,' to lead his personal and professional life with a view to contributing to society as well as to his own satisfaction. His feeling was that he was going to be Prince of Wales for many, many years to come. He regarded his approach as modern, while Edward felt it was inappropriate."

Charles's humanity, however, did not always sit so well with the Buckingham Palace Old Guard. It threatened to embroil him, and through him, the Monarchy, in a welter of controversial and unpredictable scenarios. This was not the *modus vivendi* of traditionalists of any complexion, and most certainly not traditionalist courtiers. They never, but never, advised any action unless they were completely confident of the result. They avoided controversy like the plague. They refused to waste their or their employer's

214

time unless they were assured that the returns of any action were favourable in terms of kudos and public reaction.

Charles, however, had other ideas. He was testing various waters, trying to ascertain where his influence could be best put to good use. It did not please all the members of his staff, on whose shoulders the lion's share of the work devolved. And it did not thrill his conservative Private Secretary. According to a like-minded member of the Royal Household, "He was forever commissioning reports. He'd get an idea about something, put everyone to a great deal of trouble compiling data about it, then he'd give the report—several weeks' or months' work, mind you—no more than a cursory glance. He'd lost interest. He was on to yet another project, inspired by yet another idea. That was frustrating and annoying for all of us, and drove Edward crazy. He felt, if we've gone to all that trouble and it's a good idea, it shouldn't be allowed to die on the vine. It should be implemented, put to good use. And if it wasn't a good idea, it shouldn't have been pursued in the first instance."

That, however, was only the tip of the iceberg. The problem went deeper. The crux of it seemed to turn on the question of whose judgement should dictate Charles's actions. Should he follow his instincts, as is the right of any mature and reasonable human being? Or should he put himself into a position of deference to his Private Secretary? The traditionalist view of the Private Secretary was that his role allowed him to be an arbiter, and that he, rather than the royal he worked for, was better at keeping the Royal Family out of trouble. This was obviously a view held by Edward Adeane. But The Prince of Wales is independently minded, not a typical, run-of-the-mill royal. For all his dyed-in-the-wool traditionalism where his rights as a royal are concerned, he is also a maverick. He is independent and spiritual, an electric combination that is bound to create sparks as he overturns orthodox approaches and forges new ways. In my opinion, what he needed was a Private Secretary who was in tune with his heartfelt beliefs, who also possessed the unusual blend of traditionalism and heterodoxy, who wanted to preserve, conserve and change.

Instead, he had someone who understood only "preserve and conserve," who was uncomfortable with change, and did all in his power to discourage his "charge" whenever Charles had one of those brainstorms that seem like inspiration to the mass of the British populace and have done so much to make the less privileged and the disadvantaged feel that their future King is in sympathy with them.

"The trouble with The Prince of Wales," according to the same courtier, "is that he's basically a thinker. He's not a doer. He gets an idea, goes with it to the point of implementation, then loses interest. In other words, he goes with it only as long as it remains an idea.

"Edward felt very strongly that that was a waste of our time and effort. An example of what I mean is the reports that were done on Kennington, which is a part of the Duchy of Cornwall south of the river. It's very run-down. Well, The Prince of Wales commissioned the usual reports, then once he had them, did absolutely nothing about them. Although Kennington could be a very nice area with a bit of initiative, it's still run-down. I used to tease him about it and tell him he's a slum landlord. I believe they've now taken the decision to divest themselves of the property rather than improve it.

"It's that sort of inaction, the dichotomy between Charles saying one thing and doing another, that drove Edward wild. He didn't approve of the Prince's sudden enthusiasms followed by his equally sudden indifference, nor did he approve of him breaking new ground and entering controversial areas."

Time, however, has shown that The Prince of Wales has carried through many of his ideas. He has nursed such projects as Business in the Community, the Youth Enterprise Scheme, the Prince's Youth Business Trust, The Prince of Wales Community Venture, The Prince of Wales's Advisory Group on Disability, and The Prince's Trust from germ to fruition. In the process, he has gained the respect of the many people he benefits as well as the nation in general. He has forged a new, more relevant role for the Heir to the Throne than opening factories and shaking the hands of this Lord Mayor or that industrialist.

He has, indeed, become enmeshed in controversy. His views on alternative medicine, on plant life, and on architecture have excited ribald commentary in the press. Time, moreover, appears to be on his side. Scientists are already proving the wisdom of his views on biology and medicine. And the populace likes his concept of what constitutes a desirable house for its members to live in, even if his taste is curiously akin to Hitler and Stalin's, and at serious odds with Lord Palumbo and modernist elitists.

For Charles, staying home with Diana and taking care of William was a welcome respite from the problems he was having with Edward Adeane. "It was a genuinely happy time for him," says a cousin. "He read up all the baby books he could get hold of, and became quite the expert." Diana herself described him as "a doting Daddy," and together they were so preoccupied with the baby that Barbara Barnes often had nothing to do.

There was an additional reason why Charles retreated from public view. Diana suffered badly from post-natal depression. This was partly hormonal and partly due to her resuming her dubious dietary methods. As the bulimia once more took hold, and her eating pattern went from merely having a large appetite to starvation followed by gargantuan binges leading to vomiting, she exacerbated her condition by taking laxatives. "That way I can eat more and still lose weight," she commented to a member of the Household. Like an alcoholic on a prolonged bender, she could not be induced to give up habits that were seriously undermining her health and her marriage. "As far as she was concerned, she had no problem. If something was wrong, it was wrong with those around her." "Often, she was in quite a state for no reason at all," says a courtier. "One second she'd be perfectly normal, and the next she'd be upset. It was quite disconcerting." Seriously concerned by his wife's physical and emotional condition, The Prince of Wales consulted several different medical experts. Diana, however, still stubbornly refused to acknowledge that she had a problem or that she needed help. So he settled upon the alternative course of action they suggested as a palliative, and gave her the patient understanding and loving care which he hoped would bring her to her senses.

It was not until 1988, when her former flatmate Carolyn Pride, now Bartholomew, threatened to go public with her problem that Diana actually sought help. Typically for someone who must always hold the reins in her own hands, Diana did not consult the Royal Family or their doctors. Instead, she turned to her family's general practitioner, who referred her to Dr. Maurice Lipsedge. He is well known within fashionable circles, where eating and other emotional disorders are so prevalent, as something of an expert in dealing with even the most recalcitrant patients. "He has a great bedside manner. He never lets you feel there's anything wrong with you. Your illness is always a manifestation of something healthy within you that's gone wrong. That's his secret," says David Hornsby, a descendant of the famous Marquis of Reading who was Viceroy of India.

Ministered to by such a wise and sympathetic doctor, Diana gradually began to relinquish a pattern of behaviour that had destroyed her marriage and made serious inroads into her health. She is still not cured, and is subject to bouts whenever she is under stress or has to do anything she does not wish to, but at all other times, she now has sufficient control of her diet and appetite to eat normally.

CHAPTER FIFTEEN

Polishing the Image

*T*he halcyon days in the Wales marriage continued as the infant William grew into a toddler.

Despite her shaky health, Diana was happier than she had been since the first fortnight of her honeymoon. She saw more of her husband. They finally had something to talk about. And it looked as if Charles had willingly settled down to her version of a happy marriage. Both mother and father remained besotted with their little bundle of joy, although even here they were laying down foundations for future conflict.

One bone of contention was the difference between Charles's and Diana's attitude to the Crown. "Diana refused to be awed," says the noblewoman whose brother-in-law is a top-ranking courtier. "Those of us who are familiar with the royal scene know only too well that everyone connected to the Monarchy treats it with awe. Even The Queen herself, who really does believe that she reigns by Divine Right. And definitely The Prince of Wales. In my opinion, it's quite ludicrous the respect they endow the whole business with. All that reverence, as if it's something sacred. As if, if you even look at it too long, you might break the spell or blind yourself or God knows what else—make the magic disappear, I suppose. The whole Royal Family and all the courtiers I've ever come across treat 'The Monarchy' almost like a religion of which they're devoted followers. But Diana wasn't having any of that. It's not that she didn't respect the institution. She did. She simply refused to be awed by it. I believe that was a healthy response."

Diana's sense of proportion coloured her behaviour in many ways, not all of which were conducive to peace. Unlike Queen Mary, whose reverence for the institution of monarchy had been so absolute that George V and her children were first actual and potential kings, and only afterwards her husband and children, Diana viewed William as first and foremost her son. Somewhere down the line in her list of priorities he was the Heir in Line to the Throne, and while this approach would later cause problems with discipline, it allowed the young Prince to breathe the fresh air of naturalness and to expand in the spontaneity of unsuppressed emotion.

One of the sacrosanct items on the royal agenda is the Royal British Legion's Annual Festival of Remembrance at the Royal Albert Hall. Charles and Diana were both expected to attend in November 1982, and, as a list of royal engagements is always published beforehand, it would not have been possible for Diana to wriggle out of it without an excellent reason. She, however, decided that she did not feel up to it. She wanted to stay home and play with William instead. As only death or its near neighbour would have been acknowledged as a valid enough excuse for being absent, The Prince of Wales put his foot down and insisted that Diana honour her commitment. This she refused to do point-blank, causing a huge row and forcing him, in the end, to depart without her.

Despite her stubbornness, though, Diana is not stupid, nor is she a revolutionary. She has a reflective turn of mind where her conduct is concerned, and, after thinking about it, decided that she might have behaved rather self-indulgently and irresponsibly. So she quickly hauled on some clothes and turned up at the Albert Hall, fifteen minutes late, after The Queen had arrived. This was a solecism of the highest order, for no one is meant to arrive at an engagement after or depart before the Monarch, whatever the reason. This Diana knew full well. Someone who was born at Sandringham, raised in royal circles, and married to a Prince, could not have failed to appreciate the disrespect she had shown. But The Queen, I am told, ignored the slight. She thought it was wiser to do so than acknowledge it and give it a weight it would not otherwise possess.

With good cause, The Queen was still nervous of Diana's emotionalism, still intent on placating her wherever possible. By this time, Diana had ceased limiting her differences of opinion with The Prince of Wales to the privacy of whichever palace they happened to find themselves in. This new mode of behaviour was causing grave disquiet, for the Palace was worried about the effect it would have upon the public if news got out. Diana, however, did not seem to care, and in one famous incident managed to provide the press with a glimpse of how wilful and unco-operative she could be when she set her mind to it. This was when she and Charles joined Prince Franz Joseph and Princess Gina of Liechtenstein for a skiing holiday in January 1983. Pointedly sulking, she refused to pose for the photographers when they tried to snap her on the slopes. Not even Prince Charles's entreaties could induce her to budge, and the result was a flurry of newspaper commentary and needless conjecture, all of which could have been avoided with five minutes' co-operation.

Diana, of course, should have remembered that elusiveness incites the eluded, whether Prince or press, to chase the quarry that is in danger of slipping away. By acting up as she did, she induced the photographers to turn what should have been a relaxing holiday into a press rout. It was therefore with relief that she and Charles returned home to prepare for their six-week tour of Australia and New Zealand in March–April 1983.

This also precipitated behind-the-scenes scenes. In defiance of the custom of royal parents never taking their children on official tours, Diana wanted William to go too. "She would not listen to how impractical it was," says a royal cousin. "She didn't care that her programme was so full she'd be lucky to see him for ten minutes every third day—and that's no exaggeration. She wanted her baby with her, and come hell or high water, that was what she was going to get. Our Diana can be very dogged when she sets her mind to it." Yet again, The Queen was confronted with the choice of failing to oblige her determined daughter-in-law or giving her her way, and in so doing break with previous custom. "The Queen is a very flexible mother and mother-in-law. If she has a fault," says the royal cousin, "it is that she does not put her foot down enough. Yes, she does have a reputation for being stern, but that could not be further from the truth." So Her Majesty consented to William being taken. In accordance with the way official invitations are issued, the Palace then advised the office of the Australian Prime Minister that an invitation including the baby Prince would be appreciated. Malcolm Fraser himself duly wrote a charming letter to the Waleses saying how cognisant he was of the needs of a new family, and Prince William officially became a part of the tour.

That, however, was not the end of the matter. Diana also wanted William to fly out on the same aeroplane with them. This was yet again in direct opposition to the royal custom of an heir and his heir never travelling together, lest there should be an accident and they both die. But, to everyone's surprise, The Queen waived the rule, showing just how accommodating a mother-in-law she could be. "Since she's so keen to take him, let her," she said. "After this trip, she won't want to make that mistake again."

Experience had taught The Queen wisdom, and soon it was Diana's turn to drink from that chalice as she, William and Charles headed down under for her first foreign tour. Royal trips are a gruelling round of public appearances. You have to get up early in the morning, down a quick breakfast and get dressed in full royal togs. There can be no skipping the expected hat and gloves, which see you through a tight schedule that lasts from mid-morning until late afternoon. Lunch is invariably a working meal, as is dinner, though you do have the opportunity to bathe and change into your evening dress and possibly tiara before heading off into the night. The day that starts at 6:30 or 7:00 am ends at midnight, and no matter how tired or ill you feel, the following morning you have to be up at the same time, ready to shine and make everyone you meet feel as if you have been waiting your whole life for this one, brief encounter.

The tour of Australia and New Zealand was a success. Even the increasingly republican Antipodeans were enchanted with the royal couple and baby, and, while Diana quickly learnt why babies never travel with their parents—there were times when she did not see him for days on end—bringing William along was a public-relations coup.

Although Diana was delighted with the reception she was accorded, she did not enjoy the exhausting round of duties. She was still worn down by the stress of marriage, the changes in her identity, motherhood, and post-natal depression. She was also caught up in the cauldron of physical and emotional turbulence caused by the return of her bulimia. Moreover, "in the early days she hated making public appearances," says a former member of the Royal Household. "We all had to coax and cajole her from the moment she left her bedroom until the second she stepped out of the car. It was always the same. 'I hate this,' she'd complain. 'Why do I have to do this? My God, it's so boring I could die. I can't stand it. I hate it. *Hate it.*' Then the car would grind to a halt. Diana would hop out. She'd be all smiles, saying how marvellous it was to be there, how wonderful everyone was. Everyone who had been with her in the car would be just stunned by the total about-face."

Royal public appearances, of course, are performances of a sort, as Diana has said on many occasions. Like the actress who vomits before going on stage to give a bravura performance, she was working off her negative feelings, then stepping out and giving the public the full benefit of her positive sentiments. And the public were clearly loving it. Far from interest in Diana waning after her marriage, as everyone, herself included, had expected, it continued to increase. The public seemed incapable of getting enough of her. Wherever she went, she was greeted with the enthusiasm reserved for the reigning rock star of the moment. And not a day passed without each of the popular papers devoting several column inches to her activities, her clothes, and her photograph.

* * *

Like most people who are new to celebrity, Diana was preoccupied with her public image. "Each and every day she would get cuttings of everything all the papers had said about her," says a connection of the Royal Family. "She'd pore over every word, pausing to savour the praise and getting really upset about any criticism. Let me tell you, she read each and every word and inspected each and every photograph as if she'd never seen a picture of herself before. She became obsessed with how she looked. Dresses and hats had to be photogenic. They had to make her look pretty and above all *slim*. She practised smiling and getting in and out of cars, so that the photographers wouldn't get bad photos of her. She was just like a model. Absolutely professional about the visual."

Gliding gracefully in and out of cars with a smile on her face, however, was not enough, not if Diana wished to look her best at all times. To do this she had to maximize her every asset. "She started looking at herself the way a director looks at a movie actress," says a Spencer cousin. With consummate professionalism, the perfectionist Princess approached the public image of herself as an object to be burnished to the maximum brightness. Her hair was treated to the best care money could buy, and combed out every morning by her hairdresser, who came to the Palace to tend to her, or travelled with her if she went abroad. Her face, which never saw the light of day without being fully and expertly made up by Diana herself (she was taught by the make-up artist Barbara Daly), now began sporting heavier and heavier cosmetics, to such an extent that she later had to modify her techniques. But it was in the area of clothes that she excelled.

"She has an undoubted flair for clothes," opines Elke Hundertmark, the eminent fashion journalist and PR/marketing consultant, whose expertise has been in part responsible for the considerable success of the Mary Quant empire. "What she has is a gift. It's natural. It's innate. It's instinctive. You can't teach what she has. Anna Harvey and the *Vogue* crew polished up her act. They made her more sophisticated. But they didn't give her the eye she's always had. Just think of her pre-wedding photographs. Remember that Inca jumper with the one black sheep that she wore, that was then knocked off worldwide. That was pure Diana: stylish, unusual, flattering. Or her combinations: ruffles beneath jumpers, jodhpurs when no one else was wearing them, strong, unexpected colours. Anna Harvey only gave Diana the benefit of her knowledge and gave her access to designers. Diana did all the rest herself. From the very beginning, she chose clothes that were different, that were interesting and eye-catching and exciting. Sure, she made mistakes. We all make mistakes. But, when you stop to think that all hers were made in the public eye, and that she was very young, she made relatively few."

Elke Hundertmark believes that Diana's talent for picking the most flattering and eye-catching clothes enhanced her natural physical attributes and thus her reputation as a great beauty. But there was an unexpected and major side-effect. "Diana gave the fashion industry the benefit of the flair she was born with. She has been grossly underestimated over the years. She has been consistently trivialized. Yet her accomplishments in fashion terms have been considerable. Her impact on the British fashion industry is hard to exaggerate. Thanks to her, British designers throughout the Eighties had an international platform. She also singlehandedly changed the way royal women dress. Until she came along, they all dressed in a regimented way. Even the more glamorous ones, like the Duchess of Kent or Princess Michael, dressed in subdued colours, with hats that were off the face, and the inevitable white gloves. It was boring, boring, boring. Now they all wear stylish hats and exciting and dynamic colour combinations. They've even discarded the hackneyed white gloves. Even The Queen wears black gloves or red gloves or whatever colour is appropriate to the outfit she's got on. It's been a fashion revolution, and it's all due to Diana."

At the start of her revolt, however, before she had properly manned the barricades, she had to rely upon the men and women who created the clothes. Choosing which designers would dress her was a happenstance affair. Whenever she ran across someone whose creations she liked, she had Anna Harvey get in touch with them. This, for instance, is what happened with Britain's answer to Balenciaga, the immensely stylish Murray Arbeid, who is also one of the designers I use. He says, "The Princess of Wales attended a gala evening at Goldsmiths' Hall. My clothes were shown there. It was shortly after Prince William was born. She liked what she saw. Anna Harvey rang me up and asked me if I could take around some selections Her Royal Highness had made, to the Palace. This I did.

"The Princess proved to be a real pleasure to work for. She's a dream of a client. She's beautiful to look at, beautiful to know. She has a perfect figure, knows what she wants, and wears clothes fabulously. What more can a designer ask for?"

Murray Arbeid also clears up a popular misconception about Diana's behaviour towards her designers. The press and previous authors have often maintained that she invariably addressed them as Mr. or Mrs. Whoever, and that they always had to enter the hallowed confines of Kensington Palace through a side door. "No, no, no, that is absolutely not so," Murray Arbeid says. "I never used anything but the front door. She always received me in her sitting room. At first, she called me Mr. Arbeid, but when we got to know each other better, she called me Murray. I, of course, always called her Your Royal Highness followed by Ma'am, as one normally does with royalty."

The form of address Diana employed, and which door the designers used, is significant because it reveals whether Diana was pompous and disrespectful or down to earth and respectful. Had she given her staff instructions that these men and women, who are celebrities in their own right, should enter through a side door, or had she called them by anything but their Christian names once she got to know them, she would have been reducing them to the status of tradesmen. This would have stripped them of their dignity, and would have been a sorry reflection upon her. It would not have been, as some writers seem to have thought, showing respect; quite the opposite. But the nuances of royal and aristocratic behaviour are often lost upon the scribes who write about a world they do not inhabit.

Diana, indeed, gets along well with all her designers, as Bruce Oldfield and David Shilling also confirmed to me. Like everything else in her life, she knew what she wanted, and set out to get it. She was diligent, thorough and painstaking. Her approach was professional, the effect dynamic, and within a year she was the world's most famous cover girl.

By 1983, Diana's appearance had also altered radically. Gone was any residue of teenage or pregnancy chubbiness. Gone too was the unpolished presentation of Lady Diana Spencer. The Princess of Wales now had the patina of a professional beauty. Nothing was allowed to interfere with the highly finished look. She took every contingency into account. As with most famous beauties, her make-up, hairstyle, clothes, shoes, bags, and jewellery were all carefully thought out. Nothing was ever left to chance. The wind, the rain, the sleet, the snow, the cold, the heat, the press, the public, standing up, sitting down, bending over, leaning forwards, getting in and out of cars, even walking were all factors which were weighed before she chose her look of the day.

There were only two provisos laid down by the powers that be at the Palace limiting what Diana and the designers could do. At all times she had to look dignified, which meant no miniskirts or plunging necklines. And in public she had to wear British. What she did in the privacy of her own home, or when she was out of the range of public scrutiny, was her own business. Naturally, no wealthy woman who loves fashion can limit herself to the English side of the Channel, and in her private life Diana often wears clothes by St. Laurent, Valentino, Armani and the other Continental designers.

Diana's interest in fashion, as Elke Hundertmark rightly points out, soon had a profound impact upon both the British fashion industry and her own image. Due to the tremendous amount of publicity she generated, Diana's reputation as a stylish beauty grew apace with the fame of her designers.

There was a very good reason for this phenomenon, of course. All but the most exceptional magazines and newspapers have an insatiable appetite for celebrated women who are good-looking. If you then consider that certain publications are directed particularly at women or the fashion industry, you begin to appreciate why the media needs its stars. Without women who will sell magazine after magazine, newspaper after newspaper, who are of unending interest to a vast readership, these publications would soon go out of business. The stars need the publications as much as the publications need the stars, and in this most symbiotic of relationships, each flourishes only if the other does well.

On the other hand, publicity is a double-edged sword. Once a star is established in the firmament, the negative effects of stardom can quickly make themselves felt. In this obtuse game called life, few things are more perverse than the rules governing fame. The biggest attractions are invariably those who initially use publicity to further their own purposes, but become reluctant to play once they realize that the fame game has its downside. This, as we have seen, had already started to happen with Diana, with the standard effect: the tantalizing of both the press and the public, who refused to be shut out.

But Diana's attitude towards the press wavered, and during this period, according to a friend, "she started enjoying her celebrity again. She was chuffed by her newfound status as a great beauty." Diana herself was open about how she felt. "It's fun to see yourself in the papers and to know that everyone thinks you're great-looking," she told one friend, while she said to another, "I just love it when I arrive somewhere and everyone is waiting with their tongues hanging out." She also told a relation how much she loved "seeing everyone drool," and agreed that "it's fantastic when everyone thinks you're hot stuff."

The inevitable backlash did not come until after Prince Harry was born. When it did, the press chose the most convenient chink in Diana's armour with which to berate her. They criticized her for extravagance. They also began accusing her of vanity. "She got very upset about the bad press," a friend says. "She couldn't see why she shouldn't be allowed to buy new clothes and look her best, like any other normal woman with a well-off husband. She began resenting the press once more. She felt they were trivializing her, using her clothes to get at her unfairly."

Hating the adverse publicity, Diana attempted to change it by wearing certain dresses again and again. This, however, only inspired yet more criticism, and Diana was driven to complain, "I just can't win. They either accuse me of spending too much on clothes or of wearing the same outfit all the time. I wish everyone would stop talking about my clothes."

The wheel had gone full circle. But this time the consequences of press intrusion, which is how she saw the criticism, were more than merely being inconvenienced on a ski slope. The media had sullied her public image, turning the uncritical praise to which she was used, into accusations of wastefulness and vanity.

Diana, of course, was only experiencing what every famous person learns sooner or later. Fame has teeth, and the British press especially enjoy biting until it hurts. Thereafter, her press would be as patchy as her feelings about it, until Sarah Ferguson made a welcome entrance on to the stage. At that point, Diana was relieved from the harsh and heated glare of the spotlight, as the media enthusiastically picked up Fergie, raised her to great heights of public approbation, then just as suddenly sent her crashing down.

During her banishment, though, Diana learnt a valuable lesson. "She discovered she couldn't do without the attention. She'd become a fame junkie. She hated it when Sarah became the centre of attention. She was jealous," says a cousin of the royals.

Competitive and jealous though she is, Diana is also canny, with a worldly wisdom beyond her years. As she edged back into the centre of the spotlight, she resolved to minimize the heat and the glare of fame. The aim was to take the sting out of the criticism without detracting from her glamour or professionalism as a beauty.

The main criticism had been about the amount of money Diana's vast wardrobe was costing. "Her advisers helped her. They always help all the royals with their public image," a courtier says. "The strategy devised to combat the criticism was a simple one. She therefore resumed wearing dresses the public were familiar with on official duties, while cutting down on the number of designers she patronized for new clothes. This was a shrewd move, for, by limiting herself to Catherine Walker and Victor Edelstein, Diana prevented the fashion writers from designer-spotting. A daily diet of old dresses interspersed with the odd new one by Catherine Walker was hardly newsworthy, especially when she consciously strove to present a sensible and businesslike image. She was still permitted the odd moment of sartorial glory when, in her words, she could 'sock it to them.' But these moments were chosen carefully, such as when she was at the end of a foreign trip, so that she would have the opportunity to reaffirm her glamorous image while gaining kudos for promoting the British fashion industry, without attracting criticism for extravagance."

The expertise with which Diana and her advisers took the focus off her appearance is commendable. She has successfully lived down the image of being a mindless clotheshorse and has shifted public attention to her work. As her Press Secretary, Dickie Arbiter, said, "She's aiming to be known as a workhorse, not a clothes-horse." What he did not say, but what the observant notice is that, now the glare of criticism no longer singes her, she has reverted to her old ways. She is again being seen out and about in new clothes. She has even adopted new designers, like Tomasz Starzewski. But she has so grown in stature in the last five years that the press no longer comment on such superficialities.

♔   ♔   ♔

CHAPTER SIXTEEN

Hirer and Firer

After the birth of Prince William, both Diana and Charles were anxious to provide him with a sibling at the earliest moment. They did not want him to be an only child, not just because he would grow up isolated, but because he would also become spoilt.

Getting pregnant the second time around, however, was not as easy as the first. Fame, marriage, motherhood, her royal status and constant weight-watching had all conspired to make the previously fecund Diana unimpregnable. When attempt after normal attempt resulted in repeated monthly disappointments, she and Charles resorted to reading a thermometer before making yet another try at conception. "It's just as well the Windsor men are always ready for action," says a former fancy of Charles, explaining why The Prince of Wales had no trouble performing upon demand, before going on to explain why Diana would also have welcomed his attentions. "All that German blood has come out where it counts. He is, shall we say, a richly blessed man who uses his considerable hidden wealth with great sensitivity. I should think Diana had an awful lot of fun getting pregnant." History does not record her verdict on these forays, only that she was delighted when she was finally able to announce that she was pregnant once more.

Diana's second pregnancy was a rerun of her first, except that she made sure she did not gain any more weight than was absolutely necessary. Being an acknowledged beauty was still new to her, and she did not intend to jeopardize her reputation by swelling up the way she had with Prince William.

"I haven't felt well since day one," Diana said shortly after the announcement of her pregnancy was made on Valentine's Day. "I don't think I'm made for the production line." Nevertheless, she continued fulfilling a light but visible array of public engagements, ending, appropriately enough, with the opening of the Birthright Centre at King's College Hospital in London.

At 4:20 on the afternoon of Saturday 15 September 1984, Diana gave birth to her second son. Once more, her husband was with her, and once more the birth took place at the Lindo Wing of St. Mary's, Paddington.

But this time around there was an important difference. Charles and Diana were not alone. There were William's feelings to consider, and Diana handled his introduction to his little brother with laudable finesse. When he arrived with Charles and Barbara Barnes on Sunday morning, she scooped him up into her arms in the corridor, and took him into the room to look at Prince Henry Charles Albert David, as the baby was already called. Barbara Barnes stayed outside, to give Diana a chance to handle this delicate moment without distraction. The fact that William thereafter was invariably solicitous and playful with his little brother is a testament to the success of the incorporation.

This time Diana was even more anxious to return home than the last. She did not stay in the hospital for the full day, but left at 2:30 on the Sunday afternoon. Charles drove his elegantly attired and carefully made-up wife and his infant son to Kensington Palace, before heading off to the Guards' Polo Club, Smith's Lawn, Windsor, where he played in a match specially arranged to celebrate his second son's arrival. He even toasted the birth in champagne: an unusual activity for someone who loathes the stuff. Diana, meanwhile, was at home resting, the baby in good hands. Sister Anne Wallace, who had also nursed William for the first weeks of his life, was taking care of Harry, though Diana would yet again prove to be very much a hands-on mother once she got over the physical exhaustion of giving birth. She breastfed Harry, changed his nappies, bathed him, played with him, attending to all his personal needs as they arose. This time, though, Barbara Barnes felt less redundant than she had the first time around. She had William to occupy her, and William was already proving to be a handful.

Once more, Prince Charles was an active and devoted father. He cut down on engagements the way he had with William, involving himself in every area of the baby's development. This did not please his father, especially when the press began commenting on the dearth of public duties Charles was fulfilling. "You'd think The Prince of Wales could find more gainful ways of employing himself than bathing his son, when the boy already has a nanny to do such monumental tasks for him," The Duke of Edinburgh cuttingly observed to a relation.

Nor was Prince Philip the only member of the family to be disenchanted with Charles's post-feminist fatherliness. Diana also was not thrilled by her husband's constant presence. "From shortly after William's birth, she felt that The Prince of Wales was trespassing on her territory. Motherhood was her role, and he was usurping it," says a friend of hers. "William preferred his father and Baba (Barbara Barnes), which was a constant source of distress to her. Given the choice, William always ran to his father or nanny. If they were out, he wanted to be in their arms, not his mother's. Diana blamed Charles for this more than Barbara Barnes. She felt that he had used his influence with his staff to clear his diary and make himself available to be with William, but did nothing to stop them forcing her to go on official engagements. Diana has a very jealous and possessive nature, and it just drove her crazy that her son should not love her more than anyone else. She bitterly resented The Prince of Wales for allowing this to happen, and felt fully justified in doing so. She also resented Barbara Barnes. While she recognized that her feelings in this direction were not entirely reasonable, she couldn't help herself. I think it pained her to not be able to be more kind towards Baba. She likes being a warm and considerate em-

233

ployer. But in this instance it was beyond her. She was too eaten up with jealousy."

Without a good reason for getting rid of the nanny who was "stealing" her son's love, Diana was stuck with Barbara Barnes, at least for the time being. She was saddled with something else she hoped would be equally transient: her husband's presence. So fed up did she become with what she saw as his encroachment that she went public with her complaints. "My husband knows so much about rearing children that I've suggested he has the next one and I'll sit back and give advice," she commented acerbically, giving honest vent to her feelings. However, people only hear what they expect to, so the significance of what she was saying was lost on her audience.

The children, who should have been a unifying factor, were now a bone of contention in the Wales marriage. Their parents even had different attitudes towards discipline. "He was inclined to think she allowed William to run wilder than was good for him," says a relation of the Prince's. "He was an extraordinarily energetic and boisterous little boy. He had lungs Pavarotti would envy. The Prince thought it would be better if he were taught moderation—and modulation—from an early age. As much as he loved his son, he did not think it was appropriate for William to have a free run of the place. He was forever butting in on the adults, making noise at all hours of the day and night, and generally being a little tearaway. But his mother took an opposing point of view. She thought it was perfectly normal, and refused to allow anyone to 'suppress' him."

It was almost inevitable that Charles and Diana would think differently about discipline. All his life the Prince had been treated with firmness tempered with consideration. There had never been any question of his avoiding a duty because he was not in the mood, or of indulging a desire if it was inappropriate. Brought up by a series of adults who were not his parents, with The Queen and Prince Philip perpetually absent on official business whether at home or abroad, Charles's only childhood indulgences had come from Queen Elizabeth The Queen

Mother and Princess Margaret. Kindly though they were, neither was a slouch where the future King's conduct was concerned, and by the time he was a toddler discipline and restraint were already an integral part of his make-up.

Diana, on the other hand, had been raised in a relatively relaxed environment. Even while her parents were together, she was not subjected to the restraints which Charles always took for granted. The Althorp children were an integral part of the household. There was none of the old "children are seen and not heard" way of doing things. And once their parents split up, and they became the battleground on which Johnnie and Frances waged war, the boundaries of discipline were shifted even further in the direction of indulgence. No one, after all, could call a household disciplined when a father and grandmother stood by impotently, as did Johnnie Althorp/Spencer and Ruth, Lady Fermoy, while one daughter, Diana, threw her nanny's clothes away, and another, Sarah, neatly updated the eccentric Emperor Caligula's ennoblement of his horse, and brought hers into the drawing room for tea.

To Diana, there was no more important role in life than motherhood. Whatever the differences between her husband and herself, she approached motherhood with conscientiousness and indeed with passion. Once Harry was old enough for her to resume her round of official duties, she tried to arrange her schedule so that she was with the children for the more important parts of their routine. Breakfast, lunch, bathtime and bedtime were especially important, but there were times when she departed so early and returned so late that she did not see the children at all. This was a source of great annoyance and disturbance to her, but it was the unavoidable price she had to pay for being royal, and dislike it though she did, she was not keen to swop the status or its rewards.

One compensation, however, was that Harry was closer to Diana than William had been. "He is gentle and introverted, like The Queen and his father, but without Prince Charles's irritability or stubbornness," says a courtier. "William is a bit of a bruiser, like Prince Philip. He also has a lot of his other grandfather in him. But not Harry. He's a real sweetie-pie, good-natured almost to a fault."

From the moment Diana returned to KP with Harry, he adored his mother. "They have compatible personalities," a cousin says. "It's a yin and yang thing. That's also why William was so drawn to his father but not his mother." Diana, however, did not care about the reason. The fact was all that concerned her. "Harry has been a source of constant and never-ending delight to his mother. I can't ever see anything coming between them. They are just so good together."

Fearful that Charles and Barbara Barnes would snatch Harry's love away from her, Diana did everything she could to marginalize their influence. But, Barbara Barnes was not used to being sidelined. Throughout her fifteen years with the Tennants, with whom she was and still is friendly, she was at the centre of a happy, vibrant, somewhat bohemian family. The thrill of being nanny to the premier family in the land had long worn off with the onset of a chilled atmosphere. Nevertheless, Barbara Barnes was not precipitate. She gave the situation a chance to improve. Since it had not by the time Harry was eighteen months old, she took the decision to depart at an opportune moment. She would not leave Charles and Diana and the children in the lurch, but when something else came up, she would go her own way.

Diana, however, beat Nanny Barnes to the punch. The cause of the trouble was a birthday party given by Colin Tennant, now Lord Glenconner. In December 1986, Colin hosted a huge costume party on his island, Mustique. All his close friends were there, including Princess Margaret, Mick Jagger, Jerry Hall, Raquel Welch—and Barbara Barnes. The party received widespread publicity. Photographs of Colin dressed as an Indian prince, of Princess Margaret in costume, and of the many celebrity guests, including Barbara Barnes, appeared in publications throughout the world. "The Princess hit the roof when she picked up the papers and saw her nanny portrayed as a celebrity," says a connection of the Royal Family who is friendly with the Glenconners. "She was furious. She thought it utterly inappropriate for a servant to be mixing with her, Diana's, social equals, as if she too were a social equal. If you carried it to its logical conclusion, that made Barbara Barnes *her* social equal."

Diana was not having any of it. She was not from a long line of aristocrats for nothing. She might be nice and kind and approachable. She might speak to little old ladies as if they were her equals. But she was not going to step over that invisible dividing line with her own nanny. There was a difference between good manners, politely assuming equality, and going that step further and turning it into reality. Barbara Barnes was getting above herself. It was time for her to go.

Diana had found the reason to rid herself of the nanny who had stimulated so much jealousy within her. No sooner did the tanned Baba return to Kensington Palace in January 1987 than Diana called for her. She made it plain that the time had come for Baba to depart. She astutely suggested that the announcement be made on William's first day of school. The press, she reasoned, would not notice Barbara Barnes's departure. But Diana was wrong. The following day, all the newspapers were full of both William's first day at Wetherby and of Nanny Barnes's sacking.

Although not all the reasons for Barbara Barnes's departure were known, there were enough rumours flying around for Diana's reputation to take something of a knocking. Up to that point, the public had been led to believe that The Princess of Wales was a sweet, rather shy little flower who could not say boo to a goose. The facts that she was tough and determined, that she was absolutely adamant in achieving a goal once she had it in her sights, were not yet known outside the royal circle.

There were, of course, clues. One was the way Diana dealt with filling Barbara Barnes's void. Having divested herself of the nanny, the Princess now needed a replacement. She got the word put out to the more pukka agencies and on the nanny grapevine, then sat back to await developments. These were not long in coming. She turned down various applicants, including an otherwise suitable

237

girl on instructions from the Palace when it emerged that her religion was Roman Catholic. No such problems presented themselves with the nanny next door, however. Forty-year-old Ruth Wallace had an impeccable provenance. A State Registered Nurse from the prestigious St. Bartholomew's Hospital, London, she was nanny to Lord Frederick and Lady Gabriella Windsor, the children of Prince and Princess Michael of Kent, and had previously worked for King Constantine and Queen Anne-Marie of the Hellenes. All her charges were well-behaved, with excellent manners and good attitudes. Moreover, she knew William and Harry. The Wales and Kent children and their nannies were forever running into each other in the courtyard shared by their parents' respective apartments at Kensington Palace. William and Harry liked Ruth Wallace, and, after some delicate negotiations, Diana offered Ruth the job.

Poaching servants is one of the greatest solecisms a well-bred person can commit. I know of several people who have stopped speaking to cousins, friends, even siblings, because they enticed their staff away. It is almost better to sleep with your best friend's spouse. "Princess Michael was not particularly pleased," says a friend of hers. "But she put a good face on it and reacted generously. She could have created a big fuss. It's to her credit she didn't. She let Ruth go and wished her well."

William and Harry now had a nanny their mother could live with. She knew her place, did not try to move away from the sidelines into the centre of the show, and had never pre-empted Diana the way Baba did with William. Charles, for his part, also approved of Ruth Wallace. She was more of a disciplinarian, and that, from his point of view, could only be to the good.

With or without William and Harry, with or without nannies, there were still problems within the Wales marriage. These went deep, right to the core of both Charles's and Diana's personalities, and it is my considered opinion, after speaking to several people who know them well, that they are simply incompatible.

One of their problems is communication. Verbal skills are not Diana's strongest point. She has never been particularly articulate, not in public, not in private, not at parties, nor in tête-à-tête. When she is upset, she does verbalize, but it is her distress that she communicates, not the underlying causes for it, so, instead of winning sympathy, she antagonizes. Charles, on the other hand, is articulate. But his verbal skills wither on the vine at the first sign of personal conflict. Rather than put into words what is troubling him, or arguing through a problem, he retreats into himself, voicing neither his distress nor the underlying causes.

Had communication difficulties been the only problem keeping The Prince and Princess of Wales from enjoying the support and companionship they both insist they yearn for, their marriage might have maintained the intimacy and affection it had at its outset. Yet, even putting aside the difficulties which her bulimia caused, it is doubtful whether their marriage would ever have flourished. However, both are stubborn. They like their own way, and resent it when they do not get it. She, moreover, is a dominant personality, and while he is not exactly dominant—he is selfish but happy to give others their own way as long as they allow him his—he passionately loathes being dominated. This combination was hardly conducive to an equitable and fulfilling union, even if there were excellent communication between them. Their personalities are too similar where they should be different, and too different where they should be similar.

Between 1983 and 1986 the marriage eroded in gradual but perceptible stages. Who held sway with the children was only one of the problems within the marriage. The old issue of intellectual compatibility and its fruit, companionship, was one of the first issues to rear its head again. "If I must tell it like it is, he thought she was an airhead," says a former courtier. "He was bored with her. Bored out of his mind. I can't blame him. She never had anything at all to say for herself, ever. She wasn't interested in anything except clothes and babies. If her life depended upon it, she couldn't come up with an interesting or original thought. Sure, she was sweet enough. But once she'd asked you how

239

you were and you'd said 'Fine' or 'Not so well,' and she'd said 'How marvelous' or 'That's awful, tell me about it,' you'd exhausted the conversational possibilities. I'm not denying she's a nice person and superb with children and old people. But a civilized, sophisticated, mature and intelligent man isn't a child or a poor old person who's in awe of royalty and has never met anyone above the rank of knight. He needs more from a wife than a sweet smile and a kindly word. He wants thoughtful conversation, intelligent companionship. But she didn't want to know."

When their engagement was announced, Charles and Diana told the press that one of the things they had in common was their sense of humour. Undeniably, they do both have good senses of humour. Hers is witty and suggestive, his witty too, though with a greater sense of the ridiculous. As their marriage slid down its uncompanionable course, though, neither any longer saw the amusing side to anything the other said. "He never laughs at my jokes," she said, while he greeted her witticisms with stony silence in private and grimacing appreciation in public.

Who had the power, who was calling the shots, who was in control, who was going to be the dominant partner, were the real issues in the marriage. As neither partner was capable of subservience, it became a protracted battle.

Even before Harry's birth, Diana was complaining to friends. "The Princess told me she had no control over her life," says one of her closest friends. "She said The Prince of Wales was always underfoot with the children. He prevented her from freely exercising her rights as a mother, he controlled the office, their house, the apartment [at KP]. Everything official had to pass through channels, which meant that people he appointed ran her professional life. There was not one area of her life that she felt mistress of."

As we have seen, Diana did in fact have a considerable amount of control over her life. She had been given far more latitude than any other royal, had been cosseted and protected in a way no one else was, and had not hesitated to wield the influence she had, as soon as she was married. "What she was after was total control," says a cousin of the

Prince. "She can't handle opposition. Having her own way is a compulsion with her." The goal of total control, however, was not compatible with royal life. Royals perpetually have to look over their shoulder and think what effect their actions will have upon their station in life and the people for whom they are responsible.

"Diana's problem," says a courtier who knows her well, "is that she is temperamentally unsuited for the restraints of her role in life." She was also, by all accounts, equally unsuited for her relationship with Prince Charles.

Neither experience nor example had prepared Diana for the kind of marriage she had or the type of man to whom she was married. Raine and Frances had both ruled their households. Johnnie Spencer and Peter Shand Kydd were both men who sat back and let their women get on with things. Indeed, one of Frances's complaints against her first husband had been that he left everything so entirely up to her that she felt used, like a servant. Although her second husband was more appreciative and easygoing, he too lived by the tradition that a woman's domain is the home and that a good wife takes care of her husband. Raine and Frances were both strong, dominant women, and while they took their husbands' points of view into account in the running of family life, there was never any doubt about who was in charge of the everyday details.

Having expected that she too would hold sway in her own home, Diana was shocked to discover as a newly-wed that Prince Charles wanted to have rather more of a voice in their home life than she was used to or considered appropriate. Moreover, Diana is a person who needs to be in control. While some people who know her well attribute this to the long line of strong women from which she springs, others think it is a manifestation of her troubled childhood. They believe she needs to hold the reins because she basically does not trust anyone else. Having been privy from an early age to the savagery that loved ones can perpetuate upon each other, she does not have a benign basis from which to observe life. This tremulousness and the horror of the unexpected means that she is never secure unless she is in complete control.

There is, however, yet another point of view about her conduct. She herself says, "I am a perfectionist," and there is no doubt that she is an extremely capable person when she puts her mind to a task. That, allied to her stubbornness and determination, make her a difficult person to be with on a day-to-day basis, for, if things are not done her way, her good nature vanishes.

Whatever the motivation for her need to be in control, one event more than any other shook everyone around her: the departure of her Private Secretary, Oliver Everett. It caused a huge amount of ill-will, some of which has never cleared up, and it cast Diana in the most unflattering light in which she has ever been seen.

"Ideally, she would have liked to get rid of Prince Charles's influence, but since that wasn't possible, she went after the next best thing," says a cousin of the Prince. "She went off Oliver for a variety of reasons," says someone who worked with him at the Palace. "She blamed him for the professional pressure she felt was ruining her life. Of course, he was not to blame. Even though she did not see it, she was not exactly overworked." Her schedule was not particularly arduous and she did have more time off than most working mothers. The fault lay not in the work.

"He is a wonderful person," says that same member of the Royal Household. "He is warm and friendly, good-natured and witty. He had been a close and affectionate friend to her as well as a patient and good-humoured, albeit effective, Private Secretary. He had a difficult time with her from the very beginning. First there was the never-ending battle of getting her to read the reports. Then once she settled into the role [of being Princess of Wales], she wanted an unacceptable amount of flexibility. You know the royals' diaries are filled six months in advance. Well, one of Diana's Sloane Ranger friends would ask her to lunch or dinner, she'd say yes, then she'd want Oliver to rearrange her diary. But that was not possible. He couldn't very well let people down when they'd been waiting four or six months to see The Princess of Wales, just because she wanted to see a friend instead. So he'd put his foot down and tell her no, she couldn't do what she wanted, she had to honour her commitments. She didn't like that. Not one bit. She can be very self-willed.

"Oliver had to put up with a lot, but he took it all in his stride. His attitude was, 'She's young'. He never forgot that no twenty or twenty-two year old likes being burdened with responsibility, and he never allowed her turns to affect their relationship. Nor, to her credit, did Diana. Not until the very end. They were very, very close—a lot closer than she and The Prince of Wales. They really got along like a house on fire, and she was always popping into his office to have a chat with him. They were more like conspirators and friends than Private Secretary and Princess."

To onlookers, Diana's change in attitude towards Oliver Everett was as sudden as it was inexplicable. "She turned against him, for no apparent reason," his colleague continued. "It was dreadful. It was so embarrassing I cannot tell you. One day they were as close as cheek and jowl, the next she wouldn't speak to him or take his calls. If he spoke to her, she ignored him. It was as if he didn't exist.

"No one knew what to do. At first, everyone, The Prince of Wales included, hoped it was a passing thing and she'd get over it. But she didn't. As far as she was concerned, Oliver Everett had ceased to exist, and she was going to freeze him out."

Oliver Everett, however, was not Stephen Barry. He had been one of the rising stars of the Foreign Office. He had returned from a posting in Madrid to act as Private Secretary to The Princess of Wales, with the promise that the job was his for life. "The Prince of Wales was distraught at what was happening," says the member of the Royal Household. "He felt responsible for Oliver's career. He tried to get the Foreign Office to take him back. But they said, no way. As far as they were concerned, Oliver Everett had made his bed, let him lie in it. So then there was a flurry to try to find another position for him in the [Royal] Household. The best they could come up with was Librarian at Windsor Castle. The whole thing mortified the Prince, and contributed to the erosion of the marriage. It deeply offended his sense of justice. He loathed what she did. He was furious that she forced him to stand by ineffectually while she did what she did."

"I left The Prince and Princess of Wales in December 1983 and came to Windsor in January 1984," Oliver Everett, whose warmth and humour are immediately apparent to anyone who speaks to him, said to me. His comfortable sinecure is hardly a great height for someone who was assured of reaching the diplomatic Everest until he was ill-advised enough to leave the security of the Foreign Office for the instability of The Princess of Wales's office. Even today, the departure of Oliver Everett causes behind-the-scenes comment. "Of all the moves Diana has made in her life," says the Royal Household member, "the destruction of Oliver Everett's career has got to be the most dubious. I only hope, now that she's older and wiser, she regrets what she did. For, make no mistake about it, she destroyed his career. And for no good reason at all."

To Diana, of course, there was a very good reason for ridding herself of Oliver Everett. He was Charles's man. He was doing Charles's bidding. She wanted someone who would do hers. And what she wanted, she got. For the next two years, Anne Beckwith-Smith handled many of the duties of Private Secretary, while also remaining the premier lady-in-waiting. What she did not deal with, The Prince of Wales's staff did, which was an efficacious solution to the problem, as it was not deemed safe to appoint another Private Secretary for Diana.

In November 1986, Anne Beckwith-Smith's role was formally recognized when she was appointed the *de facto* Private Secretary. Officially she became the Assistant Private Secretary, a position from which she has since resigned, reverting to being purely a lady-in-waiting. "Anyone who works for either The Prince or Princess of Wales as a Private Secretary is going to have a hard time maintaining an amicable relationship with them. They are both very wilful. Anne did the smart thing. She gave it up while the going was good. If she hadn't, there would have come a point when she and the Princess would have fallen out," says a former member of the Waleses' staff. "It would have been as inevitable as night following day."

The next person to be left gasping was Edward Adeane, but this was not Diana's fault, though the trait of self-will which she shares with Prince Charles was what caused his departure. Two immediate factors, I was told, precipitated his leaving, and as The Princess of Wales's office operates under the umbrella of the Prince's, and she was unfairly blamed for what happened, it would be derelict not to look at what transpired.

The first factor arose as a result of Prince Harry's advent and the dramatic reduction in the number of engagements Prince Charles was prepared to accept. The second revolved around the arrangements for the Waleses' tour of Italy, which included what the traditionalist Private Secretary regarded as an unconscionably low number of official engagements. "Edward felt the Prince wasn't pulling his weight," says a colleague. "He expected The Prince of Wales to have a full series of engagements, not to spend the majority of his time playing with babies or planning tours of Italy that took more account of his interest in music, art, and architecture, or attending *musicales* and visiting art galleries and churches while he was there, than fulfilling his duty opening trade bazaars and doing all the things one does on official tours to promote Britain's culture and trade. He felt he should be earning his keep, not swanning off on a contemporary version of a Grand Tour paid for by the British and Italian taxpayers."

Unbeknown to Edward Adeane, however, Charles was not being as self-indulgent or as self-willed as he appeared. He had a valid reason for planning the tour as he did. He was trying to save his marriage, which was in deep trouble by this time. Recognizing that one of the problems was a lack of companionship and shared interests, he hoped to awaken an appreciation for the finer things of life, aside from shopping and ballet, in Diana. Admittedly, he was also fulfilling an old ambition. He had never been to Italy, the land of the Renaissance, the birthplace of so much that is great in art and architecture, two of his great passions. But he was hoping, "almost against hope," according to a friend, "to find a basis from which companionship could grow."

Edward Adeane, however, was not privy to this aspect of Charles's thinking. Faced with a boss who, over the years, had refused to accept his advice, who often did the exact opposite of what he counselled, who commissioned reports which were seldom acted upon, who was playing househusband instead of heir to the throne for the second time in as many years, and who was compounding that dereliction by using an official tour of a foreign country to satisfy his personal tastes at the expense of his professional obligations, the Private Secretary resigned.

"The erosion was gradual even if the departure wasn't," a colleague on the Prince's staff said. "The trouble was that Edward Adeane is a perfectionist while The Prince of Wales is a failed perfectionist. Edward set himself moderate goals which he achieved. Prince Charles set himself high ideals, got everyone excited about them, then didn't carry through. After a diet of that, Edward had simply had enough."

So sudden was Edward Adeane's departure, in late 1984, that Charles was left without a Private Secretary. David Roycroft, an Assistant Private Secretary, filled the role while the task of finding a replacement was farmed out to professional headhunters. They came up with three names. Charles selected the Eton- and Oxford-educated Northumbrian baronet, Sir John Riddell. Aged fifty-one, he was the Executive Director of Credit Suisse First Boston Bank and the Deputy Chairman of the Independent Broadcasting Authority. He had much to recommend him aside from his social and professional background. He had never held a royal post before, he had two young children, and he was sociable, easygoing and agreeable company.

The departures, however, were not at an end. David Roycroft soon left to work for Independent Television News. He was replaced by two Assistant Private Secretaries. The Hon. Rupert Fairfax was on secondment from the Hanson Trust and Humphrey Mews (who recently died at the age of forty-eight) was a career civil servant from the Foreign Office; both were charming and delightful men.

There is a popular misconception in fashionable circles that Rupert worked for The Princess of Wales, possibly because they have remained friends since his departure, and he is sometimes seen in her party at events such as polo. But he told me, "I never worked for her. I only ever worked for him." He enjoyed his time with The Prince of Wales, which is rather more than could be said for Humphrey. "From The Prince of Wales to Robert Maxwell is some progression," he once told me, meaningfully rolling his eyes to the sky. That gesture said it all, for the late publishing tycoon was a renowned monster, and though The Prince of Wales is known to be a kind and decent person, he has long been notorious in fashionable circles as a difficult employer.

Diana was not blamed for Humphrey's departure, but, by 1987, she was acquiring a reputation as something of a hirer and firer. When the press finally cottoned on to the ebb and flow of office and household staff, responsibility for Edward Adeane's departure was mistakenly laid at her door. This was unfair and inaccurate and she is, in fact, an easier employer than Prince Charles. As long as things are done her way, and staff live up to her expectations, she is warm, kind, generous and understanding. This is something Fay Marshalsea, her dresser, and Inspector Graham Smith, her detective, would attest to, for she was kindness itself when they both had cancer. "Smudger" Smith even went along as a guest on the Mediterranean cruise the press dubbed her "second honeymoon" in 1991.

CHAPTER SEVENTEEN

Diana the Good

*H*ad the turmoil in the Wales household been reserved to their staff, The Queen, her advisers and the senior members of the Royal Family would have been most relieved. By 1986, however, the Wales marriage had broken down to such an extent that Diana was seriously considering leaving Charles.

Two people were primarily responsible for her staying, but before discussing the roles they played, it is useful to examine the world in which Charles and Diana function, for its values are the ones by which they live, and these ultimately were also relevant in keeping her in a marriage that was now causing her great unhappiness.

The conventions governing royal and aristocratic alliances are not the same as those relating to middle- and working-class marriages. There is only one other segment of society which is so firmly tied by worldly bonds. The very poor are often as much prisoners of circumstance as the upper class, the former because they do not have enough money to leave if they want to, the latter because they have so much at stake in the marriage that it is usually better all round to stay within it.

Great fortunes and great estates would not remain intact for long if a husband changed his wife every time he changes his bed companion. There has long been the recognition that ex-wives are expensive propositions. Furthermore, women who enjoy the benefits of great position and

248

wealth are seldom keen to swap the source of their privilege for the poorer rewards of divorce.

Out of these worldly realities, the convention of aristocrats and royals remaining married for the duration of their lifetimes has arisen. Time has not made serious inroads into that code of conduct, nor has it significantly altered the basis on which most genuine grandees marry. Even today, most well-bred girls, having been brought up to marry suitable men, select someone whom they love or like with money and position.

All the old values still hold sway. Only the most unmaterialistic of young girls discount the desirability of marrying rich young men who have, or are heirs to, titles and family estates. The acceptability of divorce as an intrinsic part of contemporary life has not changed the basis for marriage. It has simply provided people with a way out of marriages that have become so intolerable that divorce is the only alternative to death. Even then, divorce is invariably a last resort, undertaken only if you have to choose between your marriage and your sanity.

Staying in a marriage when romance has gone is not unknown to middle- and working-class women, of course, but there is less incentive. Before you exchange a castle or a palace for a manor house or a single residence in town, before you relinquish a great rank for the uncertainties of life on your own, you think long and hard.

The Victorians recognized the damage that divorce caused to the aristocratic and royal way of life. They discouraged it so firmly that ostracism was the inevitable result of any official break-up of a marriage. Being practical, however, they had accommodations, and these have continued as integral but unwritten aristocratic and royal codes of practice down to the present. Every Lady, Duchess or Princess knows that her duty is to provide an heir and a spare, and to be a good hostess and a social asset to her husband. Social life is not always merely a question of seeing one's friends. It is often the venue in which a woman reaffirms her position. If you have provided your husband with his heir and his spare, and romance has fled and you are no longer sleeping together, as long as you continue to solidify (or advance, if you are unfortunate enough to be a lower aristocrat) the family's social position, your husband has no reason for divorcing you, even if you both have lovers. Only if you so completely loathe each other that you cannot be in the same room is there a valid reason for dismantling the structure of your life together. And even then, I know of more than one couple who have managed things so well that they remain legally married, despite actively disliking each other, by resorting to the simple expedient of never being in the same place at the same time.

To expect people to spend the rest of their lives in personally unfulfilling marriages without external nourishment would be unreasonable, so the unwritten rule that, having done your duty, you can sleep with whomever you please as long as you are discreet, has long been viewed as a realistic necessity, not as a condoning of immorality. Nor does class necessarily govern the choice of a lover: I know of one countess who had an affair with the chauffeur, and another who slept with the gardener. The former Viscount Weymouth, now the Marquis of Bath, has had a string of "wifelets," and these have included the black Jamaican singer Nola Fontaine and Jo-Jo Laine, the ex-wife of former Wings musician Denny Laine. But the more typical arrangements have been between gentlemen and ladies. The former Tory minister Lord Lambton, for instance, has lived in Tuscany in unmarried bliss for well over a decade with the Hon. Mrs. Claire Ward, mother of the Marchioness of Worcester and the actress Rachel Ward, while Lady Lambton reposes in domestic harmony in the splendid marital home in Durham, her position inviolate.

By this code of practice, the only reasons for shattering a civilized arrangement are if it has become redundant, or if it threatens to harm the parties involved. Redundancy was the reason for the writer and broadcaster John Julius (Viscount) Norwich changing Viscountesses. For over twenty years his extra-marital arrangement flourished, but when it was no longer necessary, he and his first wife were divorced, and his inamorata became his second wife. The threat of harm to the monarchy, however, was what broke up the marriage of Princess Margaret, thereby introducing divorce as a viable alternative to traditional arrangements, albeit only if it serves the interests of the royal partner. For years it had been an open secret amongst the cognoscenti that Princess Margaret and the Earl of Snowdon were leading separate lives. What was less well known was that they almost loathed each other. Not even those sentiments were adjudged good enough reasons for parting, however, until Roddy Llewellyn's relationship with her threatened to tarnish the image of the Royal Family. At that juncture, the ever scrupulous courtiers at Buckingham and Kensington Palaces took the decision to end the marriage, and tried to do so in such a way that Lord Snowdon would receive the blame. They did not even have the courtesy to inform him that an announcement of his divorce was imminent, and he arrived in Australia, as his PR, Robyn Hall, confirmed to me, to discover that everyone in the world but he knew that his marriage was to end.

Divorce is even more a last resort for royals than for aristocrats; people at the Palace confirm that there is no way The Queen's advisers would have allowed The Princess Royal to move for a separation if they had not known that Captain Mark Phillips was vulnerable to paternity claims by an Antipodean one-night stand. But courtiers are nothing if not pragmatic, and their intention is to use this as justification to dissolve the Princess's marriage at an opportune moment.

As a result of the breakdown in those two Princesses' marriages, a new rule with regard to the dissolution of royal marriages has come into being. They can divorce, but only if absolutely necessary, and only if they can be presented as the injured party. Mud can be slung. But it must not stick to the royal, only to his or her partner.

Charles and Diana, of course, are only too intimately acquainted with the ground rules. This is their world. They know that the moral conventions must be observed. Nevertheless, the rules do recognize that royals are also human. This means that they are not always willing to share some of the more personal aspects of companionship with their spouses.

Out of this need for companionship has grown the institution of the confidant (or confidante if it is a woman). In many ways, this has been the saviour of the royal way of life. Royals have as great a desire as anyone else for companionship, understanding, compassion, affection and the many other human needs that constitute satisfaction. They too want to plumb the depths of human interchange, to feel close to one special person, to know that there is someone who understands them, who is with them through thick or thin. Discretion may dictate that that person has to remain in the background, forever out of the public view, but the main *raison d'être* is not perpetual physical proximity, nor public confirmation of the individual's private standing, but freedom to pursue this most nurturing of friendships behind closed doors. Custom by the way has evolved a structure that makes it impossible for the parties involved to indulge in any wrongdoing as they pursue their relationship.

By 1986, Charles's and Diana's marriage had deteriorated to such a point that he had returned to his old love, Camilla Parker Bowles, for the companionship he was not receiving from his wife. When Diana discovered this, she was understandably gripped by jealousy and began throwing scenes. These took many forms. Always vigilant where her husband's movements were concerned, Diana began policing Charles with the tenacity of a private eye. Wherever he was going, whether it was on official business or not, she demanded to know precisely when he was due back. If she received an answer (she often did not), she would telephone the Parker Bowles residence over and over again once the time that he was due home had passed, each time hanging up without speaking, until he came back home. On the other hand, if the Prince refused to divulge the projected time of his return home, she also telephoned the Parker Bowles residence repeatedly, again hanging up without speaking, though on these occasions the calls cascaded down, from the moment she estimated the Prince to have arrived at Middlewich House until his return home. "It was horrid for Camilla," a friend of hers said. "Most of the time Prince Charles wasn't even there. But she'd have to put up with these nuisance calls." On the odd occasions when Charles was at Middlewich House, to which the Parker Bowleses had moved from Bolehyde Manor, he heard for himself what his insanely jealous wife was doing to his friends. And when he did return home, whether he had visited the Parker Bowleses or not, it was invariably to a row and to threats of what Diana would and would not do to him and to herself. Sometimes she would even lose control to such an extent that she would hit him.

"He was heartily sick of her antics by this time," a Royal relation said. "Ever since their marriage he had had to endure the most unbelievable histrionics and hysterics. No man can stand a daily, sometimes hourly, diet of dramatics that are more suitable for an operatic stage than a home. Even in the early days of the marriage, when they were meant to be happy, she was always pulling scenes to get her own way. Once, when he was going riding and she wanted him to stay with her and to tell her how much he loved her, she created the most dreadful scene for everyone at Sandringham to hear. The whole family, the houseguests, the [domestic] staff all heard it. Later that same day, she slipped down the last few steps of the staircase. It was an accident. A servant saw it."

Indeed a servant did, and recounts, "She must have missed her footing. She slid down the last four or five steps. She was pregnant with Prince William at the time. About three months. I was wondering if I should go and help her when she got up. She was fine. She wasn't hurt at all. She walked off out of sight for a few seconds. She came back and lay down at the bottom of the stairs. I was surprised. Yes, it is fair to say she draped herself at the bottom of the stairs. A few minutes passed. I was wondering what I should do when she got up, went and had a look around the corner. She came back and lay down again. She could only have been there for a minute or so before Queen Elizabeth The Queen Mother came along. She was dreadfully upset. She was worried that HRH might have hurt herself and the baby she was carrying."

A doctor was duly called. The Princess was not bruised, despite subsequent reports to the contrary, nor was she indisposed in any way at all. In fact, so well was she that she was able to attend a family barbecue two hours later. Recent attempts to turn it into a suicide attempt in which she hurled herself down the stairs are simply incorrect.

This, however, is not the end of the story. That episode was but one of the many dramas which the Princess instigated and which had the effect of turning the Prince off her. "He very quickly came to distrust her. He could never tell when she was telling the truth and when she was play-acting." That, indeed, was a characteristic which her own brother Charles commented upon elsewhere, recounting how the young Diana had had such a slim grip on the truth that the vicar's wife was once compelled to stop the car and warn her that she would be forced to drop her off if she told one more lie.

"She must always be the centre of attention," the Prince's relation continues. "That's why she's always manufacturing moments which feature her as the central character." Whatever her motivation, there is no doubt that Diana became a deft hand at creating scenes. "Their rows were loud and sometimes violent. He never struck her, but she was always going at him," the relation said. "Yes, hitting him. Once, she wanted to prevent him from going on an official engagement. An *official* engagement, mark you. People sometimes put in months of work for an official event, as you know only too well from your own experience. She wanted him to disappoint everyone who had done all the work they'd done, so that he could stay home and watch television with her. He rightly refused, and she accused him of being selfish and of always putting his Royal duties before love. Now, I ask you, is that reasonable? Who was being selfish? When she realised that he was really going to leave her to fulfill his obligations, she rushed to his desk, picked up the penknife, and ran to the door. She blocked his way, brandishing the knife and screaming that she felt like killing him and herself. She did not try to use it, either on him or herself. She has never cut herself on her chest or thighs, but even if she had, how could that qualify as anything but a tantrum? You can't kill yourself by scratching yourself on the chest or thighs, and

254

anyone who did that would be grandstanding, not trying to kill herself. But how can I be sure she didn't do it? I know it from Prince Charles. But more importantly, I've seen with my own eyes. She's never ever had marks anywhere on her body. I've seen her with great regularity over the years. I've seen her in everyday clothes, in evening wear— some quite revealing—and in a bikini. I tell you, she does not have one mark on her body. Who did genuinely try to commit suicide was Queen Alexandra when she was Princess of Wales. She slit her throat. That was why she had to wear chokers. Not because of the after-effects of any illness, as historians will say. But Diana, never."

There were other, memorable temper tantrums, some of which have been presented as being quasi-suicide attempts. One that has never been previously revealed involved yet another row, this time at Balmoral. The Prince had promised to meet his mother. Diana, however, wanted him to stay with her. "She dug around in her glad-bag of tricks," his relation recounts, "and pulled out the whole lot. First there were the usual tears—she's like one of those movie stars who can cry on demand—and when that didn't work, there were the threats. Everyone in the house could hear her, which says something about her lung-power. He stormed off in a puff, telling her that he was not going to let his mother or anyone else down to accommodate her childish and selfish whims. She followed him out of the room, and when he started down the stairs, she gave him an almighty shove. She pushed him from behind, on his shoulder, and shrieked that she hoped he'd break his neck. He took it to be nothing but a temper tantrum, but if her other tantrums are now being presented as suicide attempts, which is nonsense, it would be equally fair to categorise that as an attempt to murder him."

There were other tantrums that were nothing but hysterical histrionics. One involved a lemon slicer. "Once more they had one of their stand-up, drag-down rows. She picked up the lemon slicer and threatened to stab him with it. He told her not to be so dramatic, and walked out. He hates rows and always walks out first. Neither of them was wounded in any way in that incident, and it is beyond ludicrousness for anyone to claim that she tried to commit suicide. How do you kill yourself with a lemon slicer? Do you peel yourself to death? And all of this nonsense about her dramatics being cries for help. They were shrieks for attention. She's a glutton for attention. She can't get enough of it. No matter how much he's given her, it's never been enough. If he spent twenty-four hours a day with her, she'd demand that he make the day twenty-five hours. And if he told her he couldn't, she'd begin ranting and raving about him never giving her what she needs. That's the sort of wife she is. A real nightmare, or, as the Americans say, hell on wheels."

Brenda Stronach had her own opinion about the suicide claims. Married to the Prince's valet throughout the period they were supposed to be happening, she was quoted in several newspapers saying that Diana had never tried to commit suicide, nor had she ever wounded herself. This was further corroborated by Diana's fellow West Heath alumna and former flatmate Carolyn Bartholomew, who spoke to the *Daily Mirror* and said, "She has never mentioned the word suicide to me." The implication was clear: if one of her oldest and closest friends did not know about the supposed suicide attempts, how could they have taken place?

"The Princess of Wales has never slashed her wrists," a former member of the Wales Household says. "I'm incredulous that the press and the public could have fallen for the story that she did. I've seen her ever since her engagement. She has never, not once, had a scratch or a mark or a bandage on her wrists. They are clean, completely clean. But people don't need to take my word for it. Let them think it through for themselves. She has never once, throughout her years in the public eye, been photographed with a bandage around her wrists. And she has never been out of the public eye long enough for cut wrists to have healed without the bandages being seen."

In fairness to Andrew Morton, the original purveyor of the suicide stories, it should be noted that he does not allege in his book that she slashed her wrists. He actually alleges that she slashed AT her wrists, whatever that means. To award such an activity with the status of a genuine suicide attempt is like giving Diana a trophy for swimming across the Straits of San Francisco just because she once got in a car that drove over the Golden Gate Bridge.

Nevertheless, the story does have a footing, albeit a tenuous one, in the truth. "She did pick up a razor blade and threaten to kill herself with it during a row with the Prince," his relation informs. "She also threatened to slit his throat. Was it attempted suicide, attempted murder, or a simple temper tantrum? I am sure all reasonable people will come to the same conclusion the Prince did. She was merely being a drama queen. She has a great gift for that. Once, she telephoned him at Highgrove and told him that she wanted him to come to London immediately. He said he couldn't, as he had an official engagement that evening. She accused him of wanting to stay to see Camilla Parker Bowles. She said he preferred Camilla's company to hers. I should think he does. I certainly do. Camilla is a far more interesting person than Diana. She knows how to behave, which is rather more than Diana knows how to do when she's out of the public gaze and the cameras are turned off. Anyway, she began one of her screaming rages, which ended with her slamming down the phone. Five minutes later she phoned again. She said she'd tried to kill herself. He didn't think she really had, but he couldn't be sure. You can't when she's in one of those states. She's so volatile she can do anything, and you can't rely upon what she's saying. So, even though he was fed up to his back teeth with her histrionics by this time, he was sure to keep his head and very gently asked her what she'd done. She said she'd taken an overdose of paracetamol, but that she'd thought better of it and had vomited it up. She doesn't know it to this day, but the evening before, he'd had a headache and gone to the medicine cabinet in search of some paracetamols. There were four left. He took two and left two. You can imagine his disgust when she tried to trick him like that. But even then he didn't take any chances. He got on to their doctor and had him go round to KP to check her out. She was perfectly okay and went out that same evening. The following day all the papers were full of the sparkling and radiant Princess of Wales. She thrives on scenes and dramas, but he hates them. Most men would. Only a deeply disturbed man would not be turned off by dramatics like that."

"Diana is nothing if not resourceful," says the sister-in-law of the top-ranking courtier. "Once she realized that he was not going to stop seeing Camilla Parker Bowles, she decided to knock her off her perch." The institution of confidante, being an honoured one, is the source of a tremendous amount of kudos and social influence. If The Prince of Wales has one confidante, she occupies a position in society that is superior to most duchesses and only marginally below that of Diana herself. On the other hand, if he has two confidantes, this duplication reduces the influence and prestige of both. "So," continues the aristocratic sister-in-law, "she asked Dale Tryon to lunch at San Lorenzo."

San Lorenzo in Beauchamp Place, Knightsbridge, is Diana's favourite restaurant. Asking Dale to meet her there was a masterful public relations move. Diana knew, as all of us know who frequent that most fashionable of Italian restaurants, that the *paparazzi* photographers' spies always tip them off when anyone famous is eating there. It was therefore a safe assumption that Richard Young, Dave Bennett or Desmond O'Neill, and most likely all three, would be round there to record this most public of rapprochements for posterity and the readers of the following morning's popular papers before Diana and Dale even had time to finish their starter. Which is precisely what happened. A photograph of the two women at their table, huddled together deep in conversation, was flashed all over the world—despite the fact that the proprietor, Mara, is very vigilant and cameras are never allowed into San Lorenzo unless the patrons agree.

Diana was well aware that Charles and Dale were no longer exchanging the closest secrets. Dale was therefore no longer a cause for jealousy. But she could be useful. By reintroducing her into the public consciousness as Charles's other confidante, Diana was diluting Camilla's standing at the same time that she was elevating Dale's.

Quite deliberately, she was making Dale, who no longer technically held the position, the publicly accepted confidante. By doing so, she was undercutting Camilla, whom she declines to acknowledge either privately or publicly. It was a brilliant ploy, one which covered Dale in prestige, though it has not, in the end, made any difference to Camilla's stature. The truth always comes out, and even if the world at large does not yet know that she is the prime confidante, insiders do.

These games did nothing to improve what was happening within the Wales marriage. By this time, Charles and Diana were barely talking. They would have a blistering row followed by days, sometimes weeks, of silence. Both were deeply unhappy about the state of their marriage. "They both suffered terribly," says a connection of the Royal Family. "They recognized that they were tied together for life. They were like two Olympic runners whose feet are set in cement. Much as they'd like to get up and run, they're stuck where they stand, forever.

"He felt he'd been conned, that he'd been deceived into marrying someone he didn't get. She felt disappointed. She'd sincerely believed that, by marrying The Prince of Wales, she was going to have a wonderful, romantic marriage. You can see how a young girl would fall into that trap. He is the nicest man imaginable, and she sincerely believed that his kindness, sensitivity and love for her would provide her with the means to change him into being more the sort of man she wanted. It's always a fatal mistake, but one which so many of us make: believing you can change a man, especially one who is already set in his character and way of life.

"When Diana first got married, she used to joke and say she kissed the Prince and got the frog. Now she was saying it again, and it wasn't a joke," says one of her closest friends. She also felt that she was swamped with responsibilities she did not want and chores she did not need. In the years since her marriage, she had become, to a large extent, isolated from her old friends. Although Kitty Waite Walker had attributed this entirely to the courtiers whom Diana described as being "condescending beyond belief" and told how they "meant to cut off all of her old friends so that she doesn't know what she is missing," the truth was marginally more complex.

"The courtiers undeniably played a large part in isolating Diana. To them, she was not a young girl who needed friends, but a Princess of Wales who would carry the banner of monarchy into the next century," says the noblewoman whose brother-in-law was a top-ranking courtier. "She herself withdrew from her old life and her old friends. It was an inevitable part of the process of adjusting to being royal. But she got tired of being surrounded by older people, of having tea with Lady Susan Hussey, of missing out on the fun she knew her contemporaries were having. In my opinion, she would have sacrificed her old friends willingly, if her marriage had brought her the satisfaction she hoped it would. But, because it didn't, she needed her friends. She needed fun. She needed to be young. It was a case of, if I can't be fulfilled, then I want to have fun."

Not being a rebel, however, Diana did not look far afield for new friends. She sought companionship from within the limited royal circle. One friend she made was Sarah Ferguson, the daughter of Prince Charles's racing manager, Major Ronald Ferguson. "Fergie was fun," says the courtier's sister-in-law, "and helped Diana while away the many boring hours involved in watching the men chase about on a polo field. She was also familiar with royal protocol, and while that did not matter to Diana, it did to the courtiers, who strongly objected to the familiarity with which Diana allowed her old friends to treat her. To them, Fergie was a good egg. She knew when to curtsey and when to crack a rude joke. She was safe, or so, at least, they thought."

After her marriage to Prince Andrew, the courtiers would learn to their cost that Fergie is also an individualist, and that she is not as malleable as they would like. She has a strong character and is indeed a good egg, far nicer and much better value than the press give her credit for being. Even though she tried the patience of the courtiers (no bad thing too, in my estimation), she is warm, down-to-earth, amusing, and loyal. She is far more dignified and gracious than the press make out. But because she has an animated manner and an expressive face, they manage to get unflattering photographs that catch her "on the wing," choosing to publish the one out of maybe fifty that makes her look ridiculous. In person, however, she is anything but.

In June 1985, a deeply disenchanted Diana asked Fergie to join her party for Royal Ascot, thereby changing both their lives for ever. Until then, Diana had been miserable and querulous, her life on a downward spiral with no hope of climbing out of the hole she had, in part, dug for herself. Fergie was also at a low point in her life. "She was the girl all the guys left," says one friend. "Kim Smith-Bingham had dumped her. Paddy McNally had effectively done so. She'd given him an ultimatum to marry her—or else. It was 'or else'."

During lunch at Windsor Castle, the saucy Fergie and the amorous Andrew engaged in a meaningful exchange over a profiterole, prior to setting out for Ascot racecourse. So began their romance, which was consolidated very quickly, as romances between two passionate people invariably are.

Sarah Ferguson was the first of the two people who would dramatically alter Diana's life. As Princess Michael of Kent said prior to the marriage, "She will have a great effect upon all our lives. She's a very strong personality. They [the dreaded courtiers] won't be able to control her. Through her, things will change for the better."

Even before Sarah became Duchess of York and Princess Michael's prediction had a chance of coming true, things did change for the better, but only for Diana. Through Prince Andrew, Fergie had become privy to the secrets within the Wales marriage, and she encouraged Diana to stand up for herself and do what she wanted. "Until Sarah came on the scene," says a famous beauty connected to the Royal Family, "The Princess of Wales felt alone and adrift. She was a great public success but there were her marital problems and she was hemmed in by the traditions of the Crown—and that load of old fogeys who run things. Whether they're four, forty or four hundred, they're all the

same: born old. It's terrible if you're young. The Duke of Edinburgh went through it. So did Princess Margaret. They destroyed her life. And nothing had changed in the thirty years since. They were still standing over the royals, like Sadducees at the gates of the Temple. They were more prison wardens than guardians, especially to The Prince and Princess of Wales. But Sarah came along and said, "Hey, come on—you don't want to do anything that's wrong. You only want to have a life. So you want to have lunch at Ménage à Trois with your friends. Big deal. That's not a crime, it's not undignified. So go, have lunch with your friends in a public restaurant. This isn't the Victorian Age. This is 1985." She gave the Princess back a lot of the confidence which she'd had when she married The Prince of Wales, but had lost in the intervening years."

After Sarah Ferguson became The Duchess of York, her effect upon the other members of the Royal Family was, as Princess Michael had predicted, dramatic. There were now three contemporary females influencing the royal way of doing things, and, for the honeymoon period at least, the press allowed the public to be enamoured of the Duchess's naturalistic way of behaving. She was perceived as being a breath of fresh air, and even her unregal past, with acknowledged live-in boyfriends and the freewheeling style of the chalet way of life, were accounted attributes.

Thanks, in part, to her new sister-in-law, Diana now had more scope. The trouble was, she did not yet know it, and even if she had known it, she was so dispirited that she would not have known what to do with it.

One person alone would not have been enough to catapult her out of the misery she was now in. The second person who would have a dramatic effect came into her life through her brother-in-law, Prince Andrew. Early in 1986, the photographer Gene Nocon and his wife had a dinner party. Their guests were Prince Andrew, Sarah Ferguson, Simon Best and his wife, Penny Thornton. During dinner, the conversation turned to astrology. Upon learning that Penny is what Mrs. Henry Ford II calls "a very gifted astrologer, no question about it. She's one of the best,"

Prince Andrew seized upon her as a possible source of help for his sister-in-law.

The potential for disaster was great, of course, as many astrologers are crackpots. But Prince Andrew steered Diana to someone who is one of the unchallenged mistresses of her field. According to Cathy Ford, "Astrology as practised by Penny is not for nuts. Her approach is very learned, very scientific. It's for intelligent people, and she's one of the best. I had her do a chart before she knew who I was. She had typewritten her analysis. You know, people are always saying someone knows you better than you know yourself. Well, I think that's nonsense. No one knows you better than yourself. But when I received her analysis, it took me two weeks to get back to her. I had to think very carefully about what she'd said, because in some ways she knew me better than I know myself.

"She is so good, I had her calculate when Henry and I should get married. When you're getting married, you want everything to work in your favour. She chose the date and time. It was a good calculation. Our marriage worked well.

"Penny has a gift of using language. She doesn't speak about the moon in Pisces or equally unintelligible things that no one but another astrologer will understand. Her choice of words is always so good that you decipher what she is saying in an intelligent way."

Penny Thornton, who is a prolific writer and sees clients only one day a week, was in the middle of writing a book. She discouraged Prince Andrew from having The Princess of Wales get in touch with her until she had finished her book. But knowing Diana's desperation, he nevertheless gave her Penny Thornton's telephone number.

According to a source close to Diana, "She phoned Miss Thornton herself. They made an appointment for Miss Thornton to come to the Palace for tea." At 4:00 pm on Thursday 6 March 1986, Diana had her first meeting with Penny Thornton. "They were together for nearly three hours. They were in Her Royal Highness's sitting room. Miss Thornton had a headache, and Her Royal Highness herself went out to get some Disprin for her. At teatime, the meeting was interrupted by Prince William. He was wanting a biscuit."

Diana was distraught. "She was in desperate straits, at the end of her tether. She needed someone she could talk to, someone she could trust." She wanted to leave Prince Charles. She could stand neither her marriage nor her way of life any longer. The former had reduced her to a terrible state of despair, the latter had left her feeling oppressed and imprisoned. She could see no other solution to her problems than to leave her husband. "Of course she didn't want to give up being Princess of Wales," says a friend. "She just didn't see what other choice she had. Leaving him, escaping from him and the royal way of life, seemed the only solution to her problems. But Diana is a staunch royalist and she loves being The Princess of Wales. She hated the idea of damaging the monarchy and of giving up her position."

Penny Thornton pointed the way to a solution that did not involve departure. "Through astrology, she showed her that her suffering would come to an end," says someone to whom Diana confided. "She told her that her problems weren't insoluble. This period could be replaced by great happiness and she'd eventually find fulfilment. She told her to use her suffering to make herself more substantial, that it could have a strengthening purpose if she, Princess Diana, used it wisely."

At times of crisis, human beings are more readily open to suggestion. Because people often turn to astrologers only when under great stress, astrologers can have great power over their clients. This proved to be the case with Penny Thornton and The Princess of Wales. "Penny Thornton had a profound effect upon her. She is very spiritual, and she made Princess Diana aware of her spiritual path. She helped Princess Diana get in touch with the spiritual part of her personality. She helped her to see that her role, as Princess of Wales, was important," says the friend.

One of the many problems was that Diana felt belittled by Prince Charles. She also maintained that she "had been desperately in love with him at the time of their marriage, but that he had not been in love with her at all. His treatment of her was very callous and cruel," at least in her eyes, "and he had hurt her terribly. He had humiliated her. Penny Thornton somehow managed to make her feel that she could live with these feelings, instead of making them force her into a course of action she didn't really want to take," says the friend.

On more than one occasion, Penny Thornton was called as a last resort. "Once, Prince Charles was the one who arranged for the call to be put through to Miss Thornton. Princess Diana had her bags packed and was ready to leave. Miss Thornton managed to calm her down. According to the Princess, she showed her that there was light at the end of the tunnel," says the source close to Diana.

Penny Thornton's special talent does seem to be therapeutic. A well-known aristocratic beauty, who has experience of Miss Thornton's talents over nearly two decades, says, "What she gives you is faith and hope. She is a very positive person. You come away feeling that things will eventually be good—not merely better, but good. What she does is to give you the means to find the tools within yourself to cope with the issues and problems within your life that are causing you pain."

Over a period of a year, during which Diana and Penny Thornton were in close and constant touch, the astrologer managed to "encourage Princess Diana in her increasing spiritual development." Miss Thornton was observed popping in and out of Kensington Palace, acting, by all accounts, more as a spiritual guide and therapist than an everyday astrologer. With time, her efforts bore fruit and the shaky and desperate Princess did begin to see the light at the end of the tunnel. Thereafter, the visits wound down, to be substituted by telephone calls which still go on to this day.

When I telephoned Miss Thornton for corroboration of all I had learnt, she was very obviously taken aback that I had discovered her link with Diana. "This is all very difficult," she said, the panic plain to hear. "I don't know how you found out. No one knows. I've never told anyone. I want to protect her." At that point, she checked herself and said, "I'm not confirming anything. Anything at all. I'm not even admitting that I've ever met The Princess of Wales. You can't say that I know her at all, because I won't corroborate that I do." By the end of the telephone call, she had so affected to know nothing that anyone listening in would have believed that she had never even heard of The Princess of Wales.

Despite this discretion, the fact of the relationship cannot be denied, nor can the importance of her influence be exaggerated. It was she who kept Diana from leaving Charles, a debt which The Prince of Wales himself has privately acknowledged. Moreover, it was she who showed Diana that she could turn her suffering into something useful and life-enhancing, thereby banishing futility and bringing joy into her own life as well as the lives of others. It was thanks to Penny Thornton that Diana found her way. The Royal Family's answer to Mother Teresa had been safely delivered after a long and arduous labour. Diana the Good was born.

♛ ♛ ♛

CHAPTER EIGHTEEN

Charity for the Charities

*T*he transition from deflated Princess of Wales to Diana the Good was a straightforward affair, though it did have its setbacks and was not always easy. The way any woman of status, heart and conscience makes a valid contribution to the world at large is through charity work. Even if she is a busy artist, such as the sculptress Shenda Amery (Sheikha Nezam al bin Khazal kabi al Amery, Chairman of the Ladies' Committee of Help the Aged), a prolific writer such as the novelist Una-Mary Parker (organizer of the Royal British Legion's Poppy Ball), or a busy widow and mother such as Beverley, Lady Annaly (founder and trustee of SIGN, the charity for the deaf which is spearheading the campaign to create communities for the deaf and to make signing available to all), she still finds the time and energy to do charity work. There are thousands of good causes, all needing help. It takes a stony heart and a vacuous head to bear a grand name, to have all the access and connections attendant upon it, and to refuse to recognize that you have the capacity to make a contribution to society, and that the positive effects of your endeavours will far exceed the effort you put into them.

Diana, of course, was already familiar with the charity world. In common with most of the other royals, the vast majority of her official engagements revolved around one charity or another. Few of her official duties were state engagements: she might occasionally have to meet a visiting head of state at Victoria Station with Prince Charles, or once a year have to attend the State Opening of Parliament. She might have to take part in the odd state banquet at Buckingham Palace or Windsor Castle, or put in an appearance at one of the annual garden parties at Buckingham Palace in London and Holyroodhouse Palace in Edinburgh. But she would never be the Queen Regnant, and only the Monarch's diary is filled primarily with state engagements. All the other members of the Royal Family, from the Consort downwards, earn their keep by doing good works. Even the Annual Festival of Remembrance, which is so much a fixture of the royal calendar, is affiliated with a charity, in this case the Royal British Legion.

Until Diana's spiritual transformation, her attitude towards her public duties had been a problem. With the intervention of the astrologer Penny Thornton, however, Diana became motivated into changing her perception of her work, and began to view tasks which she had previously thought onerous as opportunities for personal enrichment. "Once she realized that her work could really mean something, that it had a purpose beyond meeting pompous dignitaries and snobbish socialites, she really took an interest in it," says a friend.

Up to this point, Diana's public duties had been primarily involved with the two segments of society with which she had had childhood and adolescent links: children and old people. There had long been the suspicion that this was because she was unable to cope with anything more demanding. Once her work became an interest, however, Diana's approach changed dramatically. Even though she would never become a voracious reader like The Prince of Wales, where she had previously been prepared only to glance at a condensation of reports for charities such as Birthright, now she faithfully read them. More to the point, she digested the details and began asking for more information. She was finally developing her mind, intermingling its diet of fantastical romanticism with useful information. Prince Charles was finally getting the wife he had wanted from the very outset. It remained to be seen whether too much conflict had arisen for them to enjoy the fruit of an enlightenment that would have enhanced their marriage had it come sooner.

Eager to break new ground, Diana used her resourcefulness and initiative to discover fields in which she could utilize the unique package of gifts she had to offer. Privately she said, "I want to do what I can to help, to make life better for people, to relieve suffering and distress," while she was publicly quoted in 1990 as saying that where there was suffering, that was where she wanted to be.

One charity Diana looked at was WomenAid. Founded in 1986 by Pida Ripley, who has headed the fund-raising endeavours of the United Nations Association since the mid-seventies, WomenAid was conceived as an organization through which the women of the developed world would help their sisters in the Third World, who are responsible for 90 per cent of the work, including crop-tending, relating to survival. "The Princess of Wales chose us," Pida Ripley says. "She wanted to become involved in something that was making a meaningful contribution, something that was small and had just started, the way she did with Birthright. She's chosen her charities carefully. She wanted to grow with them. She had seen a leaflet about WomenAid, I believe lying around at one of her friends'. She asked about it, heard that it was women working for women, and said that's something she'd like to get involved with. We'd just started, and the Foreign Office said she couldn't become a Patron yet, not until we were more established and had more of a track record."

That, however, did not stop the Princess from becoming involved. One of her contributions to WomenAid was to attend the luncheon to celebrate World Food Day on 16 October 1989, at which she presented the Women of the World Awards. "I was surprised by her," Pida Ripley continues. "She was a lot deeper and more knowledgeable than I had been led to believe she would be."

With her customary thoroughness, Diana approached her newly awakened interest with dogged determination and commendable efficiency. "She picked her areas carefully—babies, old people, women, AIDS—all areas that were notoriously difficult and unsympathetic until she got involved with them," Pida Ripley says.

Dancing had long been one of Diana's greatest passions, and she did not neglect it once she turned her attention to the good she could do. Adding it to her burgeoning list of charitable interests, she became involved with growing companies such as the London City Ballet and the English National Ballet.

Nor were her contributions merely cosmetic. As Diana knows very well, the charity world is a complex one. At every level, it is interwoven with social life. The more successful a charity becomes, the more prestigious it is. And the more prestigious it is, the more royal links it has. Inevitably, that also means that a fair number of the people who support charities do so either partly or purely for the social opportunities arising. Without being cynical, one soon learns that people do not always give money or support merely because a cause is worthwhile. What counts is that people want value for money, which has to be stressed at committee meetings when the naïve threaten to ruin the success of a venture with misplaced faith in the altruism of others. Good entertainment, fun, glamour and gratification of the basest instincts of the snobbish are all factors to consider in spearheading a successful charity.

Because Diana has a worldly streak that was much in evidence even before her marriage, she has proven to be an invaluable asset in fund-raising. According to Jamie Jeeves, the fund-raiser for the English National Ballet, "She has a knack, a real instinct, for saying the right thing to the right person at the right time, to get them to loosen their purse strings and give money."

Raising funds, however, is only one part of charity work. Getting along with the people you work with, and the people for whom you are working, is also a necessary part of the whole. On an official visit to the Mildmay Mission Hospice in East London in November 1991, Diana impressed 32-year-old Michael Kelly. He told her, "Now I am known as a man with AIDS, I'm worried someone might throw a brick through my window." She commiserated with him

270

and observed, "Unfortunately you have to live with their ignorance."

"She's truly incredible," Jamie Jeeves said. "She's fantastically co-operative and always willing to oblige, to do what we all know has to be done to make things a success. She's such a delight—really wonderful. Very down-to-earth, no airs and graces. I'm a complete fan. It's difficult to exaggerate how great I think she is."

Pida Ripley also has only praise for Diana's human qualities. "She is a real delight. I think the secret of her success is her approachability, her informality, and her sense of humour. It's not a wicked sense of humour, it's nice and gentle and fun. She's also so informal. But it's her approachability that wins everyone over. You feel you can say anything at all to her. I have a lot of time for her."

Even before her conversion, Diana's impact upon the charities with which she was affiliated was dramatic. Her two main charities from her earlier period, Birthright and Help the Aged, are a case in point. It was her name, her popularity, her prestige, and the quite remarkable interest shown in anything relating to her that catapulted them from insignificance into being two of the best-known and most successful charities in the country. Bunty Lewis, whose husband Tom has enjoyed an immensely distinguished career as an obstetrician and gynaecologist, was one of the founders of Birthright, and she tells me, "We could never have done what we did without The Princess of Wales. It was a relatively new charity and she helped to put us on the map. She became involved with us through knowing George Pinker (who was her obstetrician and delivered her sons), and because she is one of the members of the Royal Family who is an Honorary Fellow of the Royal College of Obstetricians and Gynaecologists."

Association with Diana also furthered the cause of Help the Aged, which I remember well from the late seventies, when I went to see Peter Laing, who was running the charity, and Marion Alford, who was working as their fund-raiser and has since gone on to become the most successful fund-raiser in the country. Help the Aged was struggling. No one, but no one, wanted to know about it. The old were perceived as embarrassments, not as people with needs and desires who could still make a valid contribution to society, or whose presence could enrich it. Then along came The Princess of Wales. Whatever the motives for her interest, and whether or not she chose the aged because she was more comfortable speaking to them as a result of having learnt to do so at West Heath, the fact is her association with Help the Aged turned it into one of the most fashionable charities in the land. Nowadays, their annual awards luncheon is one of the fixtures of the social calendar. The ladies who lunch turn out in force to see and be seen. Whatever else the charity organizes, it is assured of success, as long as the invitations contain the words "In the presence of Her Royal Highness The Princess of Wales."

Without those magical words, as Birthright discovered to its cost in spring 1991, the most appealing event loses its sparkle and tickets become impossible to move. The charity organized a Sixties ball and cabaret at the Royal Albert Hall. Every renowned act from the Supremes through Gerry and the Pacemakers to the Searchers performed. Stars from the social and musical firmaments such as Jane, Duchess of Roxburghe, the Marquis and Marchioness of Worcester, Bill Wyman, Petula Clark, and Patti Boyd Harrison Clapton committed to attending or were on the committee. The evening was full of promise, not only musically but also socially. Once word got out that Diana was not going to be there, however, the tickets, at £250 per person, moved as slowly as treacle. On the evening itself, there were large sections of the box tier filled with nothing but air. And all because Diana, with her tremendous drawing power, was not there.

Diana, of course, is aware of this. "She realizes her presence at something will enhance the occasion," says John Coblenz of CRUSAID, the tremendously effective AIDS charity started in 1986. "For instance, in January [1991], she attended our reception in the House of Commons, although it is unusual for a royal princess to go to the Commons—because she realized her presence would give a certain prestige to the occasion."

Since her conversion to spiritually motivated work, Diana's contribution to such initially unpopular causes as AIDS has been invaluable. Her work for CRUSAID has been extensive, and has covered the full spectrum from very private to very public. "She's very helpful, willing to devote as much time as we need. What she did when she opened the Kobler Centre for us in September 1988, took much of the sting out of the prejudice surrounding the disease," John Coblenz said. "At that time, AIDS was so unknown by the general public, and The Princess of Wales's involvement so newsworthy, that the event had high coverage on television. She purposely went in without gloves and shook the patients' hands without protection, which made a profound impact. She was quite deliberately showing the public that you can't catch this disease by normal physical contact. It did a lot to reduce fear and prejudice."

Not everyone, of course, approves of Diana's interest in controversial causes such as AIDS. One titled lady, a friend of her father, says, "All of this jiggery-pokery with buggers just isn't on." Another friend of her father's, also titled, says, "Spending all day with Adrian Ward-Jackson [the art dealer and board member of the English National Ballet, of which Diana is Patron], rushing to be there at the moment of death, spending however many hours afterwards with his family, then going to his funeral was appalling. I'm convinced she did it for the publicity and because she thrives on drama. He was a horrid, sycophantic poof who used people ruthlessly. He was a true opportunist and a great flatterer. I used to go to his lunches, which were frightfully grand. I was told that Basia Johnson [the Polish-born widow of the Johnson heir] got him launched. He blew hot and cold with people. Once I realized what he was really like, I distanced myself from him. I didn't go to his memorial service because I no longer liked him, and I thought it was pretentious in the extreme that his friends had to apply for tickets. Did you know he gave The Princess of Wales his diamonds? Why leave her diamonds when so many of his friends are in need? The whole scene made me sick."

Whether narcissism and public approbation do play a

part in Diana's motivation, only she can say for sure. But what is indisputable is that she is as committed to her work when the press and television cameras go away as when they are in evidence. She is aware, of course, as are all people working for charities, that the grander you are, the more of an opportunity you have to motivate others, and she uses her position to great effect. I personally think she should be commended for this, not criticized, for the presence of royal involvement always inspires everyone concerned with a project, and royal visits are both a reward and a fillip to greater action.

With this in mind, Diana now does a great deal of visits and openings. "She's been to many wards in the hospices," says John Coblenz. "Recently, she also went with Barbara Bush to the Middlesex Hospital, which we support." When she is not giving quiet words of encouragement and comfort to the ill and dying, her official engagements revolve around such milestones as the opening of projects. For CRUSAID, says John Coblenz, "She did the official opening of the Rodney Porter Ward at St. Mary's Hospital [where her sons were born]. She opened the FACTS Centre in North London earlier this year. This is a neighbourhood health and drop-in centre for HIV-positive people. She's also opened the offices of a group called Positively Women for us. It's a self-help group of women who have tested positive. They run a children's fund directly to benefit the children of HIV-positive mothers. We administer the fund."

All this work might seem frightfully worthy but awfully depressing to outsiders, and Diana was recently accused in the *London Evening Standard* of being something of a disaster-groupie. Her compassion was dismissed as co-dependency, her spiritual qualities equated with malfunctioning. Anyone who has actually done charity work, however, knows that great suffering and great joy are intermingled. Some of the most humorous and good-natured people are those whose circumstances would lead you to expect the opposite. Being with the disadvantaged, the needy, the infirm and the terminally ill is always moving, frequently inspiring, and often joyous. As no one has ever put it better than the Duchess of Norfolk, the founder of Help the Hospices, I shall let her speak: "I was so surprised by the feeling of trust, dedication and happiness, the first time I went to visit a hospice—St. Joseph's in Hackney—that I decided, 'This is what I want to do with my life.' I was astonished to see so much happiness in such a place," she told me once when we were speaking about what motivated her to begin her hospice crusade.

Penny Thornton had been right. Diana could turn her own suffering to advantage. She could use it to help others, and it could lead to fulfilment and, ultimately, to happiness. "She became much happier. She'd found her purpose in life," says a friend. "Needless to say, the courtiers didn't want her dragging her name into controversial and distasteful areas like AIDS. But she didn't give a stuff. She'd learnt from Prince Charles and Sarah [York]. You can do what you want, and there's not a damn thing they can do to stop you. Or, at least, not much. So, they hassle her about lending her name in an official capacity to AIDS charities. They think it would be impolitic for her to become a Patron. Inappropriate, they call it. But she does the work nevertheless. And there's nothing they can do to stop that, short of tying her to the bedpost and keeping her prisoner at KP."

Fortunately for the courtiers, especially her brother-in-law, The Queen's latest Private Secretary, whose influence has grown apace with his sister-in-law's celebrity, not all Diana's interests revolve around birth, death and dying. The courtiers enthusiastically encourage her associations with such safe but worthy charities as the English National Ballet or the British Youth Opera. "Her AIDS publicity makes them nervous," says the sister-in-law of the top-ranking courtier. "On the one hand, they love her being presented as Mother Teresa in a tiara. On the other hand, though, they can never quite forget that not everyone in the country sympathizes with AIDS victims. Of course it's prejudice. They believe no one can decry her for her links with cultural charities. But I'm of the opinion that they're mistaken. You mustn't forget they're an arrogant and insular lot. They judge everyone by themselves. They think ev-

275

eryone has *their* values. They don't see that a substantial proportion of this country's population doesn't give not a fig for anything cultural. I'd say the number of people who have objections to the royals supporting the arts is about equal to those who aren't in favour of them supporting AIDS. You can't please everyone, so you may as well do what you think is right. But then I'd say that, wouldn't I? I'm not a courtier. I don't inhabit an ivory tower and I'm not blind. All I can say is, thank God the Waleses are always defying their advisers."

Whatever the potential for criticism from the populace at large, some of Diana's strongest detractors have been from the very segment of society in which only admirers might be expected. As her renown has grown, it has not only evoked the disapproval of elderly ladies like her father's friends, but has also triggered off the competitive spirit of some of the celebrities who cross paths with her. I was recently at a luncheon where her hostess, a certain Princess, barely rose out of her chair to greet Diana when she arrived, late, at the table. The Princess's attitude was, "She was meant to be on time. If she hadn't been so busy talking to all her admirers, she'd have kept to her schedule. I'm not going to bob up like a jack in the box just because she's become such a superstar that everyone wants to meet her."

Nowhere was this competitive spirit more clearly illustrated, though, than in the build-up to "A Royal Gala Evening," which was held at the Departmental Auditorium on Constitution Avenue in Washington, DC, on Thursday 4 October 1990. It should have been the gala to end all galas. Conceived as a trans-Atlantic venture in aid of the London City Ballet, the Washington Ballet and Grandma's House, a home for abused and abandoned AIDS babies, it had a glittering committee of social and media luminaries such as Mercedes Bass, Judy Taubman, and Kari Lai. Tickets started at $3500 per person, going up to $5000 per person. According to a Palace source, Barbara Walters expected an exclusive interview with the Princess for the price of her ticket. It was not forthcoming and she felt unable to attend the event.

In addition, enough people associated with the event, had the media connections to throw a spanner in the works. "There was some adverse prepublicity about the price of the tickets. By then, the tide had begun to turn [in America]. Such expensive galas were becoming unpopular. They were uncomfortable reminders of the excesses of the Reaganite eighties. And the tickets *were* expensive."

Once the floodgates opened, a wave of bad publicity washed over the organizers. "It was easy to get the Americans annoyed. The organizers were shipping everything over from England: the food, the chefs, the flowers, the florists, even the gilt chairs. It stirred up a lot of latent colonial feelings of antipathy."

Some committee members, with a practised eye on public opinion, deserted the chairman in her hour of need. "A lot of the socialites didn't like having to go to Washington. They behaved like schoolchildren who set out to cut someone out, to ostracize someone. They gleefully tried to ruin the evening. They were on the committee, they'd made all these promises. Usually, when you're on a committee, you take a table. That's your unspoken commitment. Once the knives were out, they didn't honour their commitments with their tables."

Some committee members, like the cosmetician Georgette Mosbacher, went one step further. Having already paid for their tickets, they demanded their money back. "It was unheard of. No lady behaves like that. But these people didn't expect it to get out. They thought they could put the knife in, and someone else would come along and clean up the blood."

Diana flew into Washington to board a sinking ship. Preparatory to doing so, she met fifty of the people who had helped launch what threatened to be a social Titanic, at a reception at the British Embassy. In attendance were committee members such as Judy Taubman, Mercedes Bass, and the Canadian beauty Kari Lai.

The saboteurs, however, had reckoned without several factors. Diana still had more clout than they. Many of the people who had committed to attending still planned to, either through a sense of obligation to Diana or through adherence to honour and decency. Dr. Armand Hammer, Pamela Harriman (the Hon. Mrs. Averell Harriman), and Barbel Abela (whose husband was Prince Alfonso Hohenlohe's partner) bought tables for which they paid themselves. Evangeline Bruce, finding herself unable to come, nevertheless paid for her tickets. "The Palace and Diana came out looking brilliant," a committee member recalled. "There were wonderful pictures of her cuddling AIDS babies at Grandma's House and looking spectacularly beautiful at the Gala. She wasn't touched by the adverse publicity at all. She was regal and magical and no one could fault her. An enormous amount of good came out of it, despite the manoeuvrings to sabotage the event, and all the leaks to the press fomenting adverse publicity. It made $100,000 for each charity plus $20,000 for an organization which promotes British-American cultural exchange. And Princess Diana's favourable publicity with the AIDS babies raised public consciousness yet another degree. She was helping to take a lot of the fear out of AIDS."

The skill and facility with which Diana managed to rise above the stink is but one of many attributes she has displayed, as she has settled down to doing serious, constructive charity work. The social scene has even more snobs and arrogant imbeciles than it has bitches. It is therefore only natural that a reasonable proportion of them would attach themselves to various charities, and that some of these would cross paths with Diana.

The noted operatic impresario Alan Sievewright masterminded a unique opera and ballet gala in the presence of The Princess of Wales to raise funds for an arts charity in 1991. He said, "The whole evening was suggested by Prue Waterhouse and Chrisanthy Lemos [well-known charity fund-raisers]. I thought of asking the distinguished choreographer Ronald Hynd to create a new ballet specially for the occasion. The subject that seemed most appropriate was Sylvia, which is of course the story of the Goddess Diana, the chaste goddess of the hunt. As the gala was going to be held on 18 May, I suggested we dedicate it to the memory of the late Dame Margot Fonteyn, whose birthday would have fallen on that date. I asked

Montserrat Caballé, the great Spanish soprano, and Samuel Ramey, the great American baritone, to perform for nothing. Then some of the people associated with the charity arbitrarily informed us that they had changed the date and venue and said in that haughty, plummy way that brainless snobs have, 'You can inform MONT-serrat Ca-BARL-lay and Samuel RAH-meR of the new arrangements.' They didn't even know how to pronounce their names properly.

"It was outrageous. They're so pompous, those people, full of their own importance. Montserrat Caballé and Samuel Ramey were donating their services to a British charity —two foreigners, giving their time. Of course, it fell on my head, as I'd asked them. But I wasn't about to allow such disrespect to be shown to such great and generous artists. I spoke to Prue and Chrisanthy, and we decided to approach the Princess, who understood perfectly and said she was happy to go along with any changes we made." Not all royals are as accommodating or as flexible as Diana, whose co-operativeness and refusal to stand upon unnecessary ceremony have been much remarked upon by everyone who has ever worked with her.

Keeping the same date, and with the drawing card of Diana as their guest of honour, Alan Sievewright, Prue Waterhouse and Chrisanthy Lemos switched both the venue of the event and the beneficiaries. They renamed the event "Serenade to a Princess," and acquired the splendid Banqueting House in the Palace of Westminster, with its magnificent ceiling by Rubens in the Banqueting Hall, where dinner would be served and the performances staged. They also managed to enlist the services of some of the ballet world's greats, including the Royal Ballet's Bryony Brind, Sweden's Petter Jacobsson and Laurent Novis from the Paris Opéra Ballet. The charities became the English National Ballet, one of Diana's babies, and the British Youth Opera, an area in which Diana was developing an interest. The evening itself was a great success. It was captured on video and Diana happily gave her consent for it to be sold to raise further funds for the charities.

Ever resourceful, the mature Diana now never misses an

opportunity to connect either professionally or personally if she is moved. So it proved that evening in May 1991 at the Banqueting Hall. "As a result of that event," says Alan Sievewright, "she is now Patron of the British Youth Opera. She even attended a special performance of *La Bohème* in a new production at Sadler's Wells Theatre for them."

Alan Sievewright also learnt that Diana has a budding but genuine interest in opera (one of Prince Charles's passions). "Of course she loves dance, but she's also warmed up to opera. She listens to it. That's how we've all learnt, commoners and royalty alike—you have to listen to learn. She's building up a record collection of operas as well as her ballet collection and other music. At the British Youth Opera performance of *Bohème,* I drew her attention to a wonderful performance by the great English conductor, Sir Thomas Beecham. That's now been added to her collection. She'd never heard of it before. She already had a performance conducted by Karajan. She wrote me the most delightful letter. She definitely appreciates it."

Like everyone else who has worked with her, Alan Sievewright has the utmost respect for Diana. Nor is he easily deceived. He has known or worked with the most eminent names in international music. Everyone from Maria Callas to Grace Bumbry has been his personal friend or his professional colleague. "The Princess of Wales has a lot of perception. When you're in the glare of the public world, you've got to catch up fast. In terms of the arts, it's important that they get as much encouragement as possible. It's a tremendous fillip that the opera and ballet need. She's marvellous at this. She really does seem to care and she really does do her homework. And no, she doesn't strike me as being in the least bored by her work, nor does she come across as someone who is simulating interest. With her, what you see is what you get. And what you get is a lovely woman. You really do feel this caring nature."

Sad though it is that Diana had to find meaning through suffering, no one can deny that she has been a force for good. Beneath the beautiful packaging lies a tender heart, and it has made a great deal of difference to the quality of the lives of very many people throughout the world. If she did nothing else, or had no other virtues, she would still be an admirable and adorable person because of those contributions alone. That in itself is all the commendation she needs. But it is not the only commendation she deserves.

CHAPTER NINETEEN

Friends and Relationships

*I*f man does not live by bread alone, woman needs rather more than good works to fulfil her. As Diana gingerly climbed out of the black hole of despair, she was faced with a less than ideal personal life; her prospects were anything but inviting, unless she turned her gaze outwards, as her husband had done.

The Prince of Wales, unsurprisingly, was not about to recommend such a course of action to his wife. Few men are prepared to encourage the notion that the goose should live by the same set of rules as the gander. Despite ample precedents to the contrary, and the existence of an aristocratic and royal code of marital conduct, most men find that their pride alone prevents them from surrendering the atavistic rights of control and exclusion. Aristocrats and royals are as human as anyone else, with the same impulses as their less privileged brothers and sisters. Coming to terms with the rigours and civilized demands of a marriage that has lost its lustre is seldom painless for anyone. The nob in the castle is as gripped by jealousy and possessiveness as the beggar at the gate, and Prince Charles was as reluctant as any other man would be to countenance his wife's right to freedoms he was already enjoying.

Moreover, the well-being of the monarchy is never far

from the Heir to the Throne's thoughts, and there were dangers concurrent with any Princess of Wales living a full and active life. If word of this got out, it might, with dire consequences, alienate certain people.

Nevertheless, Diana was a young woman, still in her twenties. "She is very sensual and needs a lot of affection," says a friend. "She's very needy emotionally. She can't live without love."

True love is not always on tap when one needs it, but if one is young and beautiful, glamorous and charming, and The Princess of Wales, one can be reasonably sure of having a wealth of admirers. It was from amongst this number that Diana chose The King of Spain as confidant. "He's well known to be a great appreciator of women," says a European aristocrat whose husband is closely involved with the Royal Family. "To put it politely, he's a tremendous flirt. It's not as if to say he has to try very hard. He's a good-looking fellow and women appreciate him as much as he appreciates them."

King Juan Carlos was an ideal choice for a confidant: first of all, he is royal and could therefore be trusted to respect the boundaries of good taste. Secondly, he is a relation and keeping things in the family has long been the royal and aristocratic way. This applies not only in a personal sense, but also in a professional one. For example, The Queen rewarded Andrew Parker Bowles for distinguished service by extending his tenure as Commander-in-Chief of the Household Cavalry for a period of three years to five before making him Silver Stick in Waiting. Other royal servants have been similarly rewarded. Thirdly, his wife, Queen Sofia of Spain is well used to the displays of admiration surrounding her attractive husband and the prospect of a jealous outburst, indulged in by a consort of a later confidant, was therefore out of the question.

Their privacy protected, the two families joined forces in August 1986 for the first of their summer holidays at the Marivent Palace in Majorca, where King Juan Carlos and Queen Sofia spend each summer. There were cruises on the Spanish monarch's dazzling yacht *Fortuna*, excursions to exotic beaches and places of interest, water sports and all manner of other delights. Sometimes The Prince of Wales even left Diana to her own devices, going to stay with José Luis de Villalonga, Marquès de Castelvell, the aristocratic writer, who has a house in the village of Andratx.

By this time, the Prince had not only returned to the warm companionship of Camilla Parker Bowles, but had also come across a whole new crop of women who were anxious to share his close confidence. One such was the Marchesa di Frescobaldi, Bona, to her friends, a willowy blonde beauty. A decade or so older than Charles, she is married into one of the oldest and grandest families in the Florentine aristocracy and the family palace, bursting with fabulous treasures, became the setting for many intimate dinners and amusing lunches which Bona organized for her intellectual and sophisticated circle of friends. There they could talk about art, architecture, and all the other subjects to which informed and intelligent men and women of the world are drawn. Bona Frescobaldi was just the sort of woman The Prince of Wales regarded as an ideal confidante.

Bona Frescobaldi, however, also had a young and beautiful daughter, Fiametta. When the press got wind of Charles's interest in Italy's rarer treasures, they hurtled down a blind alley. Fiametta was portrayed as the woman in whom Charles had an interest, despite the fact that their relationship did not go beyond the loose parameters of family friendship. Nor would the Marchese and Marchesa di Frescobaldi have been pleased to find The Prince of Wales paying too much attention to their unmarried daughter. All was resolved when Fiametta became engaged to one of the d'Arenberg princes and has since become a princess herself. Her mother, meanwhile, remains on cordial terms with The Prince of Wales, although their friendship is no longer so close as it was.

As Charles and Diana pursued independent lives, Charles practised safety in numbers, spreading himself thinly amongst several confidantes. Camilla Parker Bowles still reigned supreme, but there were other women with whom he could discuss the deeper meanings of life, and who brought him amicable relief as well as companionship. Most, ironically, were older than he, but then experience has always been more attractive to Charles than naïvety.

There was Patti Palmer-Tompkinson, with whom the Prince skied and who nearly died with him during the avalanche at Klosters in 1988 that claimed Major Hugh Lindsay's life. She was badly injured and hospitalized in Switzerland, where he returned to visit her on several occasions. By that time the warmth and affection between them was in marked contrast to the iciness that typified his relationship with Diana. Someone who witnessed this said, "After the accident, Diana went bounding up to him, in full view of everyone, as if to say, 'Thank God you're alive.' He brushed her aside without a word. His attitude was clear to see. Rightly or wrongly, he felt that she was making a show for the benefit of onlookers. He wasn't having any of it."

There was also Candida Lycett-Green, daughter of the late Poet Laureate Sir John Betjeman and something of an expert in the field of architecture. She and Charles tour churches together, when they appear as engrossed in the glories of architraves and pediments as each other.

Lady Sarah Keswick, daughter of the Earl of Dalhousie and another woman a few years the Prince's senior, shares a love of music and laughter with Charles. The wife of banker John Keswick, and as such a member of the fabulously wealthy Jardine-Matheson families, Sarah Keswick was the *raison* for a scene that took place in the Royal Box at the Royal Opera House, Covent Garden. Despite Diana's acquisition of her own independent sources of companionship, she was still presenting a façade to her husband that belied this. That posture presented her with the justification to indulge in as much pique as she wished, and, in high dudgeon at Covent Garden, she screamed at Charles and Sarah Keswick, to the consternation of the people in nearby boxes. One of them says, "It was quite something, I can tell you. She didn't give a damn who heard her. She behaved more like a fishwife from Billingsgate than a royal Princess. Having seen her in action, I'll never again be taken in by that sweetness and light act. She could ride roughshod over an elephant."

Sarah Keswick, however, was not the only friend of Prince Charles's whose existence triggered Diana's feelings of jealousy and possessiveness. Two years ago, I was at polo at Smith's Lawn, Windsor. So too were the Prince and Eva O'Neill, a striking-looking blonde some years older than the Prince who was voted one of the most elegant women in the world at *The Best* Awards in Paris in 1989. Although I have only ever met Eva glancingly, London at a certain level is a small place and secrets are hard to keep—not that Eva seemed intent on keeping any that day: she was conspicuously in attendance upon The Prince of Wales.

Knowing that polo is a very seductive sport, The Princess of Wales has turned up unexpectedly at the polo ground on several occasions. "She [Diana] is very jealous and territorial," says a famous socialite who knows Eva O'Neill. "Even though the state of her marriage has long since ceased to give her the right to be possessive, she feels she's entitled to keep competition at bay. In her opinion, she's his wife, and that in itself gives her the right."

One incident that resulted from Diana's predilection towards jealousy is amusing. This took place in the changing rooms of the Guards' Polo Club, where The Prince of Wales and Eva O'Neill were discussing the finer points of play when a polo-playing friend of Charles's noticed that Diana had arrived and was on her way to join them. Appreciating what her interpretation might be, he set about averting a contretemps. This resulted in Anthony Taylor—who is married to brewery magnate Lord Daresbury's heiress daughter, the Hon. Susan Greenall, whose brother's wife is also Princess Beatrice of York's godmother—helping Eva to jump out of a window, and thereby avoiding a potential upset. Charles stood outside engaging Diana in conversation, keeping her well away from trouble.

Diana, for her part, has not found the path to confidential relationships easy. By nature she is too emotional to adjust herself easily to the restraints that such civilized accommodations require.

* * *

Although by no means complete, Diana's life had altered dramatically since the arrival of Sarah York, and this was nowhere truer than with regard to her friends. "Gone were the days when she was isolated in the Palace," says a former member of the Royal Household.

Until The Duchess of York's arrival, Diana had spent her time mostly with older people like Lord and Lady King, the Husseys, or her in-laws. She was good friends with Prince Andrew and Prince Edward (who is still the most frequent weekend visitor to Highgrove), as well as being close to her sisters, especially Jane, and, to a lesser extent, Lady Sarah Armstrong-Jones.

But these friends and relations were never enough. To her credit, Diana did not wish to be restricted to this tight little group from the upper reaches of the establishment, and with the Duchess came Diana's opportunity to expand her circle of friends. Sarah York knew an extensive network of people, who were young, fun-loving, and in some instances, racy. Generous by nature, she happily introduced Diana to all her friends, much to the Princess's delight and the Palace's consternation. "Some of it [the disapproval] was nothing but old fogeyism," says a Spencer cousin, "but some of the Duchess's friends did give them real cause for concern. They didn't like either of them mixing with Lulu Blacker, for example. Not after there was all of that awful publicity about her ex-boyfriend's [Jamie, Marquis of Blandford] problems with drugs. She burst into print admitting that she'd 'tried all kinds of drugs' herself. That sort of thing was bound to make the Palace nervous. Though, I daresay, if you stop to think of it, all the young people in that generation dabbled with exotic substances."

This was not strictly true. Diana and most of her circle had never experimented with drugs. But they were members of a generation that had been raised during the drug culture of the 1960s and 1970s, so they neither condemned nor spurned those who dabbled or developed problems.

Drugs aside, the Palace were soon frothing at the mouth because of some of the antics the naughty but nice Sarah and the newly daring Diana started to get up to. These were all harmless things, such as poling Major Hugh Lindsay and Lulu Blacker in the bottom with an umbrella at Ascot, or turning up at Annabel's dressed as policewomen with comedienne Pamela Stephenson and Elton John's wife Renate, but they seemed to horrify the press almost as much as the walking cadavers at the Palace.

Like just about everyone else in the country, in fact in the world, Diana now wished to choose her friends from amongst her peers: people of similar age, background and interests. Tired of being a prisoner in her gilded cage, ordinary in her tastes and egalitarian in spirit, she did not agree with the courtiers who believed that royalty must always set itself apart from mankind. She was really living for the first time in years. It felt good to have a peer group, to be a part of a crowd, and, now that she was out and about, she was adamant in her refusal to return behind bars. In her opinion, there was no valid reason why she could not relax and enjoy herself in the same way as other young people of her age, irrespective of rank or background. There was nothing wrong in eating and laughing with people you liked. Nor was there any valid reason why a contemporary royal should not be allowed to swim at public pools or play tennis at private clubs. She cared not a jot that The Prince of Wales and all the other born royals, with the exception of Princess Margaret, led sheltered lives behind the closed doors of their friends, in the age old tradition of reigning royalty. She intended to be a part of the mainstream of life, both professionally and personally. Kensington Palace was her home, not her prison, and like millions of other women all over the world she planned to leave it in the morning to go to work, and return to it at the end of the day, after she had lived in the real world. Princess Michael had been right. Fergie's influence was proving to be decisive.

Through her sister-in-law, Diana acquired new friends, including Kate Menzies, daughter of the newsagent magnate. They started to play tennis at the Vanderbilt Racquet Club in London's Shepherd's Bush, a seven-minute drive from KP, and sometimes were joined by Julia Dodd Noble, another of Fergie's introductions. However, a point came when Diana realized that she would have to be careful not to become too caught up in Fergie's world. "As soon as The Duchess of York settled into her role as a royal, she and The Princess of Wales drifted apart. It was a mutual thing," says a well-known beauty with royal connections. "Once the novelty of having a compatriot wore off, they went their own ways. They're still good friends, just not as close as they were. But they have their own lives to lead. They're busy women. And you can't have two bulls in one pen in any way. All the royals are so used to being the centre of attention that they like having their own show on the road."

As a result, not all of Diana's new friends came through Fergie. Another tennis partner was the Marchioness of Douro, wife of Lady Jane Wellesley's brother and a royal princess in her own right. Then there was Life Guards' Major David Waterhouse, the handsome nephew of the Duke of Marlborough and a bridge partner-cum-walker. The beautiful American-born Queen Noor of Jordan also became a friend, not only to Diana, but to Charles and his parents. Norton Romsey and his wife Penelope had been friends (and cousins) from the very beginning, but property developer Ben Holland Martin, Philip Dunne's sister Camilla (Millie), wife of Lord Soames's son Rupert, Viscount Bearsted's son the Hon. Michael Samuel and his wife Julia, sister of Sabrina Guinness, and Catherine Soames appeared to swell the ranks. Catherine was due to play an important part in Diana's life. Queen Elizabeth The Queen Mother's great-nephew the Earl of Strathmore and Kinghorne is married to the former Catherine Wetherill's sister Isa, and he says, "They're the closest of friends."

To her credit, Diana has chosen her friends for strictly personal reasons. She has not fallen prey to the royal trap, which is to choose your friends according to rank or convenience. As a result of criteria which she applies to her friendships, a surprising number of people, whom one would expect to know Diana well, barely know her. The Queen's godson, the Duke of Northumberland, says, "I don't know her well. I've only ever met her a few times." Mikey [Earl of] Strathmore, the Queen Mother's great-nephew, echoes Harry Northumberland: "I don't know her well at all. I've only ever met her about three times." She has also distanced herself from some of the friends she had when she was first married: Susan Hussey is no longer the bosom buddy she was, nor is Tally Westminster, whom Diana dismissed as being "too grand." Yet I distinctly remember Tally's cousin Janet, Marchioness of Milford Haven, who is incidentally Diana's cousin by marriage too, telling me on one occasion how very down to earth and ungrand the Duchess of Westminster is. "Mark it down to Diana's competitiveness," says a schoolmate of hers. "She was always like that. If someone was competition, she always came up with some reason to discount them." This could also account for the fact that all Diana's girlfriends and ladies-in-waiting are plainer than she is, in marked contrast to Fergie's entourage—two of whose ladies-in-waiting are stunning.

As with almost everything else in their lives, The Prince and Princess of Wales do not have similar taste in people, and this has become more pronounced with time. "He finds her friends boring and mindless. He says it's impossible to have a proper conversation with them. Or, for that matter, with her. They're not interested in ideas. Only in gossip." On the other hand, "Diana finds him and his friends stiflingly boring. Real downers. They're always pontificating about weighty matters when they could be enjoying themselves."

Because they value different qualities in people, Charles and Diana have wildly different opinions of people, a case in point being Diana's good friend Catherine Soames and her former husband. The Hon. Nicholas Soames, Tory MP for Crawley since 1983 and Sir Winston Churchill's grandson, had long been one of Prince Charles's closest friends. Indeed, so close were they that the Prince was best man at the couple's wedding. Yet Catherine Wetherill Soames's cousin, James Buchanan-Jardine says, "The Princess of Wales couldn't stand Nicholas Soames. She though he was loud. Always booming, the way all the Churchills do."

The end of the Soames marriage showed the extent of

change in the Royal Family's conduct. In a repetition of what had happened with Diana's parents and the Shand Kydds, the Soameses went on a skiing holiday where Catherine became intoxicated with the thrice-married ex-Olympic skier and fashionable antique dealer, Piers von Westenholz. She promptly bolted, though the object of her desires did not act reciprocally. In years gone by, such a series of events would have been enough to ensure the sudden cooling of a friendship between the figure of attention and the royal friend. But nothing has changed between Diana and Catherine Soames, who remains a close friend.

While Diana was reassessing her attitude towards her friends, she took another look at those friendships she had made prior to her marriage. Having distanced herself from them while she adjusted to her new life as a royal, she now decided it was both safe and desirable to rekindle those friendships whose fire had never entirely died out: Carolyn Pride, Sophie Kimball, and Laura Greig were only three of the many friends who were enthusiastically readopted. So too were others, including her old boyfriend George Plumptre and her good friend Rory Scott, who subsequently married the daughter of Sir Roderic and the Hon. Lady Brinckman, with Diana in firm and solitary attendance. The Prince of Wales never goes to her friends' weddings, receptions, or parties, and she seldom goes to his.

There was one old friendship which had never caused the Palace any problems and which was never discouraged. This was with Alexandra Loyd, whose father was The Queen's Land Agent at Sandringham. Her childhood friend with whom she shared beach holidays at Brancaster, and spent her farewell picnic to that way of life, prior to the move to Althorp when Viscount Althorp became Earl Spencer in 1975, Alexandra Loyd was viewed by the courtiers as "one of us." "Had Alex Loyd been her father's fifty-second cousin twenty-seven times removed, they would have preferred her to a duke's daughter without courtier connections," says the worldly-wise sister-in-law of the senior courtier. "They're so insular. As it is, she's a sweet girl." So profoundly was Alexandra Loyd approved of that she was soon appointed a lady-in-waiting.

This was indeed progress and showed to what extent The Princess of Wales had gained almost absolute control of her life. With the increase in her workload since her change in attitude towards work had come the need to have a full complement of ladies-in-waiting. Gone were the days when Anne Beckwith-Smith could virtually handle everything single-handedly with the help of Lavinia Baring and the former amateur jockey Hazel West, who had been on Diana's staff since the early days. The first supplements to the lady-in-waiting roster had been not Diana's personal friends, but Palace choices: Viscountess Campden, whose husband is heir to the Earldom of Gainsborough, and Jean Pike, whose uncle is the Duke of Norfolk and whose father, Major General Lord Michael Fitzalan-Howard, was Marshal of the Diplomatic Corps. Ironically, both are members of leading Catholic families, but religion, which had been so much a factor in disqualifying nannies for Prince William and Prince Harry, was fortunately immaterial when choosing public companions for The Princess of Wales. By the time the need arose for more additions to the roster, Diana was so firmly in command of her life that she was able to push through her demand for the appointment of two friends: one was the Palace favourite, Alexandra Loyd, the other her former flatmate, Laura Greig, now Mrs. James Lonsdale. And in 1992, she added a figure whose behaviour had previously caused severe discomfiture in palace circles: her unpredictable, strong-willed and highly emotional sister, Lady Sarah MacCorquodale.

The days when the Palace could dictate to Diana are over, and this is supported by the way ladies-in-waiting are chosen now. The Dowager Lady Torphichen's daughter, Anne Hodson-Pressinger has been "friends with Sarah Campden since childhood. She never speaks about her work at the Palace, and I, of course, would never embarrass her by asking about it. But I do know that the Palace had their eye on her for about five years before they asked her to become a lady-in-waiting. They had to be absolutely sure that she was discreet and suitable in every way. They're very strict about who they have." But ladies-in-waiting spend so much time with the royal they wait upon that Diana will never again have anyone who is not already her friend.

CHAPTER TWENTY

Whisper in My Ear

With her friendships and professional life sorted out, Diana could now turn her attention to finding herself a confidant who was more conveniently situated for the exchange of secrets than Juan Carlos of Spain. Confidential friendships conducted across the water force even the most independent of personalities into postures requiring too much resilience, and with the passage of time, Diana had realized that her need for companionship was not being met by a king in Spain. What she needed was an admirer in London, someone accessible, with whom she had something more than royalty and admiration in common. She wanted a bosom buddy, someone warm and affectionate with whom she could share her deepest secrets.

In 1987 Diana alighted upon Philip Dunne. He was Princess Alexandra's godson and the son of the Lord Lieutenant of Hereford and Worcester. An Old Etonian merchant banker, he also had a girlfriend: the Hon. Katya Grenfell, daughter of Lord St. Just and ex-wife of Sir Ian Gilmour's conductor son Oliver.

The prominent merchant banker and novelist Richard Szpiro, whose family virtually own the hugely successful publicly listed company, Wintrust, has known Philip Dunne for many years. "I met him skiing in Switzerland," he says. "We were in the same houseparty. In those days [the early 1980s] he was with Warburgs [the eminent merchant bank]. All the girls were after him, and I could see why. He's very good-looking, charming, intelligent. The classic tall, dark and handsome type. But there's a lot more to him. He's street-smart as well as civilized. He's got it all. When we got back to London he asked me to lunch. I was astonished when we were ushered into Warburg's private dining room. Just the two of us. I thought, This guy has more to him than meets the eye. How is it that someone who's so young, and has no seniority, can have the dining room to himself? He's worth watching. You can judge for yourself whether I was right."

Richard Szpiro was not the only person who had a high opinion of Philip Dunne. A fashionable socialite observed Diana and the banker lunching at Ménage à Trois. She noticed how interested each of them was in what the other had to say and left with the impression that they were deriving great pleasure from each other's company.

Philip Dunne joined Charles and Diana's party for skiing at Klosters, proving that The Prince of Wales did not disapprove of his wife's friendship. Back in England, gossip spread like wildfire on account of society's ever efficient version of the bush telegraph. Exclusive dinner tables everywhere clattered to the sound of approval for the way in which the Waleses were handling their differing approaches to companionship.

Diana went to stay with Philip Dunne at his parents' house, Gatley Park, near Leominster in Herefordshire, for the weekend. This excited a certain amount of comment because old-fashioned decorum had not been maintained. There was no chaperone. Philip Dunne's parents were skiing at Meribel while The Prince of Wales was away elsewhere. No one seemed to notice the anomaly of treating The Princess of Wales as if she were an errant fourteen-year-old virgin in nineteenth-century Spain. She and Philip Dunne were not alone in the house. There were the staff and the other members of the houseparty, who included his sister and her good friend Millie (Mrs. Rupert Soames, sister-in-law of her other good friend, Catherine Soames).

The ski season ended and Royal Ascot rolled around. Diana's friendship with Philip Dunne continued to bloom. He was a member of the Royal Family's party and accompanied her on her peregrinations to the Paddock, to the

Winner's Enclosure, and back to the tearoom in Her Majesty's Representative's Box.

One person, however, who was not witnessed dancing attendance upon Diana was Lord St. Just's daughter Katya Grenfell, Philip Dunne's official girlfriend who predated his meeting with the Princess. It takes no great feat of imagination to figure out that no woman is ever pleased when her boyfriend is known to be spending time in the company of another woman. Because the friendship between Diana and Philip Dunne was conducted mostly in full view of those closest to them, it became inevitable that there would be a certain amount of comment. This in itself is not unusual as all royal friendships excite interest. This is what happened at the dance to celebrate the marriage of the Marquis of Worcester to the actress Tracy Ward.

The Princess of Wales is well known for her flirtatiousness which was in part responsible for igniting the gossip that subsequently ensued. She was observed dancing for much of the evening with Philip Dunne and was seen to run her hands through his hair and even pecked him on the cheek in full view of everyone. The mere fact that this was done in public should have afforded her a measure of protection, but by this time it was obvious that she and the Prince were not getting on. He spent much of the evening huddled in conversation with Camilla Parker Bowles, studiously ignoring Diana, and at two o'clock departed without her. She remained behind and spent the rest of her time happily dancing the night away.

Immediately after the Worcester wedding dance, speculation about Diana and Philip Dunne arose in the press. This rumbled on throughout the summer. In July Charles and Diana spent their sixth wedding anniversary apart, in keeping with the way they had spent most of the preceding year. This separation did not pass unnoticed in the press, which erupted in an explosion of speculation during October, when The Prince of Wales flew down from Balmoral, where he had spent thirty days away from his wife, to join her in Wales for a visit to the victims of the Carmarthen flood. No sooner was the visit over than he fled straight back to Balmoral, without even bothering to pretend that he wished to spend any time with her. It could not have been clearer that they were leading separate lives, news which seemed to excite the press beyond belief.

Diana, by all accounts, was stunned by the adverse publicity she was now receiving. She knew, as do all members of royal and aristocratic circles, that she was not guilty of any wrongdoing. Confidential relationships, by their very nature, preclude the participants from indulging in anything that could be dubbed dubious, and she was therefore distressed that behaviour that had traditionally been adjudged correct should now cause her such problems. Ever since Fergie had married Prince Andrew and gone on to enjoy a brief romance with the press, during which she knocked her popular sister-in-law off the front pages, Diana had changed her attitude towards publicity. She had seen the threat and did not like it, with the result that she had been assiduously courting the media. Gone were the days when she complained about their attentions. She had even resorted to the other extreme, at Balmoral the previous winter, by purposely taking the children into the range of the cameras, so that she could begin receiving some more of the favourable publicity on which she was now hooked. Then, to her chagrin, just when she thought she was in for a smoother ride, along came the stories about her friendship with Philip Dunne as well as about the supposed disintegration of her marriage.

"To The Prince and Princess of Wales, this was unwarranted intrusion into their private lives," says a royal cousin. "They don't think the press has the right to poke its nose into their private arrangements. It's none of their business and they don't have the right to sensationalize perfectly normal, acceptable, harmless everyday marital arrangements."

This, of course, is the dichotomy. If what Charles and Diana have for breakfast can be discerned as newsworthy, how much more so the way they organize their married life.

"The Queen and her advisers were appalled by the publicity about the marriage," says the noblewoman whose brother-in-law is senior courtier. "That included Diana's brother-in-law, Robert Fellowes. He had no sympathy at all for Diana. He wasn't about to have his sister-in-law affect everything he holds dear. I am told that he personally gave her the message: get yourself together. The Prince of Wales was told to make more of a point of being seen to spend more time with her, and when he didn't, evidently The Queen herself got [Sir] William Heseltine [her Private Secretary at the time] to arrange for them to come to Buck House to see her after an evening engagement. They arrived at something like eleven o'clock, and when he baulked at being with Diana more, The Queen herself hauled him over the carpet. He left with his tail between his legs. Thereafter, they were together more, though nothing had really changed between them."

Philip Dunne received a telephone call from the Palace instructing him to stop seeing Diana. Throughout the press speculation, he displayed commendable discretion. "At the height of the Princess of Wales sensation, we had a meeting arranged," says Richard Szpiro. "I got a telephone call from him asking that I meet him, I forget where. He was in hiding at the time. He'd gone to ground. We had the meeting; he was in great shape. But not once did either of us allude to the circumstances surrounding him."

"After there's publicity, these things always come to a knotty end," remarks Nigel Dempster, who is something of an expert in this area. Unless Diana wished to flout Palace convention—and she is no rebel—she had no choice but to bring her friendship with the merchant banker to an end.

This, of course, was not the first time that the newspapers had punctured Diana's balloon. At a party to celebrate Sarah Ferguson's impending nuptials at the Guards' Polo Club, which was then headed by Major Ronald Ferguson, Diana encountered an admirer. Charlie Carter was a well-known man about town, debonair and attractive, a safely married financier. They danced half the night away and when they were not dancing were deeply engrossed in conversation. At one point, unbeknown to the press, they went outside for some air and were observed vigorously arguing their points by a close friend of mine. There ensued widespread press publicity about Diana's choice of a dancing partner and this, together with Charlie Carter's basic unsuitability as a confidant for the Princess, resulted in the stymieing of any future friendship.

But Diana has a resourceful as well as a determined streak in her nature. She was not about to let the press ruin her every chance of finding a companionable confidant. The surest way of a Princess assuring herself of discretion, as Diana knew from the Princess Royal's example, was to choose a confidant from amongst the royal ranks. Anne had done so, by developing a close friendship with one of her detectives, and Diana, bruised by her forays into the world at large, now did the same.

Sergeant Barry Mannakee was a personable and attractive man, ideally situated to cater to Diana. His presence, of all people's, would not arouse undue chatter, for he had a permanent and valid reason for being with her. Palace life "is a rabbit warren of gossip, with everyone invariably knowing what everyone else is doing," says a top-ranking courtier's sister-in-law. "It is impossible to keep secrets, especially of a confidential nature, but, more than being gossipy, it is snobbish in the extreme. There is a harsh and inflexible hierarchy which only the royals themselves are willing to overlook. That means that anyone who is earmarked as being above himself is due for the chop."

This proved to be the case with Sergeant Barry Mannakee. "He was not a gentleman. The mere fact that he was The Princess of Wales's confidant was enough for the snobs to conclude that he was above himself," says the courtier's sister-in-law. "Such a position should only ever be enjoyed by a gentleman. The fact that both The Princess of Wales and The Princess Royal had ignored such prejudice did not make their actions commendable in the eyes of others. It simply meant they did not know how to conduct themselves. The snobs therefore felt compelled to deprive them of their companions." Both detectives were duly transferred away from the Royal Protection Department.

On a private occasion recently I was speaking about this particular subject to a friend of The Princess of Wales, a well-known financier. He seemed genuinely panic-stricken on my behalf: "You'd better be very careful what you say you're writing. I'm not saying you have anything to fear from the royals themselves, but MI5 are pretty unscrupulous, and will wipe you out if they feel you're writing a book that threatens the monarchy. I know as a fact that Diana was having a confidential relationship with that detective who died in an accident. When the powers-that-be found out about it, they moved him. Then, when they got wind that he was going to go public, they laid plans to get rid of him. Diana herself told me this. They were very lucky when providence played right into their hands and he was involved in a genuine road accident." Mannakee died after a Suzuki motorcycle, driven by another police officer, and on which he was a passenger, was in collision with a Ford Fiesta, whose driver was a 17-year-old, in East London during July 1987. "To this day," the financier added, "Diana believes that MI5 opportunistically used this event to rid itself of a threat to the Monarchy and is nervous that they could target one of her other friends, were they also to be regarded as a threat."

One person who would never be tempted to speak publicly about his friendship with Diana was Captain James Hewitt of the Life Guards, who became the next and so far the most enduring confidant. Moreover, he is eminently suitable for this honoured mantle, being a gentleman by birth, the son of a retired Army officer, Captain John Hewitt, and his wife Shirley, who run a riding school overlooking the River Exe. He knows the rules and plays by them.

"Jamie Hewitt came into Diana's life when he was posted at Combermere Barracks, Windsor," says a well-known social figure, who is the son-in-law of a duke. "Diana met him because he was chosen to teach her to ride." An excellent equestrian, the dashing Captain is not only a four-handicap polo player but also a tall, husky, charming blond. Furthermore, he is a "simple, uncomplicated chap," a friend corroborates. "The opposite of The Prince of Wales. Jamie's funloving and likes a good laugh, but he's not the world's deepest thinker."

Diana had finally found someone with the attributes

necessary for a compatible and suitable confidant. He was young, attractive, companionable. He was suitable. And he was not so grand that he would eclipse her. Gradually, Diana and Jamie developed a regard for one another, becoming closer and closer friends until finally she realized they had reached a plateau where she could safely entrust her deepest and most personal secrets to him.

The relief of arriving at such a rewarding juncture must have been overwhelming for Diana, who is an emotionally needy woman and cannot exist without the warmth and approval that only a loving male companion can provide. As she and Charles were still leading completely separate lives, this attention was something she had had to look for outside her marriage.

By this time, the Waleses' domestic arrangements accommodated their divergent lifestyles. Diana remained in London during the week, while Charles operated out of Highgrove. On weekends she took the children down to Gloucestershire to see their father. This still continues, although now Prince William is at boarding school she meets him and his father at Highgrove on a Friday afternoon with his brother Harry.

Despite the latitude between the Prince and Princess and the public show of unity instigated by The Queen, Charles and Diana were still getting along no better than they had for years. "There were frequent, cataclysmic rows," says a royal relation. "There still are. Unless there is company, they are incapable of being together for more than five minutes without screaming at each other. If they're not rowing, they're freezing each other out with icy silences. It doesn't make for pretty viewing."

This royal relation was not convinced that Charles and Diana like one another. "They're antipathetic personalities. They're completely incompatible. I don't think they like each other very much. In fact, I'll go further and say, I don't believe they like each other at all. But that's not a reflection on the worth of either of them. All sorts of mammals have natural aversions to one another. Cats and dogs, for instance, don't usually like each other. And so it is with The Prince and Princess of Wales. Each is a really wonderful person on their own. Put them together and you get a cat and dog fight."

According to this relation, each had wounded the other in ways they found unforgivable. To Diana, Charles's disinterest in her and his withdrawal from the pleasures of the marriage, coupled with his adherence to old and new confidantes, had hurt her so deeply that she could never again feel about him the way she had once felt. He, on the other hand, felt she had set him up in more ways than one. Aside from concealing her real personality until after the marriage, she had caused him to be portrayed in an unflattering and untrue light.

"The press are always banging on and on about how jealous he is of her success. That's not true," says the same relation. "He was initially delighted with it. I agree, he wouldn't have been human if his nose hadn't been slightly out of joint when the press started marginalizing him and the causes he cares about to report on which dress she was wearing. But he wasn't jealous of her. He was annoyed with the press and their lowest-common-denominator mentality. And she knew this was a sore spot with him. But she's very competitive and loves being the centre of attention, and she was playing to the gallery long before he cottoned on to what she was doing. He only realized it when things got bad between them, and she started openly sabotaging him. Once, he was making an important speech, I forget about what. He'd spent months working on it, which she knew only too well. What does she do? She elects to make a speech as well, on some sensationalist subject like AIDS or marriage guidance. She knew as well as you or I that the rarity value alone of her giving a speech would grab the headlines. And we all know that the press will always publish a picture of a pretty girl over one of any man, which gives a glamorous woman in the public eye a tremendous advantage over her male counterpart."

Rivalry became the key word to describe not only The Prince and Princess of Wales's relationship, but also that of their competing staffs. "It was impossible to remain neutral," says a former member. "You had to throw your lot in with one or the other. Then you treated the opposing team with as much suspicion as you'd treat any enemy."

That made for an unpleasant atmosphere at the offices in Buckingham Palace and at Kensington Palace, where there were further offices downstairs. "The Princess of Wales was elated when their offices were moved lock, stock and barrel to St. James's Palace in 1989," says a courtier. "She told me she was tired of living over the shop."

The move, however, has not altered the atmosphere in the competing households of Wales versus Wales. "The Prince doesn't like that state of affairs," remarks a royal cousin. "He recognizes the potential for damage. They should both be working for the good of the crown. They should be shoring each other up. But that doesn't happen. If the Princess or her staff can top the competition, that is to say The Prince of Wales, they will. As long as they don't get found out. No. Not by the Palace. By the public. It's all geared to the public and their perception of the Princess."

"The Princess of Wales has a fatal combination of faults for a man like The Prince of Wales," says a relation of the Prince's. "She is stubborn, competitive, and domineering. In his eyes, the only sort of man who can live with a woman like that without being miserable is a wimp. He's also got a strong character, and feels that any man with any character at all is going to find himself perpetually walking over a minefield."

Something else that contributed to the explosiveness of the terrain within the marriage was the children. The tussle over who should be the more influential parent has not been resolved. "Once the boys ceased being toddlers, it was easy for the Princess to marginalize him as a father. The Prince of Wales is a very busy man," this relation continues. "He has far more work than the Princess. This is not readily apparent because a lot of the work he does has nothing to do with official engagements. It's easy for someone reading the Court Circular to conclude that he's doing nothing while she's slaving away because she has three public engagements for a day and he has none. But that doesn't mean he's at home lolling about in a hammock. There's the Duchy of Cornwall work, there's The Prince's

Trust, his meetings with industrialists, and one thousand and one other things that the public never read about.

"Well, a mother who resents her husband's influence over the children can very easily manipulate things so that the father's influence is eroded. This is what The Princess of Wales has done. I'm not saying she's done it out of malicious motives, because I don't believe she has. She feels being a mother is a woman's most important role. The primary influence in a child's life should be the mother's. Being a father isn't so important for a man and he shouldn't be allowed to eclipse the mother's role. But the motive doesn't matter. It's the effect that counts. No man who loves his children and takes a real interest in them, as The Prince of Wales does, appreciates being marginalized like that. I'm sure it hasn't helped matters that he's also been accused of being a negligent father, when he's anything but. But how do you fight a set-up like that?

It is fairly common for the products of troubled backgrounds to repeat the patterns set in childhood when they become parents, and Diana has been making the mistake her father did. "She uses the children as a way of getting back at Prince Charles," a Royal relation says. "They've become a battlefield. She tugs them to and fro, jealously keeping them away from him, and thwarting him whenever she can. If those boys don't grow up to be emotional messes like her, it will be a miracle. Not only does she use them like a tug-o-war, but she spares them nothing in the way of rows. She rants and raves away at their father even when they're around. He doesn't think all that turmoil can be good for them and does what he can to keep it to a minimum. But she never stops to think they might be disturbed by the fights she has with their father. If he tries to walk away, she pursues him, accusing him of being spoiled or weak. He does his best to protect them from the worst excesses of her tantrums, but she accuses him of trying to bring the children up with a false view of life. There's no way you can win with someone like that.

"She also does something else which all of us find deeply disconcerting. She is forever telling the boys that she loves them more than their father. It's as if she's in some diabolic competition. That cannot be doing them any good. How does he respond? He tries not to get sucked in. He tries to avoid competing with her for their affection and regard. He feels it will only tear them apart. He takes the view that they can feel his love and that they need peace and stability. She furnishes them with enough friction for both of them. He was brought up in a harmonious environment and does everything he can to give William and Harry as much of one as he can provide. But it breaks his heart, for he loves those boys as much as she does. If you ask me, he loves them even more. His love is unselfish. He doesn't care if they prefer their mother to him. He only wants what's best for them. That's more than I can say for her. Mixed up with her love for those boys is a tremendous amount of ego. It's a terrible thing to say, I agree, but it's true."

Charles's relation also denies that he is a negligent father. "He doesn't spend that much time in London, but whenever he's there, he does the school run." This was indeed confirmed by Caroline Waldegrave, wife of the Tory Minister the Hon. William Waldegrave, who was quoted in several newspapers saying, "My child also goes to the same school, and I often see [Charles] there in the morning. Last week he was there twice." The Prince, however, is a busy man, and like most busy men, his schedule does not allow him to play nanny to his children any more than Diana's allows her a similar luxury.

"At times, the tensions between the Prince and Princess have been so great that he has had to get away from her. If he didn't, he'd do something he'd regret, or make himself ill. That's why he's sometimes away from the boys for long stretches. Because he has to get away from her. It's the only way he can cope and still remain married to her."

Matters within the family were not improved when Captain James Hewitt became a figure of affection in the boys' life. "She [Diana] got him to help the boys with their riding," says a famous aristocratic beauty. "They're potty about him. He's fun, and there's never any tension between him and their Mummy. This makes for a very jolly atmosphere, quite in contrast to the normal family one. They love their father, of course they do. He's their father, and a very kind, concerned, interested one, too. But which child doesn't love the special family friend who represents fun and games and laughter?"

Charles, however, had his come-back. William and Harry were attending Wetherby School in Pembridge Square, Notting Hill, having first been sent to nursery school at Mrs. Mynors nearby. "The Princess wanted the boys to stay at home until they were twelve. She did not want them sent away to boarding school at eight, the way she and The Prince of Wales and all their friends were. She said young children need their mothers. They need home life."

Had the children not been yet more ground for competition, it is distinctly possible that Prince William would have remained at home until he was ready to attend public school at the age of twelve. "The Prince of Wales hated boarding school," says a relation of his. "He would never have sent William away at so early an age if he hadn't been convinced it was for his own good."

Yet another Royal connection comments, "She's a good and loving mother, but the problems within their marriage were tilting the balance too much in her favour. This wasn't good for the boys." So the Prince decided that William would have to go away to boarding school. "Diana was not in favour, but she had no choice in the matter. The education of the Heir in Line to the Throne, and his immediate Heir Presumptive, are not purely personal affairs. She could kick up all the fuss she wanted, at the end of the day, this was one time her will was not going to prevail."

Moreover, The Prince of Wales and the royal advisers had one red herring with which Diana could not argue. "They said William had to go to a 'proper' prep school otherwise he wouldn't be on stream for one of the good public schools. Certain prep schools feed certain public schools, and they were able to use that as a reason why he should be sent away. It was nonsense. Of course it was nonsense. Even if he had an IQ of 70 and couldn't add up two and two, every school in the country would bend over backwards to take the future King as a pupil," adds the sister-in-law of the senior courtier.

William was duly accepted for boarding school, and in September 1990, The Prince and Princess of Wales took him to Ludgrove School near Wokingham in Berkshire to start his first term. He is due to remain there as a weekly boarder until he is accepted by his public school. There has been some talk that, when that day comes, he will be sent to Sedburgh in Cumbria. I, for one, am hoping that will not be the case. It is my favourite boys' school, one that I have recommended to friends and would send any son of mine to, if I had one. I should hate to see it ruined by Prince William's presence, which is precisely what will happen if he attends it, for what is presently an ideal public school free of the taint of fashion or snobbery, will become the most fashionable place for the sons of snobs. Far better to let him go to Eton, where speculation also places him, and which has long been tainted by the dual blemishes of snobbery and fashion.

Prince Harry, meanwhile, remains at Wetherby, until he too is old enough to be sent away to Ludgrove. He too will become a weekly boarder, returning home to Highgrove for weekends, during which he will see his mother, who leaves London each Friday to go to Gloucestershire until Sunday afternoon. The Prince of Wales remains there throughout the week, unless he has official engagements or other business in London.

♛ ♛ ♛
.

CHAPTER TWENTY-ONE

Damage Limitation

When he is in residence at Kensington Palace, Charles sleeps in his dressing room, leaving Diana to enjoy the peace and solitude of their marital bedroom. "They haven't slept together for years," says a courtier's aristocratic sister-in-law. "That's why she's always saying two children are enough and she doesn't want any more. Unless she wants to do a Queen Marie of Roumania or a Violet, Duchess of Rutland—which she does not—her family has to be complete. I understand from a friend of his, he'd sooner touch a barge pole than make love to her, and she'd sooner have the barge pole than him."

Queen Marie of Roumania's two youngest children, Princess Ileana and Prince Mircea, were fathered by Prince Barbo Stirbey, not her husband King Ferdinand, while the paternity of the Duchess of Rutland's daughter Lady Diana Cooper was the subject of much speculation, all of it inclining away from the Duke towards Harry Cust.

Despite the evident lack of sympathy between The Prince and Princess of Wales, their marriage did settle down into a recognizable pattern throughout the late 1980s and into 1991. Had they managed to cultivate a greater rapport, their marriage could even have been accounted a great success in royal and aristocratic terms. They had produced two beautiful children. They had successful professional lives. They fulfilled the public, social and worldly requirements of marriage so ably that each had increased the stature of the other. For all its pitfalls and shortfalls, theirs was an enduring union, secure against separation or divorce, and productive to boot. However, because of the problems between them, the marriage could only be accounted at best a limited success.

The year 1991 became the time when the limitations within the marriage came perilously close to revelation. Once more the media turned the spotlight on to the marriage, questioning not only its success, but whether it would last at all. It also became the year when Diana made her first serious public miscalculation since she had so ill-advisedly confided her desire to marry Charles to the Press Association's reporter.

The year began quietly enough, though those who knew what was really going on behind the scenes noticed that Diana was unwittingly giving away clues. These were all tied up with the Allied response to the Iraqi invasion of Kuwait, for, to Diana, the invasion was a matter of deep personal concern, and she was making no secret of the avidity with which she was following events, especially once the Allied troops in the Gulf started fighting. For instance, on one official engagement, she said that she had stayed up until five o'clock that morning, glued to the television. This was quoted extensively, strengthening her reputation for selfless concern with the lot of her fellow humans.

Although genuinely concerned about the welfare of all the British in the Gulf, Diana's actions were not altogether selfless or impersonal. "The reason why she was so interested in the fighting in the Gulf was that her confidant, Major [temporarily] James Hewitt, had been transferred there along with the men of 'A' Squadron, which he'd joined on Boxing Day when he'd taken up his post with the British Army of the Rhine in Germany," reports a well-known social figure, son-in-law of a duke and royally well-connected. "He was fighting." Dibbs, as Jamie Hewitt calls her, was therefore frantic for any news she could glean about the conflict, and when he led his men into battle against the Iraqi Army, she could not contain her anxiety. This manifested itself in sleepless nights and constant viewing of the television for reassurances of his and the troops'
309

safety. In the event, she was relieved and proud when the gallant Major and his men wiped out 300 tanks and took 8000 prisoners.

Keeping in close touch with her budding hero was a priority for Dibbs. This she did by letter as well as with television, but, regrettably for Diana, she was not the only attractive blonde to do so. Emma Stewardson was Jamie Hewitt's official girlfriend, and she too wrote and received letters. It is to the jealous Miss Stewardson, who finally got tired of taking a back seat to the competition, that Diana "attributes the blame for nearly ruining things with Jamie Hewitt," says a friend.

A similar type to the Princess, but paler and plainer, Emma Stewardson lived near Highgrove House in Gloucestershire. She herself has admitted that once, when he stood her up during the day, she kept a watch at the gates of Highgrove House. Later in the afternoon she observed him departing after a long lunch. Tired of playing second fiddle to the glamorous Princess of Wales, Emma Stewardson sought to gain vengeance and enrich herself in the process. In March 1991, therefore, she sold her story to the *News of the World*. "It was an innocuous story," says Judy McGuire, the paper's star interviewer. "We love the Princess."

The *News of the World* story rattled Diana. "She was seriously worried about the consequences," says a friend. "She remembered only too well what had happened when the story about Philip Dunne got out." She did not want to have to give up a confidant who had brought her so much comfort and happiness over the years. Nor did she look forward to the prospect of termination, with the inevitable consequence of enduring a painful period of loneliness until another suitable confidant came along. "She wasn't sure what to do though, to prevent further newspaper reports, so she did nothing," comments a friend.

"Then Nigel Dempster wrote two discreet and informed pieces in his column," the friend continues. "You wouldn't have known what he was getting at unless you were privy to what was going on, which few people are, of course, but it freaked her out. She knew just as you and I do that his sources are impeccable. He is on a friendly footing with just about everyone of any consequence, from Princess Margaret and Princess Michael to God knows who else. His wife [Lady Camilla, only child of the late Duke of Leeds] is also related to Queen Elizabeth. She just held her breath and waited for the next story to appear. It was like the Sword of Damocles hanging over her head, ready to drop and chop it off at any minute. It wasn't an easy time for her. Her friendship and her reputation were at stake."

"Her reputation matters to her. It matters a lot. The Princess of Wales is a perfectionist," a famous connection of the Royal Family elaborates. "Like most perfectionists, she cannot stand people seeing her as anything but perfect. She hides her flaws carefully and presents a perfect façade.

"She sincerely believes The Prince of Wales has forced her into the predicament she's in. She truly believes that the way the marriage has gone has been his fault entirely. As far as she's concerned, she was a blushing maiden, desperately in love with him, when he married her. He let her down. He was the one who didn't love her, not vice versa. She really believes this, as genuinely as a Rastafarian believes that the late Emperor Haile Selassie is God."

In an attempt to preserve her relationship and her reputation, Diana then made her first serious public miscalculation since 1980. "Her thirtieth birthday and tenth wedding anniversary were coming up in July," says a famous connection of the Royal Family. "She thought she could play these cleverly. Save her skin and stick The Prince of Wales at the same time.

"She overplayed her hand, and nearly brought about the very thing she feared the most. It didn't take genius to figure out that the press would go wild if she allowed her thirtieth birthday to pass unmarked. The Prince of Wales knew this too. He wanted them to have a large dance to celebrate her birthday. But she said no. She was adamant. Nothing could convince her to change her mind. No matter how much he tried to get her to see sense, she didn't want to know. She's very canny and wily, as you doubtless know. I am firmly convinced she quite deliberately set him up.

She fully expected everyone to sympathize with poor Diana, whose mean and callous husband treated her so badly that he didn't even mark her milestone birthday. In my opinion, the object of the exercise couldn't have been clearer. She was manipulating public opinion so that she would get a huge wave of sympathy at The Prince of Wales's expense. In so doing, she would distract attention away from her confidential life and give his reputation a sneaky kick under the table. It was a very clever plan, and it nearly succeeded."

On the day of her birthday, 1 July 1991, Diana did indeed wake up to a favourable press, all of which was highly laudatory of her and critical of her husband. "The way she planned the day was an exercise in self-promotion," the Royal Family's famous connection continues. Diana had accepted an invitation from Rainbow House, a proposed children's hospice in Walsall, to attend a fundraising luncheon at the Savoy Hotel, where Phil Collins the rock star was earmarked to sing Happy Birthday to her. "Her office was instructed to express her wishes that her thirtieth birthday be treated as just another day, a request which she knew as well as you or I, they'd ignore. But it would earn her Brownie points for modesty." As indeed it did.

"She was not content merely to set him up," adds the same family connection. "She had a message to deliver to the world, and the message was that there was no man in her life and that all hints about Jamie Hewitt were wide of the mark. That's what accounted for her extraordinary comment at the luncheon, when she said, 'I'm going to celebrate my birthday at home alone with the only man in my life tonight: Prince Harry.' If you stop to think of it, except as a message, it was completely uncalled for. And no matter what, it was rather tasteless. I know I'm not the only person who thought so."

The question of what Diana did on her thirtieth birthday has never been entirely resolved. There was a story around in fashionable circles that Diana was not alone, but spent the evening with a few very close friends at Kensington Palace, including Captain Hewitt, who was on leave from his post in Germany. Nor was the Palace very helpful in clearing up this mystery, when asked. They claimed it was purely a private matter and they could not comment one way or the other.

Having sown the wind, Diana now reaped the whirlwind, which struck with unseemly haste. "His [Prince Charles's] friends had had enough of her manipulation. They refused to let her get away with dropping him in it when it hadn't been his fault. They leaked the story to Nigel [Dempster] of how he'd wanted to have a dance for her and she was the one who wouldn't have it," says the royal connection. "That did it. Nigel published the story and she didn't have quite such a large percentage of the sympathy vote any longer. Though, it must be said, she's been skillful at putting her image across. He could be bound to a post fifty feet away from her, his hands tied behind his back, gagged and blindfolded, and, completely unprovoked, she could charge across and stab him in full view of a thousand witnesses. It could be filmed by dispassionate photographers, and still a good 70 per cent of the people who saw it would refuse to accept that she hadn't somehow been the victim."

Irrespective of who was the victim and who the persecutor, Diana's refusal to allow Charles to mark her birthday again focused the spotlight on to the state of their marriage. This was the second time in four years that the media were able to indulge in their favourite sport of speculating on whether the marriage was in trouble and, if so, whether it would end in divorce.

"No one cares what she [Diana] does privately," says the noblewoman with brother-in-law at court. "But everyone certainly does care if her public actions threaten to diminish The Prince of Wales, or to tarnish him in any way. Hurting him is hurting the throne. The difficulty is, if she is hurt, so too is the throne. That's the dilemma The Queen has with The Princess of Wales as well as with others. They have to be protected. To hurt them is to hurt the Royal Family and ultimately the monarchy. So on occasion you have the anomaly of the Royal Family having to protect someone whose behaviour is perceived as harming the throne."

Had Diana really expected to get away with the wilful

creation of controversy, she was in for a shock. "The Queen herself gave both of them a talking-to," says a cousin. "She warned them that they were putting the crown in jeopardy. They are the future King and Queen. Their behaviour counts. They're not like the other royals, whose antics don't really matter. The Queen told them to get their act together, to present a united front in public at all times, and to behave so that their conduct defeats the rumours. She also banned the Princess from going out without the Prince, obviously unless it's on an official engagement or something where he wouldn't ordinarily accompany her."

Diana herself has corroborated this curtailment of her activity. At her former flat-mate Virginia Pitman's wedding to Henry Clarke in September 1991, she explained how sorry she was not to come on to the reception in Chelsea. "The Queen's banned me from going to [social] things without my husband," she explained, returning home immediately after the church service.

Not content to leave her son and daughter-in-law up to their own devices, however, The Queen took other steps to ensure that they present a united and de-scandalizing front to the watching world. "She recommended a series of activities that were calculated to show that the marriage was not in trouble," says the courtier's sister-in-law. "She also said she didn't want further repetition of the conjecture in the future. As we all know, a recommendation from The Queen is an order that no one dares disobey."

Charles and Diana, only too mindful of the damage they could cause the monarchy if they did not abide by The Queen's instructions, did not need a third prompting. They immediately started to appear in public together, even on official engagements to which only one of them had been invited. For instance, on Monday, 8 July 1991, Charles accompanied Diana to the Royal Albert Hall, where she had had a longstanding engagement with the London Symphony Chorus, of which she is patron. They were as affectionate towards one another as if they were newly-weds. They also put up a good front five evenings earlier when they attended a fundraising recital and dinner at the Ban-

314

queting House for the Duchess of Norfolk's charity, Help the Hospices, to which they had both been asked, and to which they had both committed themselves some months before.

All over the world, people seemed eager to follow the saga of the Waleses' marriage, and the media, naturally enough, were happy to oblige. This was better than *Dynasty* or *Dallas* in their heyday. Would they split up? Were they on the outs? Had they touched hands in public? Did they sleep together? Did they even talk? As the Prince and Princess appeared together night after night, working hard to defeat the rumours of a rift by giving the impression that they had achieved a sudden rapproachment, all these questions, and more, were being asked around the world. But no one in the know provided answers.

With no one to provide concrete information, the press were forced to speculate about the true state of the marriage. "Nothing actually changed between the Prince and Princess," says a friend. "The only difference was that they made more of a show of being together." This pleased the press and the Palace, but The Queen made doubly sure that the glue stuck on the patch-up job. "She was behind the 'second honeymoon' cruise," a royal cousin confirms. "The Queen orchestrated the whole thing. She and King Constantine [of the Hellenes] arranged it all."

Majorca was ruled out as being an unsuitable place for such an important public-relations exercise. "He's the one [King Constantine] who got John Latsis to lend him his yacht." The *Alexander* is the third largest yacht in the world. On a par with *Britannia,* it is an ocean-going vessel with every luxury. The 81-year-old billionaire owner was only too delighted to oblige his King, whom he esteems like most of the other Greek shipowners, and who is firmly convinced that Constantine will eventually return to his crown and homeland, as Greek politics have a cyclical pattern, and practically every Greek king has endured a period of exile.

As the cruise was not really a second honeymoon for their cousins the Waleses, the King was accompanied by his Queen and younger children, as well as Princes William and Harry, Princess Alexandra (whose mother was born Princess Marina of Greece) and the Hon. Sir Angus Ogilvy, Lord and Lady Romsey and their children, including their late daughter Leonora, and detective Graham "Smudger" Smith, who was recovering from throat cancer. There was much speculation as to whether the generous Mr. Latsis, who was picking up the vast cost of running his vessel, was on board. The press were able to receive neither a confirmation nor a denial from any source, but a friend of mine who works for him says, "Mr. Latsis was not on board. He gave them the use of the boat. Full stop."

The cruise itself was a success and with the guests presented as the hosts, it achieved all its public aims. Privately, it was enjoyable. "It was fun," says a connection of the Royal Family. "They went all over the place: to Greece and Sardinia and Menorca. Diana loves the sea and the sun. Like everyone else, she's happy when things are going her way. And they were. Who wouldn't like cruising on one of the world's greatest yachts? It's every bit as magnificent as the *Britannia* and a lot more so than the *Abdul Aziz* [the King of Saudi Arabia's yacht]. That's too modern to be really chic. She likes Tino and Anne-Marie of the Hellenes and their kids. She likes her cousins 'Pud' [Princess Alexandra] and Angus. She likes Norton and Penelope and had a real soft spot for Leonora [the Romseys' little girl, who shortly afterwards died of cancer]. Aside from being cousins, these are Prince Charles's nearest and dearest friends, so he was happy too. It was a large, congenial group. The atmosphere was very relaxed. Everyone had a good time. Even Charles and Diana got along. But was romance rekindled? No, it wasn't."

For a while, The Prince and Princess of Wales were seen together more in public. "It hasn't been easy for them," says the aristocratic sister-in-law of the senior courtier. "They'd much rather not be thrown together so much. It's even something of a waste of royal time, because whenever they double up for something official, that means one of them is depriving another good cause of their presence.

"But some good might come out of it yet. They might learn to be more tolerant of each other." This optimism was shown to be misplaced in 1992. Despite undertaking joint public engagements and official tours to such places as Hungary and India, the divisions in the Wales union have become only too painfully visible. This has been largely due to Diana yearning to "go public." One notable and pointedly public incident happened in India. When he tried to kiss her cheek, she moved her head, knowing full well that the cameras would record the snub. This they duly did, and a photograph of a spurned and grimacing Prince was duly flashed across the front pages of the world's newspapers. With it went the message that all was still not well in the Wales marriage, despite the couple being on joint show in public. To further highlight this point, Diana then began creating photo opportunities in which she would project a solitary, waif-like image which would drive home the point that she was a figure worthy of sympathy. Two notable photographs were the lonely Diana at the Taj Mahal and the pensive and solitary Princess at the foot of the Pyramids in Egypt, which country she visited without Charles in Spring 1992. So obvious was her ploy in the latter instance that the *Sunday Times* devoted a full page to the devices by which she was manipulating public opinion.

Diana's manipulation of public opinion was a subject on which the *Sunday Times* was rather better qualified than most to comment upon in the Spring of 1992. It had purchased first serial rights to Andrew Morton's panegyric, a tome which portrayed the dynamic and calculating Diana as the passive, suicidal victim of a sadistic Prince and his unfeeling Royal relations.

Before that could come out, however, the original edition of this book was published. Once more the international spotlight was focused on the Wales marriage. There were some extraordinary behind-the-scenes moves in which attempts were made to discredit this work's contents, as well as the author personally. They failed. As one television commentator noted, the acknowledgements page alone reads like a veritable Who's Who of the British Establishment. Moreover, the information contained in these pages is unassailable, having come from the friends and relations of both the Prince and Princess as well as from courtiers within the Royal Household itself. So Buckingham Palace brought forward the announcement of The Duke and Duchess of York's separation in an apparent attempt to deflect attention away from this story.

Disturbing as this book was to the Press Office at Buckingham Palace, it was nothing compared to the Morton book when it saw the light of day. This, at least, has the merits of being a serious and balanced account that gives both the Prince and Princess's side of the story. The Morton book, however, was so heavily biased in Diana's favour that it read more like a propaganda treatise than a work of non-fiction.

As the facts emerged, it became apparent that the main story of the other book, the supposed quasi-suicide attempts, did not stand up. Despite the shakiness of the main story, the press reports generated a tremendous groundswell of journalistic support and public sympathy for a Princess who seemed to be beleaguered, until you stopped to think. She was not being assailed at all, as all the coverage was reports of her own revelations.

Quite missing the point, the Archbishop of Canterbury entered the fray, blaming the press for violating the Waleses' privacy. But by now the thinking part of the journalistic world were good and truly on to Diana. Sir John Junor in the *Mail on Sunday* and Lynn Barber in the *Independent on Sunday* led the way, querying whether the supposedly innocent Princess was behind the leaks about her private life. Within a matter of days they had their answer. Diana very publicly visited Carolyn Bartholomew, Morton's source for the information about her bulimia, giving the assembled photographers a ten-minute photo opportunity on the doorstep. The following day all the papers revealed that a well-spoken woman had tipped them off about the visit, and that she had even gone to the trouble of giving them Mrs. Bartholomew's obscure Fulham address.

The next twist was the identity of the mystery caller. Suspicion fell upon Diana, but Carolyn Bartholomew was quoted as saying that it must have been the neighbours, even though this did not make sense. The press had been tipped off before Diana's arrival, and the neighbours would have known of her visit only after she had arrived.

But what was Diana's reason for embarking upon this extraordinary course of action? "She was thrilled with the fuss she caused," the courtier says. "She was basking in the sympathy." A friend of hers concurred. "The public is the most important thing in her life after her children. She wants them to see her as a strong character who has had to fight to get to where she's got." Further substantiation comes from the aging wife of a producer who knows Diana and has known just about every movie star since Gloria Swanson. "She has the most extraordinary appreciation of her public of anyone I can think of since Joan Crawford. She really feels she has a special relationship with them. She often speaks about *my public* as if they're a close relative. They're one of her main reasons for being. They're her friends and a source of motivation and comfort. She wants them to know her better. She believes that they have the right to share her view of herself with her."

But Diana overplayed her hand. She started to show her cards too clearly. She organised a celebratory dinner at Harry's Bar, a smart members-only club in Mayfair, for the friends who had acted as her mouthpieces. This earned her condemnation from various commentators, including Sir John Junor, who saw through her as easily as if she were made of glass.

By this time Diana's manipulations had become so obvious that Buckingham Palace had ceased issuing denials of her responsibility for the furore. Paradoxically, however, the public seemed unable to accept that she was the perpetrator of the speculation about her marriage, and not the victim. Day after day on the radio and television, and in the letters pages of the various newspapers, the public condemned the media for their intrusiveness. Every time Diana appeared in public it voiced its sympathy and approval. For instance, at the Garter Ceremony at Windsor Castle, Diana was greeted with tumultuous applause. This was repeated over the next two days, during her two outings at Royal Ascot, when she received the loudest cheer from the general public. Only in the Royal Enclosure did The Queen and the other members of the Royal Family receive any acknowledgement at all. Even there, in one of the main bastions of the British Establishment, they were merely accorded polite applause compared with the rapturous greeting granted to Diana.

"Words cannot convey how betrayed The Prince of Wales feels by what the Princess has done," a cousin said. "He is deeply hurt and very, very angry that she could use public opinion against him like that. He would never do something like that. Never in a million years, not even to a sworn enemy. In his scale of things, conduct like that is so despicable as to be unimaginable."

"The Princess of Wales is a jumped-up little drama queen," a former member of the Royal Household said. "She's no better than one of those movie stars who starts believing her own publicity and gets too big for her boots. The only difficulty is, you can fire a movie star, but you can't fire a Princess of Wales."

"You cannot believe the atmosphere in the Royal Box at Ascot," a member of the Royal Household said. "Charles and Diana spent the whole time looking glum. They just sat there for two whole days. Not once was a word exchanged between them. Not once."

By this time, The Queen had managed to wipe the smug smile of victory off Diana's face. "She's been the prime mover in containing the damage," a cousin said. "She's been very worried by the fact that The Princess of Wales's hand has been so visible in all these shenanigans. In her opinion, this has been the worst crisis since the Abdication. She does not minimise what has happened. She can see very clearly that the prestige of the Monarchy has been threatened by what amounts to a character assassination of The Prince of Wales. She is desperately worried about the long term effects upon Charles's position and the Crown itself, and is beside herself that anyone could have betrayed her the way her own daughter-in-law has. She feels particularly acutely about Diana's complaint that she's never been given any support by the Family. That's simply not true. The Queen herself has done far more for Diana than anyone ever did for her or she ever did for her own children, or indeed anyone else. When Diana was first married, The Queen asked Lady Susan Hussey to ease her in. Oliver Everett did as well. The Queen interceded twice with Fleet Street on Diana's behalf when the pressure from the press was getting to be too much. In a country where you have a free press, that's a giant step for any Monarch to take. The Queen feels that Diana has publicly slapped her in the face, and that she's nothing but a scheming ingrate.

"The Queen met with Prince Charles on the 12th of June. They talked about what the Princess had done. The Queen has known about the difficulties in the marriage for a long time. She takes the view that they should both behave like mature and civilised people, but that's a tall order when you're dealing with a case like The Princess of Wales. The Duke of Edinburgh wasn't there, and as you know, The Queen never makes family decisions without consulting him.

"There was another meeting. This took place three days later, after the Garter Ceremony at Windsor. The Duke [of Edinburgh] was there, as were The Prince and Princess of Wales. This was the make-or-break meeting. Diana tried to pretend to be the injured party. The Duke wasn't having any of that and told her in no uncertain terms why he knew she was anything but the innocent she was pretending to be. She's always playing the martyr, you know, to such an extent that The Prince of Wales now calls her 'Diana the Martyr.' The Duke feels very bitter about the way Diana has treated The Queen. He has a great deal of respect for [The Queen] and can't stand seeing anyone abuse her. He more or less told Diana that the whole Family would be better off without her. He said that anyone who goes around telling tall tales about their husband and in-laws is nothing but a fifth columnist. They asked Diana what she wanted, and she said she wants a legal separation. The Queen said she favoured a show of unity behind which they could both lead their own lives. Prince Charles agreed at that was the best course of action, and she got them to ree to try it until the end of the year.

"The fact is, though, Diana is holding them all up to ransom. I am pretty sure she'll get what she wants. What's that? An official separation, with her own official residence, her own official staff, and the right to continue performing official duties. All these slurs against The Prince of Wales have been nothing but a calculated attempt to win public sympathy so that she can leave him and remain a functioning Princess of Wales. She doesn't want to be marginalised like The Duchess of York.

"The Family now understand that she is a very devious and calculating woman beneath that sweet exterior and that she has the power to do them a great deal of harm. If they don't give her what she wants, she'll simply pull a few more stunts like the ones she's been pulling of late. They all realise that the Monarchy can't stand many more jolts like the ones she's given it recently.

"She'll only opt to stay with Prince Charles if she feels that she has to. I don't believe that will happen. The press have taken her side. She has the backing of the public. The sympathy is with her. She's one very clever young woman, believe me."

Undeniably, The Princess of Wales is dextrous at fomenting support for herself, but it would be unwise of her to underestimate the wiliness of the Court. The institution of Monarchy has been functional for longer than any of us has been alive. The collective wisdom of the courtiers exceeds even that of a PR genius born into two lines of courtiers, as Diana was. Meetings have taken place involving the senior members of the Prince's household like his Private Secretary, Commander Richard Aylard, and The Queen's senior Staff. They've come to the conclusion that the very worst thing that could happen would be to allow Diana to get what she wants. "She effectively wants to set up a rival Court," a courtier says. "The preferred option is for her to consent to a civilised arrangement with the Prince and her leading separate lives but remaining together officially. The next preference is for a divorce. They have finally

322

awoken to what a real danger Diana is and to the amount of damage she can do. They take the view that she remains a potent force only as long as she has the royal platform from which to operate. Remove that and you remove the oxygen which fuels the fires of her fame: the official duties, State occasions, photo opportunities. It's infinitely preferable to be rid of her than to have her on board the royal ship, a loose cannon threatening to shoot a hole in the hull and sink the whole works. She's finally opened their eyes to how skilfully she's been using the press all these years."

Indeed, the Princess's uncanny knack for attracting publicity has been shared in recent years only by Elizabeth Taylor. It has long been a source of some concern to her husband, who, according to his cousin, "feels that you should do things because they're the right things to do, not because you're going to get acclaimed for them. She's always playing to the gallery. If it's not her Lady Bountiful act, it's Princess Bleeding Heart. An example is how she used her visit to little Leonora Knatchbull [Lord and Lady Romsey's daughter] when she was dying of leukemia. Diana went to see her only once, and lo and behold, she made sure the press were tipped off so that they could record her playing the saint. Compare that to The Prince of Wales, who went repeatedly. But not one of his visits was reported, because he did not tip the press off as to his presence. She's always using the press to project this wonderful image of herself, but he's like The Queen. He doesn't believe in acting. He believes in being. His advisors have tried to get him to change. They recognise that he's losing the public relations battle. As far as he's concerned, though, it's a question of integrity and sincerity. In his opinion, only fakes and demagogues play to the gallery."

At the time of The Prince of Wales's engagement to Lady Diana Spencer, someone close to the Prince commented, "I don't believe she loves him. I think she's using him. She strikes me as a very ambitious young woman." That view is now shared by the Royal Family. Any goodwill they felt towards Diana has been eroded. "She's worked herself into a position of isolation," the courtier said.

ey regard blabbing as the ultimate in disloyalty and achery. They've reacted the way any other family would. How would you feel if someone in your family knifed you in public? Of course you'd feel betrayed. Even the most humble family in the land wouldn't want another member of their family shooting off their mouth criticising everyone else."

According to the royal cousin, "Princess Margaret was her greatest supporter, but that's evaporated overnight. The one thing you don't do, if you're a member of any Royal family, is attack the future King in public. That's undermining the very fabric of Monarchy. Princess Margaret has made too many sacrifices in the name of duty to take a lenient view of Diana rubbishing Prince Charles. And she's furious that Diana has allowed her friends to attack The Queen. Queen Elizabeth, The Queen Mother and The Duke of Edinburgh feel the same way. So too do The Princess Royal, The Duke of York, and Prince Edward. They will be polite to Diana if she remains a part of the family. But they will never trust her or like her again."

It now only remains to be seen whether Diana will settle for the limited autonomy she already possesses as an independent in all but name Princess of Wales, or whether she will allow her wilfulness and stubbornness to get the better of her. No one yet knows what the outcome will be, not even Diana herself. It would be a pity, though, if she allows her failings to deprive the world of a Princess of Wales that, for all her histrionics and dramatics in private, is still one of the most popular women in public life.

As for the marriage, it is now dead. "There is no prospect of The Prince of Wales ever going back to her," his cousin says. "He loathes her, and even more important, he doesn't trust her as far as he can see her." Nor does Diana, by all accounts, want to return to him. "She feels it's too late."

But what does the future hold? According to a Royal Household member, "It's all up in the air and likely to remain so for the forseeable future. A divorce is possible. So is a separation. So is a pregnancy. There's even been talk that she should get pregnant if she stays with him. You know, to quiet speculation about whether the reconciliation is genuine or not. It would have to be by artificial insemination, for there's no way they'd do it naturally. Nothing is sure, except that the marriage is over in all but name."

Diana Today

Since she became Princess of Wales, Diana has enjoyed an unparalleled role on the world's stage. She has become the most written about and photographed woman of her time. She is undeniably popular, a media icon whose every action is assiduously followed.

The twenty-year-old girl who married The Prince of Wales was worldly but relatively unexposed. She has since seen more of the world than most of us ever will. Some of the countries she has visited include Monaco (1982); Australia, New Zealand and Canada (1983); Norway (1984—her first solo tour); Italy, Germany, Australia, Fiji, Hawaii and America (1985); Austria, Canada, Japan, United Arab Emirates, Spain (1986); Portugal, France [three times], Germany, Spain (1987); Australia, Thailand, France, Spain (1988); America, Kuwait, United Arab Emirates, Australia, Indonesia, Hong Kong, Spain (1989); Nigeria, Cameroon, Necker Island in the Virgin Islands, Hungary, America, Japan, Belgium, Spain (1990); Pakistan, Canada, and, once more, Spain, though, for the first time, not as a guest of the King (1991); and Hungary, India, Austria and Egypt (1992).

Diana's travels have not been simple affairs. Each trip has necessitated extensive preparations. There have been the clothes to make and buy, the staff to take, the people to see, the presents to get. Atypically for a member of the Royal Family, she is generous, and will not try to get away with presenting one dinky photograph of herself in a leather frame as a token of her regard, though she is sufficiently aware of her celebrity to know that that too will be a much prized addition to her hosts' photograph table.

While Diana's travels have given her a glimpse of more of the world than most of us will ever see, her work has provided her with an exceptionally wide range of knowledge about how different kinds of human beings live. She mixes with the most privileged people in the world, but she also sees how the most deprived live. Few of us will ever have the experience of touring a leper colony (and willingly shaking hands, glovelessly, with the patients), or of sitting on the bedside of adults and children dying of cancer, AIDS, leukaemia, heart disease and a host of other fatal diseases. Moreover, even fewer of us will have the knowledge that our visit can bring great joy and added meaning to the lives of these, and many other, people, who feel that they can die, or live, more happily, for having met The Princess of Wales.

The ability to bring such happiness, such meaning, to so many, is a great and precious gift. At any given time in history, few human beings in the world enjoy such celebrity, reverence, and adoration that their mere presence can materially affect so many of the people they encounter. This is something to be treasured, not a commodity to be minimized, and it is to her credit that Diana has the sensitivity, compassion, and awareness wisely to use this rarest of gifts.

Quite why Diana has become this latter-day icon is something that could be speculated upon from now to eternity without arriving at any concrete and final answer. I personally believe it is because despite her faults, she is basically a kind, compassionate and sympathetic person who loves people and loves being loved by them. Most of us have antennae and pick this up, especially the vulnerable, the weak, the intelligent, and the sensitive.

She is not perfect. She can be vain and self-centered, a hard task mistress to work for, jealous and possessive, manipulative and stubborn, vindictive and headstrong, and enjoy getting her own way to an unusual degree. But these are hardly the failings of a monster. They are normal and natural, and well within the range of acceptable imperfection. They make her all the more human, all the more reachable to the average man and woman, and, as a result, endear rather than repel. Even her greatest failing, her extreme competitiveness, does not repulse her large body of admirers, though it has caused problems within her marriage and has limited the scope of her friendships.

Diana is now a woman at the peak of her feminine appeal and popularity. "On the whole, I think she's a force for good," says Jacqueline, Lady Killearn, and I am sure most people would agree with that assessment.

Her life is set in a pleasant and agreeable pattern, unless she chooses to alter it. Four, occasionally five, days a week Diana works, making an invaluable contribution to the welfare of others and, in the process, earning the dual rewards of personal satisfaction and international acclaim. She is no stickler for protocol, nor does she ever say "No" to an engagement just because it is on an inconvenient date. For instance, on Sunday, 1 December 1991, she sacrificed the one evening most of us, herself included, hold dear to attend the Dance for Life gala in aid of CRUSAID, going on afterwards to a reception at Spencer House so that we, the committee, could justify the ticket price of £250. Admittedly, it turned out to be a magical evening, so what started out as a chore ended up a joy. But the fact remains she readily undertook an assignment that was an inconvenience, because it was for a cause dear to her heart. She really does wish to use her unique position to make life better for others. That is a large part of her beauty and a major reason for her appeal, and is ideally summarized by her cousin by marriage, Janet, Marchioness of Milford Haven, who said in 1991, "I think she's the best thing that's happened to us: to the country and the Royal Family. Where would we be without her? She's put Britain back on the map in a big way. She's been just marvellous with fashion, with her charity work, with everything. I can't think where we'd be without her. She's been the best thing that's happened to us all."

But Diana's life is not all work and no play. She has an active but private social life, with many friends and several admirers as well as the support of her confidant. Publicity has not marred her friendship with Captain James Hewitt any more than it has terminated Prince Charles's with Camilla Parker Bowles, and that, too, is positive, for all human beings need the companionship of special friends, and royalty is no less nor more human than anyone else.

For all the conflicts within the family, Diana is a dedicated and loving mother whose sons adore her. Prince William is tougher and more obstreperous than Prince Harry. He gives both his parents more trouble, and has a less peaceable time at school than his younger brother. "Hence his 'accident' at school," comments the mother of a fellow pupil, alluding to the incident which resulted in the young Prince being hospitalized after a friend hit him and inflicted a wound to his skull. But William now pays the price for his boisterousness and abrasiveness with his mother, who no longer puts up with the very sort of behaviour she was so at pains to encourage when he was younger.

"She's not namby pamby about hitting the children. William often gets a cuff about the ear," says a royal relation. "He's very strong-willed and doesn't like being told what to do. He's very argumentative. His parents don't put up with it, especially his mother. He also gets into a lot of trouble with the boys at school. He tells them they have to do as he says, as his grandmother's The Queen. You can imagine how much ice that cuts. For all that, though, he's a sweet little boy, well-mannered and well, a real little boy." Prince Harry, on the other hand, "has a much gentler nature. He never gives any trouble. He is the apple of his mother's eye. He really has the loveliest disposition. He is well behaved and has a real little sense of humour there. He's growing up into the most delightful little boy anyone could hope for."

Diana spends as much time as she can with her children, but with one at boarding school and the other at day school, as well as a full complement of staff to take care of all her household and professional needs, she has more free time to dedicate to herself than the average working mother. As health-conscious as ever, she continues to take care of herself as religiously as she did prior to her marriage. She still exercises whenever she can. She still watches what she eats. She goes for regular colonic irrigations, to the Hale Clinic at Park Crescent in London's medical district of Marylebone, and so far has not allowed the more conservative section of the medical profession to deflect her from cleaning out her system with the ten gallon enemas employed in this controversial form of treatment. For years she had weekly massages administered by Stephen Twigg, a fashionable society masseur, who came round to Kensington Palace and spent at least an hour kneading and pummelling and stroking her semi-nude body. "She is a born sensualist," says a close friend. "She needs to be touched as much as she needs to touch." This is also one of the secrets of her success, for when she meets strangers and establishes physical contact with them, she is reaching them in more ways than one. (In July 1992 she dismissed Twigg after he gave a story about her to one of the London newspapers.)

Her reputation as a great beauty still matters as much as ever to Diana. She has never got over the thrill of acquiring the reputation, despite her large nose, of which she remains conscious. Now that she has managed to deflect press attention away from her clothes, she again enhances her appearance with a succession of new dresses which flatter her without attracting unwanted comment. The pinnacle of her career as a cover girl was appearing on the front cover of *Vogue* magazine in December 1991. "She was thrilled," says a friend, though the sentiment was not shared by Buckingham Palace. "They were furious with her. The future Queen of England should not be disporting herself on the front of fashion magazines." But there was nothing the traditionalists could do. They only learnt of her intentions after the magazine was published. And Diana's attitude does not seem so out of step with modern life: *"Vogue* is a highly respected and respectable magazine. There's no reason why The Princess of Wales can't appear on its cover. After all, doing so isn't exactly letting the side down."

Aware that we have only one life to live, Diana never takes no for an answer unless she has to. Her other most recent success in ignoring Palace advice has had rather more harmful connotations for a segment of British industry, however, and shows that she still might have lessons to learn in putting duty before gratification if the national interest is at stake. The British car industry has long been in trouble, and the Royal Family have a policy of driving only British cars. But Diana has long been in love with Mercedes Benz, and she recently got around the rules by getting Mercedes Benz to "lend" her a car for an extended period. This she now drives, oblivious of the promotional advantages to the German car industry, and the concomitant disadvantages to ours. Doubtless we shall see more of these acts of stubbornness, and doubtless not all of them will be to her or our credit, though we, the public, must never lose sight of the fact that the flip side of this fault is her strength of character. And that undeniably works to our overall benefit.

Much of the time, The Princess of Wales is justly one of the most celebrated women in the world and she enjoys her celebrity. Barring a calamity, she will remain a large part of our lives for the remainder of this century and well into the next. Humanity is fascinated by beautiful and glamorous women, and this interest is invariably sustained when the woman behind the vibrant, well-defined image remains elusive, as does Diana.

At the nub of the interest in Diana lies a paradox. Here is a perfectly ordinary human being, with no outstanding talents, who, through circumstance and character, has been able to transform herself into the most outstanding success story of the twentieth century. She is living proof that ordinary human beings can lead extraordinary lives, that it is possible for the individual to realize his or her potential beyond his or her own dreams. But what makes her story even more intriguing is the knowledge that when dreams come true, they do so at a price. No one escapes the weight of natural justice, which may give with one hand, but invariably takes with the other. It is curiously comforting to know that no one is impervious to its leavening effects, not even The Princess of Wales.

INDEX

ROYALTY REVEALED

You see them at charity balls and public functions. You read about their train of designers and hairdressers and their troubled marriages. But what goes on after the polo matches, the hospital visits, and all those gala events? Two professional royal watchers take you into the royal ranks to learn the facts and fiction of the Windsor family.

From the beloved Queen Mother to the newest additions to the family, ROYALTY REVEALED is a remarkable and fascinating volume that covers each member of the Royal Family, telling who gets along with whom—and how Queen Elizabeth wields her matriarchal power over all of them.

An Insider's Look at The Secret World of Britain's Royal Family
by UNITY HALL and INGRID SEWARD
with 8 pages of color photos

She's captivated—and shocked—them all. But what is she really like—and what was it like for her to be married into the Royal Family? Close friend and professional royal watcher Ingrid Seward takes us into the private world of the madcap "Fergie," from her divorce-torn childhood and early life in jet-set London and Switzerland, to the Cinderella romance that thrust her into the media spotlight, to the sudden, sad separation from Prince Andrew.

FERGIE

From
fairy-tale
marriage to world-
shaking break-up:
Her *real* life
as a Duchess

WITH AN EXCLUSIVE NEW UPDATE FOR THIS EDITION!

by INGRID SEWARD